PRAISE FOR *OPEN BANKING AND FINANCIAL INCLUSION*

'Ellie Duncan skillfully explains the impact of finar
economies – whether as a result of geography, rac
employment status – and examines what different jurisdictions are doing to
minimize its impact. For those of us who believe that open banking should
ultimately improve the lives of all consumers, this is a well-researched and
much-needed study.'
David Beardmore, Ecosystems Development Director, Raidiam

'An essential read for anyone looking to understand the power and potential of
open banking through the eyes of financial inclusion. It's a well-crafted narrative
of how we arrived where we are today.'
Carrie Forbes, CEO, League Data

'Assesses open banking regimes worldwide and how they may help financial
inclusion across the globe with a very objective eye. I applaud Ellie Duncan's
efforts to create this study and share a range of potential outcomes from real-
world experience.'
Simon Lyons, Chief Strategy Officer, obconnect

'If you want to know about the drivers for open banking, this book is for you.
If you want to know about the implementation of open banking, this book is for
you. If you want to know about financial exclusion and gender inequality, this
book is for you. A great all-round read.'
Nilixa Devlukia, Chair, Open Finance Association

'Open banking has the potential to be the largest transformation in the history
of financial services. But why has it been slow to roll out in some countries, and
has it helped the unbanked in those that have? Ellie Duncan takes the reader on
a deep dive to find out. An excellent resource to understand the key challenges
and opportunities on the journey towards open banking.'
Kelly Stanley, Co-founder, Open Banking Expo

Open Banking and Financial Inclusion

Creating a financial system that provides security and equity

Ellie Duncan

KoganPage

Publisher's note

Every possible effort has been made to ensure that the information contained in this book is accurate at the time of going to press, and the publishers and author cannot accept responsibility for any errors or omissions, however caused. No responsibility for loss or damage occasioned to any person acting, or refraining from action, as a result of the material in this publication can be accepted by the editor, the publisher or the author.

First published in Great Britain and the United States in 2024 by Kogan Page Limited

2nd Floor, 45 Gee Street	8 W 38th Street, Suite 902	4737/23 Ansari Road
London	New York, NY 10018	Daryaganj
EC1V 3RS	USA	New Delhi 110002
United Kingdom		India
www.koganpage.com		

Kogan Page books are printed on paper from sustainable forests.

ISBNs

Hardback	978 1 3986 1241 9
Paperback	978 1 3986 1240 2
Ebook	978 1 3986 1243 3

British Library Cataloguing-in-Publication Data
A CIP record for this book is available from the British Library.

Library of Congress Cataloging-in-Publication Data
Names: Duncan, Ellie, author.
Title: Open banking and financial inclusion : creating a financial system
    that provides security and equity / Ellie Duncan.
Description: London ; New York, NY : Kogan Page, 2024. | Includes
    bibliographical references and index
Identifiers: LCCN 2023057598 (print) | LCCN 2023057599 (ebook) | ISBN
    9781398612402 (paperback) | ISBN 9781398612419 (hardback) | ISBN
    9781398612433 (ebook)
Subjects: LCSH: Banks and banking. | Financial exclusion. | Banks and
    banking–Customer services. | Social responsibility in banking.
Classification: LCC HG1601 .D86 2024 (print) | LCC HG1601 (ebook) | DDC
    332.1–dc23/eng/202312014
LC record available at https://lccn.loc.gov/2023057598
LC ebook record available at https://lccn.loc.gov/2023057599

Typeset by Hong Kong FIVE Workshop, Hong Kong
Print production managed by Jellyfish
Printed and bound by CPI Group (UK) Ltd, Croydon CR0 4YY

CONTENTS

ABOUT THE AUTHOR

Ellie Duncan is a financial and broadcast journalist. She currently works at Open Banking Expo as Head of Editorial and Broadcast, where she hosts the Open Banking Expo Unplugged podcast and writes regular news and features on the industry. Ellie also moderates Open Banking Expo's virtual Live Panel Debates and in-person panel discussions at its flagship conference in the UK, and at Open Banking Expo Canada.

Prior to this, Ellie wrote across a range of titles and on various subjects, including asset management, investment, pensions, mortgages and wealth management. She previously worked at the Financial Times Group, where she was latterly features editor at *FTAdviser*. Since then, she has written for the Financial Times Group's *Ignites Europe* and *Investors' Chronicle*, and moderated webinars and virtual live panels for those same titles, as well as *Ignites US* and *FundFire*.

Her work has also appeared in *Investment Week*, *Credit Strategy*, *Pensions Age*, *Net Zero Investor*, *ESG Clarity*, *European Pensions*, *Pensions Week* and *Raconteur*.

Ellie is the community manager of Women in Open Banking, an Open Banking Expo initiative in partnership with American Express, which aims to supercharge the careers of those who identify as a woman. She has also previously contributed content for the UN Women National Committee UK.

Open Banking and Financial Inclusion is her first book.

Introduction

When I first began writing about open banking a few years ago, I have to admit I had never come across the term before. But having written about investment and asset management for around a decade, the prospect of yet more financial jargon and acronyms did not phase me. When you write about a sector or an area of the industry every day, five days a week, what was once impenetrable jargon soon becomes a second language. Before I knew it, ETFs, OEICs and SFDR had been replaced by APIs, AIS and PIS, and PSD2.

I was especially unphased once I came to realize that I wasn't the only one who had little to no awareness or prior knowledge of open banking – and that goes for people working in the industry, as well as family and friends I spoke to about my job. Part of the reason is that open banking is still a relatively recent concept which makes it, to my mind, incredibly exciting. The industry is nascent and, as such, is yet to realize its full potential. Being able to, essentially, document an industry almost from its beginnings is fascinating. Of course, banking has been around for hundreds of years, so in some respects, open banking has its roots there. Yet it also feels like a new beginning for an industry that has a long history – more on that later.

Back to basics

Part of what motivates me, as a financial journalist, is getting to grips with the inner workings, or the plumbing, of a product or service. What is going on behind the scenes to make it happen? How does it work? However, it can be all too easy to get lost in a new technology, to be swept along by those who have worked on its development from the very start. Maybe even to be awed by its cleverness.

One rule as a journalist is always to ask, 'And what?', or 'Yes, and?'. In other words, why does this matter? With open banking, so much of the discussion and debate centres on how existing financial institutions will be affected by such comprehensive systems change and the wider digital transformation taking place, as well as the cost burden they have to bear – and quite rightly. Only by sharing experiences and by talking candidly about the investment required can the industry break down those barriers with workable solutions. But what does this actually mean, in practice, for the customers of banks? And then, what does it mean for those who are not banked or who are underserved by the financial system as it has been?

Through writing and researching, it soon became clear to me that open banking, when implemented, has the potential to open up access to financial services to create a more equitable and financially secure society. Much of the coverage of open banking tends to focus on the technology behind it, and/or the regulatory and policymaking aspects of it. So, instead, I sought to turn the focus onto the people whose lives will be most affected by it, by telling their stories.

Can open banking live up to the hype?

Once I had some of the more technical aspects of open banking clear in my mind and had understood the backstory and learned about its origins – which you can read about in Chapter 2 – other questions sprang to mind. What will open banking achieve or deliver that the banking industry, as it has been operating for decades, has been unable to? How will it improve the banking experience for the average consumer? Will the financial services industry recognize the opportunities open banking presents and embrace them? Ultimately, can open banking live up to its own potential, or will it fall short? And then, what next – how do countries make the shift from open banking to open finance, bringing consumers along with them?

Much of that untapped potential, I believe, has to do with open banking as a means, first of all, of maintaining or rebuilding trust in financial services. What open banking has in its favour – and where it departs from traditional banking as we know it – is that it essentially gives individuals control over their own financial data, whether that is account information or their payments history. In a world where we're so used to hearing or reading about how data that large institutions or corporations collect on us is being shared or profited from, there is a real sense of ownership with open banking. This, in turn, can help retain or restore trust, which is vital in an age of misinformation.

As the US's acting Comptroller of the Currency, Michael J Hsu, stated in a speech made at the FDX Global Summit, in banking 'trust is everything' (2023). He cautioned, though, that trust cannot be 'engineered, or manufactured, or bought', but that banks must earn, maintain and 'vigorously' protect it.

The relationship individuals have with their banks is a long and often chequered one. However, in researching trust in financial services, it soon became clear that banks have time on their side and that it is actually the newer challenger banks, often referred to as neobanks, and the fintechs that need to work on gaining consumers' confidence and trust – see Chapter 2.

Another aspect of this untapped potential is providing people who are typically rejected by the financial system with access to credit. Who is offered credit, and who is declined it, is typically based on archaic assumptions about the way we used to live and on historic data that feeds into a traditional system of credit scoring. It still amazes me that, even though huge swathes of the global population rent rather than own their home, rental payments history has counted for nothing in the eyes of lenders. The system is outdated and serves no one – individuals who pay their monthly rent on time miss out on other financial products that could help them start a business, or buy a car. On the flip side, lenders miss out on a new customer who is potentially loyal, financially independent, and who will likely require additional services and support further down the line.

Life-changing events

In my lifetime, there have been two significant events that had repercussions for the global banking industry and for users of financial services – which is to say, many millions of people. The first was the Great Financial Crisis of 2007–08, which brought much of the banking industry in the Western world to its knees and resulted in millions of people losing their homes, savings and jobs. Those institutions that emerged largely unscathed came under closer regulatory and fiscal scrutiny thereafter, and were expected to shore up much larger capital buffers to prevent a banking collapse of such scale from occurring again.

Taxpayer-funded government bailouts of banks in the United States, Europe and the UK, as well as the 'bankers' and chief executives of those failed financial institutions seemingly landing on their feet in top jobs, left a bitter aftertaste in the mouths of citizens, whose property and other financial assets in many cases were never recovered. In the immediate aftermath, consumers' trust in the banks that had been meant to serve them had been eroded.

Really, you hardly need me to spell out for you the Great Financial Crisis – as you either lived or worked through it, or have read enough about it since to be well informed. But, I do think it is worth pointing out that the harm it inflicted on individuals is still felt and influences people's attitudes – both positive and negative – to financial institutions to this day.

The second global event of significance is the Covid-19 pandemic. In many ways, the pandemic was the unlikely trigger of a digital banking revolution. Banks and lenders that had previously relied on face-to-face or in-person provision of services, had to make the switch to online offerings, no matter their customer demographic. While it presented many challenges, the pandemic also forced many individuals to rethink how they had accessed financial services and credit previously, and what that could look like henceforth.

Payments was, perhaps, the most transformed of all though. Government handouts that might have been collected in-person and in cash before the pandemic were sent directly to people's bank accounts. Moreover, in some countries, as you'll go on to read about, governments gave their citizens an online account so that they could receive their state funds directly. For many individuals, particularly women, this was the first time they had access to an online account and to digital payments of any kind. Many did not make the switch back to cash, although it did take some longer than others to make the permanent switch away from cash and to the digital world. It also gave women a new financial independence that has transformed their relationship with the financial services industry and their role within their own household.

The pandemic proved, if anything, that reform could happen rapidly and at scale – even in an industry that has often been perceived as slow moving and reluctant to change. Likewise, it showed that humans could adapt to a new way of banking and paying, as long as the benefits to them were clearly understood. The march of technological progress is often perceived as relentless and something to fear. Change may be inevitable, but what is also inevitable is our aversion to it, as humans. So it is natural to proceed with caution.

Financial exclusion – eyes wide open

That anyone remains without access to credit and with no formal banking services at their disposal can be quite shocking to consider, especially when the digital transformation of financial services seems so embedded in our everyday lives. Individuals on lower incomes are most often those who still rely on cash and have barely any financial resilience. Yet should banking be the preserve of those on middle to higher incomes? Should banking and the availability of a range of financial services be a right and not a privilege? After all, we all need money and credit to survive, so in that regard banking is an essential service.

Those who are pushed further and further to the margins of society are at risk of radicalization, poverty, criminalization, mental and/or physical illness – the list truly does go on. So, it is in all of our interests to ensure everyone is banked and that the concept of financial exclusion becomes, truly, a thing of the past. In pushing forward with an open banking agenda, the onus is on those working in the industry to ensure that no one gets left behind. I'm not saying that open banking and the types of innovations it has spawned are a panacea. But there is an opportunity, should we choose to take it, to provide a more equitable and secure financial system for many millions of people around the world.

How to read this book

I've written this book in a way that enables you to read only the chapters you want to read and in the order you prefer. Having said that, I do urge you to read Chapter 1 on financial exclusion to gain some perspective on just how many people across the world have no access to formal financial services and what this means for their prospects, particularly in an increasingly digital and cashless society.

If you are coming to this book with little to no prior knowledge of open banking, then Chapter 2 is a must, as it establishes what open banking is and how it actually works. It will provide context for the rest of the book and, hopefully, set you up with an understanding of this new technology and concept.

Because open banking is such a nascent industry and because it straddles both finance and technology, it is fast paced and, quite honestly, does not stand still. Developments are taking place all the time, whether regulatory or at market level, with new fintechs emerging and partnerships being formed. I hope this book has captured some of the energy that seems to characterize this industry, while also being as informative as possible by keeping up to date with the progress being made.

Whether open banking is really working for the benefit of consumers is a key tenet of this book, and only by speaking to key people across the open banking, fintech and data-sharing industry is this possible to ascertain. You can expect to read about real people's journeys from financial exclusion to inclusion, and how open banking helped. Case studies offer a more in-depth picture of where open banking in a developed market versus an emerging market has been successful in promoting financial inclusion. In spotlighting personal stories, I hope to provide authenticity and offer a riposte to those readers who are perhaps cynical about the social benefits of open banking.

But this book also considers the limitations of open banking – for example, in countries that have opted to take a more market-driven approach without regulatory oversight, are there indications that the underbanked will remain that way? Chapter 9 looks at the ultimate intention of open banking, which is to lead to open finance. The concept of open finance, or open data, is an emerging one – it is where the exchange of data, with the consent of consumers, applies to a range of industries, including telcos, investments, pensions and utilities, ultimately for the benefit of consumers and businesses. Some countries are firmly on that path, others a few years behind. It requires plenty of vision and ambition – here is the story so far.

Reference

Hsu, M (2023) Remarks at FDX Global Summit 'Open Banking and the OCC', Occ.gov, 19 April, www.occ.gov/news-issuances/speeches/2023/pub-speech-2023-38.pdf (archived at https://perma.cc/J6Y7-8GAV)

Financial exclusion: what it means to be outside the global financial system

Introduction

Before we can even consider whether open banking has the potential to create a more equitable financial system, it is important to establish what financial exclusion and inclusion look like in the 21st century.

> **CHAPTER OBJECTIVES**
>
> The main questions to be answered are:
>
> - What does it mean to be financially excluded – to be unbanked or underbanked – in the age of information and digitalization?
> - How does the term 'financial exclusion' apply to individuals in developed markets, compared to developing economies?
> - Is the financial system, as it is, designed to exclude some groups of people? Among those who choose to exclude themselves, what factors are influencing their decision to do so?

- What are the main benefits of bringing people into the financial system? And how do you ensure they remain banked, or included, once there?

This chapter will offer some definitions of these terms, by way of clarity. It will also consider some of the initiatives that aim to address financial exclusion – in particular, The World Bank's efforts in this area – find out how progress is being measured and, ultimately, assess how effective these initiatives are.

Defining financial exclusion

Let's take the word 'exclusion' and make sense of it within the context of the financial system.

At the most basic level, being excluded means being outside of something – this can be in a physical sense, such as being left out of a situation or a location, for instance. We often think of any form of exclusion as being inflicted on an individual or group of individuals – the exclusion is happening to people, perhaps due to circumstances outside of their control, but occasionally of their choosing.

It tends to have negative connotations, and is often associated with a form of discrimination – that idea of being on the outside looking in. Its opposite, inclusion, denotes being part of something or belonging – whether that is to a situation, a group or a system.

According to The World Bank's definition (2022a), financial inclusion means that individuals and businesses have access to 'useful and affordable financial products and services that meet their needs', including transactions, savings, payments, credit and insurance, 'delivered in a responsible and sustainable way'.

Leora Klapper, a lead economist in the Development Research Group at the World Bank and founder of the Global Findex Database – more on which later – explains that the World Bank's definition of financial inclusion is having an account at any regulated financial institution, whether that be a bank, microfinance institution, or mobile money service provider (Klapper, 2022).

'The definition of an account is 1) where you can store money, and 2) where you can send and receive electronic payments', Klapper says. 'People might have insurance products that are not associated with an account where they can store money in a safe place.'

She notes that in some countries an individual who has taken out a loan would be considered as included in the financial system. However, she adds that the World Bank would not use the same definition unless that person also has an account related to, or associated with, that loan.

Interestingly, the International Monetary Fund (IMF) and World Bank diverge on some of the criteria they use to define financial inclusion – and it comes down to mobile money accounts. Hakan Eroglu, former vice president, global lead, and Andrés Aguirre, senior managing consultant, both in the Open Banking and Open Data practice at Mastercard, point out this crucial difference in a report (Eroglu and Aguirre, 2023). It is important to note this difference in definitions because the two organizations' differing views on what constitutes financial inclusion skew the figures gathered in the Global Findex Database.

Mobile money, the report argues, is accessible to almost anyone, given that it requires only the most basic mobile phone with the ability to send and receive text messages (Eroglu and Aguirre, 2023). It works by simply linking a mobile phone number to a mobile money account to make and receive payments. In other words, this type of transaction does not require a smartphone or, indeed, an online bank account – and is also why mobile money accounts are not, technically, open banking (see section later in this chapter).

In 11 of the 23 sub-Saharan economies included in the World Bank's Findex Database, there are more adults with only a mobile money account than with a traditional bank account, which means that the 55 per cent share of adults with accounts in the region includes a 33 per cent share of adults with mobile money accounts (Eroglu and Aguirre, 2023). The World Bank includes that 33 per cent share in its definition of banked adults, while the International Monetary Fund (IMF) considers the same group as being unbanked – unless, of course, they also have a bank account accessible via a mobile app (Eroglu and Aguirre, 2023).

I agree with the IMF's criteria – so for the purposes of this book, I'm going to assume that those who use mobile money services, and have no current or savings account in their name, are unbanked.

So far, I've offered a rather simplistic explanation – in reality, financial exclusion is far more nuanced, taking a variety of forms. By unpacking the terms 'unbanked' and 'underbanked' we can shed yet more light on 'financial exclusion' and its widespread implications.

Who and why? The circumstances of the unbanked

The World Bank's definition of the unbanked is an individual without a formal account at a financial institution. They are someone without access to any kind of regulated financial services, which means they are generally reliant on what the World Bank considers are 'inconvenient and often risky means to manage their money' (World Bank, 2012).

Individuals who are unbanked typically face numerous barriers to accessing formal financial services. It will help to take a closer look at who might typically fall into the category of being unbanked. An obvious demographic is those who shun modern society and all forms of technology – this could be indigenous people, for example.

For some groups, their religious beliefs prevent them from, or are a barrier to, partaking in the wider financial system. In the Middle East and North Africa, commonly abbreviated to MENA, 95 per cent of adults describe themselves as 'religiously observant' and 93 per cent are Muslims. That is according to the MENA FinTech Association's November 2022 report, 'Embedded Finance in the MENA region', in which the authors write that religious 'compliance' has become a 'particularly major threat' to financial inclusion in the region. The authors reason that religion can engender scepticism of 'conventional banking solutions as they do not align with their beliefs' (Khan and Eroglu, 2022).

Then there are those who operate at the margins of society. Perhaps they get paid in cash for work – if they work at all – or receive welfare payments from the government withdrawn as cash. When we consider that more than 1 in 10 people worldwide live on less than $1.90 a day (UN Global Compact, nd), why would those individuals and households have any need for a bank account, let alone access to investment products and savings accounts?

Those same people are likely to be living 'hand to mouth' – the cash they receive in payment for work is used to buy goods (food) and services in shops, top up a prepayment meter to heat their homes, and settle a monthly or weekly rent directly with their landlord.

For some, the reason is geographical. In rural areas, often there are no banks in the vicinity and, if there are, the nearest branch could be miles away. Even in some urban areas now, many financial institutions lack a physical presence.

In many countries – both developed and emerging – being a woman is enough of a reason to remain outside the realms of the financial system. The majority of unbanked adults worldwide are women (World Bank, 2022b). This is explored further in Chapter 6, but suffice to say, many women live in places where they cannot or are not allowed to work, or where any money they do earn or assets they have are handed over to, or placed in the ownership of, their male partner or husband, or their father.

Of course, these are very general groupings and, in some cases, simplistic examples. Some of these factors are reason enough not to be part of the financial system, although for many individuals, it is likely that several of these factors will be at play.

Being unbanked in a developed market

An important myth to bust is that unbanked households are not a phenomenon of emerging economies. Take the United States: according to the 2021 Federal Deposit Insurance Corporation (FDIC) National Survey of Unbanked and Underbanked Households (FDIC, 2022), an estimated 4.5 per cent of US households, which equates to approximately 5.9 million, were unbanked in 2021, the lowest number since it began its survey in 2009. This means that no one in the household had a checking or savings account at a bank or credit union. In fact, the FDIC reports that between 2011, when the unbanked rate was at its highest level since the survey began, and 2021, the unbanked rate fell 3.7 percentage points, 'corresponding to an increase of approximately 5.0 million banked households'.

Any increase in the number of households joining the banking system is, of course, positive. However, those percentages are still shockingly high for a country that is one of the richest nations in the world.

The FDIC's breakdown of unbanked rates by 'household characteristics' sheds light on those most likely to fall outside of the financial system entirely in a developed market. Its findings showed that unbanked rates were higher among 'lower-income households, less educated households, Black households, Hispanic households, working-age households with a disability, and single-mother households'.

Perhaps the most telling statistic of all is that, according to the FDIC survey, the differences in unbanked rates between Black and White households, and between Hispanic and White households in 2021 were present 'at every income level'.

Some of the responses given when respondents are asked the reasons for not having a bank account reveal a split between those who would like to have an account in their name, but their circumstances and the expectation of the system prevent them from doing so, and those who have opted out based on certain beliefs or myths about the system.

The FDIC revealed that the reason most cited by unbanked households for not having an account, at 21.7 per cent, is 'don't have enough money to meet minimum balance requirements'. However, at 13.2 per cent – making it the second most-cited reason for not having an account in 2021 – was a lack of or no trust in the banks, followed by 8.4 per cent who said 'avoiding a bank gives more privacy'.

Who is underbanked – and why?

Just because some individuals have a current account and, therefore, no longer fall under the definition of being 'unbanked', they are by no means being fully served by the financial system. There are still numerous opportunities and circumstances for them to fall through the gaps, given that they often have little or no access to additional funds or financial services – such as savings or loans – to count on in an emergency.

This is not a phenomenon among those living in remote, rural areas in emerging countries – far from it. High-income countries are home to the 'underbanked' too. Take a walk down any high street or sidewalk in the UK or US, and it can be hard to comprehend how a household can remain so underserved by banks. After all, their presence is still felt in many urban areas and it is hard to avoid the marketing campaigns of the largest financial institutions – billboards, television adverts, online ads on social media sites – all of which seem to suggest there is a financial product for everyone. But while there are a range of products and services being offered by the largest banks that serve a wider range of people than ever before, there are myriad reasons some individuals can remain excluded from them – unable to access these offerings, even if they wanted to.

The FDIC survey (2022) paints a picture of the extent of being underbanked in the United States. As you would most likely expect in a developed country, there are more underbanked than unbanked households in the US – 14.1 per cent of US households, or roughly 18.7 million, were underbanked in 2021. Its definition is that a household is banked and, in the past 12 months, used 'at least' one non-bank transaction or credit product or service that it goes on to describe as being 'disproportionately' used by unbanked households to 'meet their transaction and credit needs'. Among the non-bank transactions included in that definition are money orders, check cashing or international remittances, and an example of a credit product is rent-to-own services, a pawn shop or auto title loans – the FDIC refers to these as 'nonbank credit'.

What about the use of bank accounts and online banking, given that these are often measures of being 'fully served' by the banking system?

Here, the FDIC survey showed that use of online banking as the 'primary method of account access' was much lower among underbanked households than among fully banked households – at 11.6 per cent versus 23.8 per cent respectively. The majority of all households – 96.1 per cent of underbanked households and 97.3 per cent of 'fully banked' households – used their bank accounts to pay bills or receive income. Tellingly, though, while 81.6 per cent of the latter group 'exclusively' used their bank accounts to conduct these transactions, only 38.1 per cent of underbanked households did so, according to FDIC.

Why is that relevant? Well, it potentially tells us that households are not making full use of banking services such as loans and investments. This could be because, as with the most-cited reason for being unbanked, households and the individuals within them do not meet the credit requirements stipulated by the financial institution. It also suggests some households' earnings/income are not enough to cover the cost of living each month, which is why underserved US households are relying on non-bank services, such as pawn shops, to cover an unexpected or short-term cost.

Financial resilience explored

Those that fall into the 'underbanked' category – whether in a developed country or emerging economy – can be said to have little financial resilience. The World Bank's Leora Klapper says that one test of resilience that is measured by the Global Findex database is whether an adult 'could come up with extra money' if required at short notice (Klapper, 2022).

The reality is that, according to the World Bank's Global Findex Database, 55 per cent of adults in developing economies could 'reliably access emergency money in a one-month timeline', but 45 per cent could not (Klapper and Gubbins, 2022). These findings were generated when the Global Findex Database 2021 edition asked adults from across geographies whether they could access extra money to the value of $3,300 in the US and $320 in India, which is equal to 5 per cent of each country's gross national income, within a 30-day period. If they were able to, the same adults were additionally asked how hard it would be to do so.

Klapper reports that Global Findex data reveals that, among poor adults across the G7 countries, 30 per cent of them say they couldn't come up with the money, which she asserts is still too high. 'One of the goals of financial inclusion should be to increase savings,' says Klapper, who refers to savings as 'a payment to oneself' (Klapper, 2022).

One effective way of doing this is through employer-driven auto-deposit saving schemes, 'when your employer deducts some money every month for your pension', which Klapper says research shows can have some success. In the UK, this is called auto-enrolment or workplace pensions and was introduced by the government in 2012. Under auto-enrolment, all employers are required by law to set up a workplace pension, put their qualifying employees into it and contribute to their pension savings (NOW Pensions, 2023). Since 2012, around 10 million people in the UK have been auto-enrolled and are now accumulating a pension pot 'with the help of their employer', according to NOW Pensions.

In Klapper's view, people's ability to set aside money in an additional savings or investment account is a 'critical piece' of financial inclusion, given that savings enable people to pull themselves out of poverty and to have the money to invest in their own businesses and education should they want to. In both emerging and developed economies, the ability to save comes back to resilience, the ultimate test of which, according to Klapper, is 'they [individuals] don't fall into poverty if there's a loss of job or death in the family'.

Financial exclusion, reliance on cash, and its links to crime

There is another, very urgent, reason to tackle financial exclusion and that is because it puts already vulnerable members of society at risk of exposure to, or participation in, illegal activities. In the case of heavily cash-based societies, individuals are more likely to be victims of crime.

Adults unable to access credit by legal and formal means in the UK – such as via their bank or another regulated lender – often turn to illegal methods of obtaining loans, called loan sharks. In England, it is estimated that as many as 1.08 million people are borrowing from an illegal money lender (Centre for Social Justice, 2022). These illegal lenders can masquerade as a legitimate business in some circumstances, or they may be part of organized crime groups. Unfortunately, borrowers are often subjected to abusive behaviour, particularly when they struggle to repay the lender, including demands for 'payment in kind'. The Centre for Social Justice reports 'numerous cases...

in which illegal lenders have demanded a borrower support their business' by delivering drugs or 'referring new clients to them' (Centre for Social Justice, 2022). Those who are able to make repayments are typically subjected to 'arbitrary' and 'extortionate' terms by the loan shark and payments can be prolonged for many years.

Let's be clear: people only turn to loan sharks as a last resort, after having exhausted other possible avenues. Among loan shark victims, 80 per cent 'who attempted to borrow from legal sources first are refused', while 44 per cent of victims who try to borrow go to a bank first and 27 per cent try a high-cost short-term credit provider (Centre for Social Justice, 2022).

Among those who have been declined a bank account, loan or other form of credit in the past 24 months, 9 per cent went on to borrow money from a loan shark (Plend, 2023). Worryingly, some loan shark debtors are already in debt to a regulated lender – 'a quarter of regulated loan holders are not confident that they will be able to pay off their current regulated loan debt so may be using loan sharks to cover these costs' (Plend, 2023).

Individuals who are completely unbanked and receive payment for work in cash are at risk of being a victim of crime in other ways. For example, if someone is paid a monthly or weekly salary in cash and must travel with this cash on their person and store it in their home, they are likely to be vulnerable to muggings or theft. Businesses that keep large amounts of cash on their premises also put employees' safety at risk.

According to research by the United Nations-based Better Than Cash Alliance – which advocates for digital payments – of workers surveyed in Senegal, 82 per cent said they felt 'more secure with digital wages, thanks to not having to travel with their wages on payday' (Chaintreau et al., 2022).

Global initiatives to tackle financial exclusion and promote inclusion

Financial exclusion is harmful not only to the individuals it affects, but to society and the planet as a whole. To that end, there are initiatives at the international, national and local levels that directly address and resolve the problems at the heart of this scourge on society.

'Financial inclusion is a movement for helping the underbanked and the unbanked make better use of financial services', says Reuben Piryatinsky, the chief executive officer of Altitude Consulting, a fin-tech consultancy that helps US and Canadian financial institutions adopt open banking (Piryatinsky, 2023).

He says that, in the case of the unbanked, inclusion is about 'ensuring they have access to financial services' and, when it comes to the underbanked, ensuring 'they have access to financial services that better suit their needs, so that they can do more of their banking with financial institutions or fintechs'.

Promoting financial inclusion is an imperative of many of the United Nations' Sustainable Development Goals, which were adopted by all UN member states in September 2015 (United Nations, 2020) as part of a 15-year plan to deliver on the goals by 2030.

The eighth goal sets out to 'Promote sustained, inclusive and sustainable economic growth, full and productive employment and decent work for all'. That in itself is a bold commitment, under-pinning which is the need to 'improve access to financial services' in order to achieve that 'sustained and inclusive' economic growth that continues to elude so many countries.

This supra-national initiative can only truly work with coordination from the bottom up. This means that financial inclusion initiatives need to start at the local government level, right up to national governments, policy makers and regulators, in order to feed into global change. It is also important to assess the impact that the Covid-19 pandemic had on financial inclusion efforts.

The World Bank's Global Findex Database – its origins and progress

Tracking the levels of global financial inclusion has, historically, been challenging. In 2011, the World Bank launched the Global Findex Database to provide a 'definitive source of data on the ways in which adults around the world use financial services, from payments to savings and borrowing, and manage financial events' (World Bank, 2022b). In addition, 'Global Findex data are used to track progress toward the United Nations Sustainable Development Goals'.

Leora Klapper, who is one of the founders and authors of the Database, says: 'When we started [the Global Findex Database] there had been country-level surveys, like the FinScope surveys in sub-Saharan Africa, for example, but they weren't really comparable across countries.'

She explains that the initial goal with the Findex Database was threefold: to collect measurements of financial inclusion that countries could compare to other countries in their region; to identify gaps in the data, such as for women, poor and rural adults and income groups; and to track progress over time.

This dataset obviously paints a picture, to an extent, but does not tell the full story. So, in 2014, the length of the questionnaire was doubled, to focus on digital payments. 'The most recent data collected in 2021 includes extensive modules on digital payments', Klapper says.

The 2021 Findex Database also captures the impact that the pandemic had on levels of inclusion – generally speaking, it was a largely positive one, given that it prompted uptake of digital payments at a much faster pace than before Covid-19.

Over the years, since the Findex Database was launched, it has shown that global levels of financial inclusion are going in the right direction. In the 10 years spanning 2011 to 2021, account ownership around the world increased by 50 per cent, from 51 per cent of adults to 76 per cent (World Bank, 2022b). This figure includes those who had an account at a regulated institution, such as a credit union, microfinance institution or mobile money service provider.

Whereas, up until 2017, the World Bank reports that this growth in account ownership was mainly concentrated in China and India, since then it has been more widespread across the developing economies.

Rise – and fall – of the machines (ATMs)

Over the past few years, the number of bank branches and ATMs has been in decline. This is largely due to a combination of cost-cutting measures by the banks (IMF, 2022) and what is seen as reduced demand for these types of services. Let's face it, in many economies banking online has become the norm and there are fewer instances where cash is required to pay for a service or purchase. In its Financial Access Survey 2022, the International Monetary Fund (IMF) reports that, within the high-income country group, European economies experienced the largest reduction in the number of ATMs, amid a rapid rise in the adoption of digital payments (IMF, 2022).

The IMF states that the number of traditional financial access points, such as bank branches, has decreased, largely due to the increased use of digitalized financial services by individuals.

It is worth noting that, once again, online banking is not the only form of digital finance being accounted for in this survey. The IMF reports that the number of mobile money agents per 100,000 adults almost doubled worldwide between 2019 and 2021, from around 450 to 880, and that this is mostly down to increases in Africa and Asia.

In Latin America, meanwhile, and in other low- and middle-income countries, bank branches have been replaced by growing numbers of what is known as 'branchless agent banking'. The IMF defines this as 'an innovation in the banking sector to expand the provision of financial services beyond traditional branch networks'. It cites Colombia, Honduras and Peru as examples, where 'the retail agent network expanded to reach more people in areas with low financial access, facilitating the distribution of social programs during the pandemic'.

So, more adults are becoming banked – but are they still underserved?

The Covid-19 pandemic and its impact on take-up of digital financial services

When the Covid-19 pandemic hit in early 2020, few people could have predicted how far-reaching the consequences of the deadly virus would be. As people's worst fears were confirmed and governments began closing borders and locking down countries, and death tolls rose, it was hard to imagine that any 'good' could come out of such horror and fear. As the nationwide lockdowns continued across the world, the effects of the pandemic – both good and bad, positive and negative – began to be better documented.

The efforts of pharmaceutical companies to develop and roll out Covid-19 vaccines at such speed and scale welcomed in a new era of science and healthcare, and saw countries collaborate as never before. The rise of working from home proved that individuals and companies could, and in some cases, should, work more flexibly – and so, hybrid working was born. Lives – both working and domesticated – were upended and underwent the biggest transformation many of us will ever witness.

Among the 'good' to come out of the pandemic were changes to the way in which money was distributed to individuals, and then stored and accessed by those same people. The digitalization of banking and payments was sped up – because it had to be. This is well documented in the World Bank's Global Findex Database 2021, which captured these changes as they happened – hence the report's title, 'Financial Inclusion, Digital Payments, and Resilience in the Age of COVID-19'.

The pandemic provides the backdrop against which levels of global financial inclusion were last measured, given that the Global Findex 2021 survey was conducted at its height. The Global Findex Database refers to Covid-19 as 'a crisis that further mobilized financial inclusion efforts across the world through several mechanisms, including the emergency relief payments that governments sent to accounts'. This is significant because, as the authors of the survey state, receipt of payments into an account is a 'catalyst' for or 'gateway' to the use of other financial services, whether to borrow, save or store money.

The number of individuals who made digital payments for the first time during the pandemic is quite phenomenal and reveals just how much the social distancing restrictions that were put in place by governments accelerated adoption of digital payments. The Global Findex 2021 survey revealed that, in developing economies in 2021, 18 per cent of adults paid utility bills directly from an account – about one-third of these did so for the first time after the onset of the pandemic. The survey also revealed the extent to which the share of adults making a digital merchant payment increased after the outbreak of Covid-19 – this is best illustrated by numbers out of India and China.

In India, 80 million adults made their first digital merchant payment during the pandemic, and in China, 82 per cent of adults made this type of payment in 2021, 11 per cent of those, or 100 million people, doing so for the first time after the pandemic started.

What is not yet known, because it has not been measured, is how lasting the effects of the Covid-19 pandemic will be on financial inclusion. The next Global Findex Database will be able to tell us more, of course. In the meantime, it is on governments, regulators and financial institutions to capitalize on the adoption of digital payments to enable further financial inclusion.

- How did your organization/company respond during the pandemic? Did it change the way you pay your employees or deliver welfare payments to citizens, in the case of government organizations?
- What learnings did you extrapolate from the pandemic to more effectively and efficiently serve individuals?
- Is digitalization of banking services still a priority or has it fallen by the wayside since the end of the lockdowns? If so, what is needed to push it back up the agenda and adapt it to a post-pandemic world?

Who is still 'underserved' and why?

So far, so positive – more individuals around the world are now 'banked', according to official definitions. However, there are still millions who remain 'underbanked'. Understanding why is going to be key to targeting those groups with specific products and services; as you'll see later in the book, open banking is helping to serve these niche demographic groups that incumbent banks are unable to cater to. There is a lot more to unpack here and I will do so further on in the book. At this point, let's start with a basic breakdown of who is still underbanked and what is keeping them there.

Women remain hugely underserved, despite efforts at all levels – international, national and regional – and despite the Covid-19 pandemic. During the pandemic, in many countries, government subsidies and loans were deposited directly into an online bank account, giving women access to an account and money of their own for the first time. The gender gap in financial access persisted in many economies in 2021, according to the IMF's Financial Access Survey (2022), which reports that women's account ownership, savings and outstanding loans were all lower than men's. For more on female financial exclusion and the gender gap and its repercussions, go to Chapter 6.

Often, individuals remain underserved by financial services because even if they receive funds digitally, into an online account, they then withdraw that money as cash. There are a few factors at play here – they need all of that money to pay for essentials, so there is no chance they'll end up with a surplus at the end of the week or month to transfer to a savings account, for example. Another reason for this behaviour is a lack of knowledge about how to make better use of online banking and other services. So there is an education piece required here – this is an area where banks can do better but where fintechs have stepped in, very often, to provide the education that individuals so often need on how to bank.

The World Bank's Global Findex Database 2021 (World Bank, 2022b) points to the need for formal identification to expand financial inclusion. After all, as the authors of the report state, 'identification is almost always a requirement for opening an account', so it is therefore 'necessary for the success of national strategies to expand financial inclusion, especially among women, rural dwellers and poor adults'.

Digital identity in India – has Aadhaar increased financial inclusion?

India is set to overtake China as the world's most populous country, with the most up-to-date estimate putting its population at over 1.4 billion. China's population is also above 1.4 billion, but while the number of people in China is in decline, in India it is growing (Silver et al., 2023). The population of India overshadows both Europe and the Americas, where there are 744 million and 1.04 billion people living respectively (Silver et al., 2023).

To its credit, then, India has rolled out a nationwide digital identity infrastructure that the Government of India claims has achieved nearly 100 per cent coverage. The Unique Identification Authority of

India, or UIDAI, states that its vision is to 'empower residents of India with a unique identity and digital platform to authenticate anytime, anywhere'. This digital identity number and platform is called myAadhaar, or simply Aadhaar. Every individual in India is issued with a card with a 12-digit ID number that is entirely unique to them. By the end of January 2023, UIDAI reported Aadhaar saturation of 94.65 per cent among all age groups, with the saturation level among the adult population of India, 'now near universal' (UIDAI, 2023).

What does this have to do with financial inclusion? Well, India has implemented this infrastructure, in part, to be able to provide 'efficient, transparent and targeted delivery of subsidies, benefits and services' to Indian residents. Its Aadhaar e-KYC – which stands for Know Your Customer – service has been designed to help banking and non-banking financial services providers deliver a better customer experience. As of January 2023, 170 entities, of which 105 were banks, were live on e-KYC, with the adoption of this service said to have 'significantly reduced customer acquisition cost of entities like financial institutions' (UIDAI, 2023).

Moreover, the Aadhaar Enabled Payment System, or AePS, 'is enabling financial inclusion for those at the bottom of the income pyramid' (UIDAI, 2023). The UIDAI reported that by the end of January 2023, cumulatively 1.6 billion 'last mile banking transactions' were made possible through AePS and the network of micro-ATMs in the country.

Rolling out the world's largest digital ID system is no mean feat. But has it really worked? After all, India is a vast country – surely, some people have slipped through the cracks in the system, as it were. And those who do fall through the cracks may end up considerably worse off, or even dead, if some reports in Indian media are to be believed. One such report claimed that 'of 42 hunger-related deaths' since 2017, 25 are 'linked to Aadhaar issues' (*The Wire* staff, 2018). These are cases where, reportedly, 'cardless individuals [are] starving to death because they could not access benefits to which they were entitled' (Thornhill, 2021).

In 2019 – 10 years on from the introduction of the nationwide biometric ID system – research was conducted to ascertain just how successful Aadhaar had been, but equally to identify its failures and where the system could improve. The subsequent State of Aadhaar 2019 report reveals the findings, drawn from 167,000 residents in India (Totapally et al., 2019). Among the positives highlighted in the report are that 95 per cent of adults have Aadhaar and use it, on average, once a month, with satisfaction levels running high – 92 per cent of people are 'very satisfied or somewhat satisfied with Aadhaar'. Importantly, the report found evidence that Aadhaar has supported inclusion, with 49 per cent using their digital ID to access services such as rations, bank accounts and social pensions for the first time. Specifically, of that percentage, 47 per cent used it to access a bank account for the very first time. The World Bank's Global Findex Database 2021 (World Bank, 2022b) reports that between 2011 and 2017, Aadhaar helped drive account ownership up to 80 per cent of adults, from 35 per cent.

However, in the most serious cases, Aadhaar exacerbated exclusion, according to the State of Aadhaar Report (Totapally et al., 2019). In the report's conclusion, the authors found that those individuals who have slipped through the net and do not have Aadhaar or 'who face difficulties using it are often those most in need of government support'. Plus, when it doesn't work and there are system errors and failures, it most affects those who are already vulnerable – the report identifies lower enrolment rates among marginalized groups, including homeless people, with errors more likely among those who are less educated.

- Both the UK and Australia have been mulling nationwide digital identity schemes. Should a digital identity scheme be a requirement for all countries, given its effectiveness in India in helping individuals to access banking?
- How can governments learn from India's Aadhaar system to ensure the most vulnerable are onboarded or enrolled – in terms of both design of the system, and communication/marketing around it?

What is mobile money and is it open banking?

Throughout this chapter, there have been a few references to mobile money. But this is the last time you will likely read about mobile money in this book because it is not a service delivered as a result of open banking.

Before embarking on the next chapter, which introduces the concept of open banking and the technology behind it, it is vital to clarify what mobile money is and why it is not open banking.

The International Monetary Fund provides a neat summary of mobile money in its Mobile Money Note 2019 (IMF, 2019) as 'a pay-as-you-go digital medium of exchange and store of value using mobile money accounts which is typically offered by a mobile network operator (MNO) or another entity in partnership with an MNO'. The IMF clarifies that while mobile banking and mobile wallets are 'linked to traditional bank accounts, mobile money is not'.

Clearly, mobile money is having a huge impact on levels of financial inclusion, particularly across Africa, as the World Bank's Global Findex Database identifies. However, there are limitations to the impact that mobile money can have. While it does help individuals access some financial products they might otherwise have not, without the need to open a bank account they remain underserved by the financial system.

As Mastercard's Eroglu and Aguirre (2023) put it, 'Access to financial services is not as simple as access to a mobile device, and a mobile phone with stored funds does not automatically equate with financial inclusion' – this is in line with the IMF's view of what constitutes being fully banked.

So, why is mobile money not open banking? Well, it comes down to the fact that it doesn't require individuals to open a bank account in order to transfer funds. Open banking – as the next chapter sets out – is all about opening up access to the data held by the major banks, with consumer permissions, in order to stimulate the provision of new financial products and services.

Summary

Financial exclusion is complex and those who are unbanked perhaps do not always fit the expected criteria. However, throughout this chapter a picture has emerged of certain demographic groups being far more vulnerable than others. Geography, race, gender, education, employment status all play a part. What is clear is that more of the global population is banked now than at any other time. Perhaps the biggest challenge is changing mindsets, from perceiving current account ownership as simply another storage system to instead using it as a stepping stone to unlock numerous other benefits through different products and services to individuals.

By scrutinizing who is affected by financial exclusion and why, the financial system – and its numerous players – can better serve those individuals through open banking (see Chapter 2). Hopefully, this chapter has dispelled the myth that those who fall outside the financial system are typically living in emerging economies or in very rural areas. While this chapter has provided a somewhat in-depth look at the various demographics and circumstances of the financially excluded and underserved, in Chapters 4 and 5, those individuals will be further brought to life with case studies.

The onset of Covid-19 clearly jumpstarted the digital financial journey for many people. But it also raises questions about why we needed a global pandemic for this to happen, particularly given that economic inclusion is one of the UN's Sustainable Development Goals. Whatever the reasons, it is vital that banks, fintechs, governments, regulators and central banks build on the progress made during the pandemic. It is on all of these institutions to continue to increase the numbers of banked individuals worldwide and also ensure they remain banked and increasingly well served. As it stands, financial resilience is the preserve of only a few in society, not all. That needs to change because, as we've discovered, without savings or access to credit, individuals have no choice and are far more susceptible to poverty, to crime and to a life of hardship.

References

Centre for Social Justice (2022) Swimming with Sharks: Tackling illegal money lending in England, www.centreforsocialjustice.org.uk/wp-content/uploads/2022/03/CSJ-Illegal-lending-paper.pdf (archived at https://perma.cc/K28C-VCSB)

Chaintreau, M, Pascal Mvondo, J and Ibrahim, F (2022) How to scale up digital wages in line with the UN Principles for Responsible Digital Payments, Better Than Cash Alliance, 30 June, www.betterthancash.org/news/learning-series-how-to-scale-up-digital-wages-in-line-with-the-un-principles-for-responsible-digital-payments# (archived at https://perma.cc/AZ6Y-LLKU)

Eroglu, H and Aguirre, A (2023) Purposeful and profitable: Financial inclusion via open banking around the world, Mastercard, www.mastercardservices.com/en/advisors/open-banking-open-data/insights/purposeful-profitable-financial-inclusion-open-banking (archived at https://perma.cc/9SKX-ZZF4)

Federal Deposit Insurance Corporation (2022) 2021 FDIC National Survey of Unbanked and Underbanked Households, www.fdic.gov/analysis/household-survey/index.html (archived at https://perma.cc/D27N-Q5YY)

International Monetary Fund (2019) Mobile Money Note 2019, https://data.imf.org/api/document/download?key=62780598 (archived at https://perma.cc/YFX8-CAXA)

International Monetary Fund (2022) Financial Access Survey: 2022 Trends and Developments, https://data.imf.org/api/document/download?key=64273606 (archived at https://perma.cc/4Z7Z-6UGZ)

Khan, N and Eroglu, H (2022) Embedded Finance in the MENA region, https://go.mastercardservices.com/Embedded-finance-report (archived at https://perma.cc/7XVH-FT82)

Klapper, L (2022) Igniting SDG process through digital financial inclusion, Development Research Group at The World Bank, 2655SDG_Compendium_Digital_Financial_Inclusion_September_2018.pdf

Klapper, L and Gubbins, P (2022) To build finance resilience, we need to promote savings, World Economic Forum, www.weforum.org/agenda/2022/07/financial-resilience-promote-savings/ (archived at https://perma.cc/3QU3-BVQV)

NOW Pensions (2023) What is auto-enrolment? www.nowpensions.com/employers/learn-about-workplace-pensions/what-is-auto-enrolment/ (archived at https://perma.cc/EC77-N6L3)

Piryatinsky, R (2023) Chief Executive Officer, Altitude Consulting. Interview with Ellie Duncan

Plend (2023) Financial Inclusion Report 2023 – The impact of a cost of living credit crunch, https://plend.co.uk/blog/plend-financial-inclusion-report-2023/ (archived at https://perma.cc/XPX3-GRHT)

Silver, L, Huang, C and Clancy, L (2023) Key facts as India surpasses China as the world's most populous country, Pew Research Centre, 9 February, www.pewresearch.org/fact-tank/2023/02/09/key-facts-as-india-surpasses-china-as-the-worlds-most-populous-country/ (archived at https://perma.cc/BK9V-QQZ2)

The Wire staff (2018) Of 42 'hunger-related' deaths since 2017, 25 'Linked to Aadhaar issues', The Wire, 21 September, https://thewire.in/rights/of-42-hunger-related-deaths-since-2017-25-linked-to-aadhaar-issues (archived at https://perma.cc/NT8T-9KT4)

Thornhill, J (2021) India's all-encompassing ID system holds warnings for the rest of the world, *Financial Times*, 11 November, www.ft.com/content/337f6d6e-7301-4ef4-a26d-a4e62f602947 (archived at https://perma.cc/5642-CAL9)

Totapally, S, Sonderegger, P, Rao, P, Gosselt, J and Gupta, G (2019) State of Aadhaar: A people's perspective: 2019 edition, https://stateofaadhaar.in/download-reports.php

UIDAI (2023) 200 crore Aadhaar authentication transactions carried out in January 2023 [Press release] UIDAI, 28 February, www.uidai.gov.in/images/Press_Release_28223.pdf (archived at https://perma.cc/9H3R-RTAB)

United Nations (2020) Sustainable Development Goals: 17 Goals to Transform our World, www.un.org/en/exhibits/page/sdgs-17-goals-transform-world (archived at https://perma.cc/G674-5AFK)

UN Global Compact (nd)) Strong markets and strong societies go hand in hand, https://unglobalcompact.org/what-is-gc/our-work/social/poverty#:~:text=More%20than%20700%20million%20people, less%20than%20%241.90%20a%20day (archived at https://perma.cc/HJ2Z-H8R8)

World Bank (2022a) Financial inclusion: Overview, www.worldbank.org/en/topic/financialinclusion/overview#1 (archived at https://perma.cc/ZZ6V-65JA)

World Bank (2022b) The Global Findex Database 2021: Financial inclusion, digital payments and resilience in the age of COVID-19 www.worldbank.org/en/publication/globalfindex (archived at https://perma.cc/R99G-MVLH)

World Bank (2012) Who are the unbanked? www.worldbank.org/en/news/infographic/2012/04/19/who-are-the-unbanked (archived at https://perma.cc/32HA-W847)

The advent of open banking: what is open banking?

02

Introduction

The term 'open banking' may already be familiar to you, or it may be an entirely alien concept. So, this chapter will explain what is meant by 'open banking', some of the ways in which it can be implemented and why countries might take different approaches.

CHAPTER OBJECTIVES

Some of the questions that need answering are:

- Why has open banking been introduced, and why do the reasons for adopting it vary from country to country?
- How does an open banking ecosystem hand consumers control of their data and why is that positive?
- Do consumers need to know what open banking is?
- How has open banking given rise to fintechs and, indeed, what is a fintech?

What is open banking and why do we need it?

'Consumer data is disparate and underused, guarded by incumbents like dragons hoarding treasure in caves' (Hallas et al, 2023).

Fortunately, we don't have to travel back very far through the annals of history – or confront any dragons in caves – to discover the origins of open banking, because it is a fairly modern concept.

In its simplest form, open banking has been designed to help consumers give consent for the data that, historically, the largest banks have held on their customers, to be shared with, and handled by, other firms. With the ability to port this data, consumers and small- and medium-sized businesses (SMBs) are able to build up a more detailed picture of their finances. Perhaps most significantly, this is real-time data, as opposed to historic financial data often relied upon by credit reference agencies, for example, to build an individual's credit score.

Having open banking-enabled data at their fingertips is useful in a number of ways: it allows individuals to be able to budget, or give permission for their data to be shared, so that financial services providers can make more informed and accurate lending decisions, for example.

It has also given rise to other types of regulated financial institutions, such as 'challenger' banks, or digital banks, as well as fintechs, and apps that provide budgeting and personal financial management tools.

The authors of a report published by UK-based independent advocacy group Coadec call open banking 'aspirational' on the basis that it does put people in control of their own data (Hallas et al, 2023).

It also spurs innovation and competition in the banking sector – the UK is probably one of the best examples of that, because it is the main reason open banking was mandated in the country (see Chapter 5). Analysis by Accenture estimates that $416 billion in revenue is 'at stake' for banking and other financial services providers in the transition to open banking (Mallick et al, 2021). This makes it even more critical that not only is it implemented effectively, but that the financial services ecosystem continues to embrace the ongoing benefits of open banking. Let's be clear, this is not a one-off exercise – open banking is an entirely new way of offering financial products and services that, done right, has the potential to cast the net wider to include the financially excluded. Importantly, open banking should not stymie innovation and profit – in fact, it should stimulate both.

Which data sets and how?

There is far more to open banking than the term 'data sharing' suggests. After all, that reads as rather generic and simplistic. It's also time to introduce the first open banking-related acronyms – it didn't take too long for some financial services jargon to come into play.

To get to grips with the basics of open banking, there are two terms to familiarize yourself with and understand: Account Information Service Providers, or AISPs, and Payment Initiation Service Providers, commonly referred to as PISPs. If open banking is all about consumers – and businesses – being able to consent to having their account information shared, then AISPs and PISPs are the conduits for moving the data.

I like to think of it in terms of plumbing: when we turn on a tap, we expect water to come out via the pipework. The AISPs and PISPs are the pipework or conduit for open banking. However, it is not possible to be both – in other words, a provider must register as either an AISP or PISP. Why? Because, essentially, they do slightly different things.

Let's start with what they have in common. Both AISPs and PISPs 'build and maintain the digital pipes that allow data and payments to be securely requested from banks using open banking APIs' (Costello, 2021).

Application Programming Interfaces (APIs), often referred to simply as open APIs, are the software or channel that allows these third-party providers to request data from financial institutions and then transport it safely and securely to whichever institution is requesting it – a lender, for example, or a financial management app.

AISPs are authorized to retrieve account data provided by banks and financial institutions, while PISPs are authorized to initiate payments into or out of a user's account (Costello, 2021).

As those definitions suggest, AISPs can retrieve the data but cannot do much with it, while PISPs appear to be doing a bit more legwork, as it were. However, it is worth reiterating that both AISPs and PISPs are only doing what they have been told to by an individual – open banking is consumer-permissioned data sharing. To some degree then, AISPs are limited in what they can do – 'they can look at account information, but they can't touch it' (Costello, 2021). This form of open banking is commonly known as read-only access.

Many countries implement open banking by starting only with read-only access, before later introducing 'read-write' access. The Kingdom of Saudi Arabia is one such example of this approach to open banking. The Saudi Central Bank issued an Open Banking Framework in November 2022 which stipulated that the first version of open banking in the Kingdom required banks and fintechs to focus on account information services, while the second version, which had a later deadline for those same financial institutions to meet, would focus on payment initiation services (Duncan, 2023a).

Top Tips

In light of this section on APIs, it might be worth asking yourself a few questions about whether your business should be using open APIs and, if so, what the right API initiative might look like:

- If a provider cannot open APIs directly, can you outsource to a third party? Weigh up the likely costs of this and whether the business has the resources to oversee this relationship and process.

- Opening APIs is not a one-off tick-box exercise, but a longer-term initiative that will need continual investment and resources devoted to it. Can you provide these to ensure successful implementation?

- Which people/job roles do you require to fulfil an open API initiative and where will you source the skillset – either internally or externally? What does that skillset look like exactly?

A paper published by independent thinktank CGAP, which stands for Consultative Group to Assist the Poor, sets out three S's for successful implementation of APIs in emerging markets in particular, although they also apply more broadly (2020):

- Ensure APIs connect to strategic business priorities, then align resources accordingly.
- Keep it simple: start small, configure to learn, and iterate.
- Aim for self-service: make the API testing sandbox open and ensure the transition to 'live' is as seamless as possible.

The alternative: Screen scraping

In jurisdictions where open banking has not yet been mandated or implemented by market participants – and even where it has – there are other ways for third parties to collect account and transaction data from financial institutions. After all, we live in an information age, and it is certainly not the case that, before open banking, consumers' data was unable to be shared. It's just that the method of gathering that data, commonly called screen scraping, is less secure than open banking. This is because screen scraping relies on the individual actively sharing their login details or credentials to a third-party provider (TPP), essentially exposing it to more risk than would be the case via open banking. There is nothing wrong with screen scraping, per se. It is another method of porting data and, therefore, being able to offer consumers a greater range of financial services and products.

Perhaps screen scraping is best thought of as a process of collecting data that does not put the consumer first – or at least, not their safety. Screen scraping can also leave banks vulnerable to security risks and data breaches.

The authors of a Capgemini article on open banking versus screen scraping put it in context of the European Union's Second Payment Services Directive, abbreviated to PSD2, which aimed to 'bolster data sharing' between banks and third parties, 'while increasing the safety standards for customers' (van Putten et al, 2022). It did this by steering banks to 'develop APIs to give TPPs with a PSD2 license controlled and safe access to their customers' bank accounts'. The key words in that explanation are 'controlled' and 'safe' – this essentially sums up the intention of open banking. If consumers' financial data is going to be shared – and it is – then it needs to be done in a way that is standardized.

The Capgemini authors neatly explain how screen scraping differs in this regard, writing that once a consumer has given their login credentials to a third party, 'the TPP then sends a software robot to the bank's app or website to log in on behalf of the customer and retrieve data and/or initiative a payment'. Ultimately, in this data-gathering scenario, banks have 'less control over the data retrieved', because it may go beyond account data that comes under PSD2 regulation to also include any customer data that is available.

If screen scraping has such a poor reputation, why is it still happening? In many cases, because it is the only way to retrieve consumers' account and transaction data if open banking has not been implemented. Or, in cases where it has but banks are yet to build the APIs, perhaps due to prohibitive costs. In Canada, where open banking is yet to be formally implemented, screen scraping remains the main way in which TPPs get access to data. It is therefore why many in the financial services industry in Canada would like open banking to be progressed with more urgency, given how insecure the practice of screen scraping is. For more on Canada's open banking journey, go to Chapter 7.

Two types of implementation: market versus regulation

Broadly, there are two main ways in which to implement an open banking ecosystem: countries can take a regulatory-driven approach, or they can choose a market-driven approach. Among the countries and continents that have opted for the former are the UK, Europe and Australia. Meanwhile, the US has adopted a market-driven open banking model, albeit this is about to change – about which, more later. The Canadian Government's Department of Finance has proposed something more akin to a 'hybrid' Open Banking implementation, often referred to as a 'made-in-Canada approach'.

Needless to say, there are pros and cons to each approach – in Chapter 5 of this book we'll go on to explore in more detail the UK's open banking implementation and, before that, we'll consider which method of adoption might be best designed to promote financial inclusion (see Chapter 3).

My own observation, having written about open banking for the past few years, is that the approach that each country takes is a combination of a few factors. In part, it reflects something of that country's culture, but it is also reflective of the region's existing banking sector – its size and reach – as well as the relationships financial institutions have historically had with the population.

Let's take the United States, which has relied on market forces to encourage uptake of open banking by banks, credit unions and fintechs. Partly, this has worked up until now because banking in the US is a vast marketplace, comprising large banks, community or regional banks, and credit unions, challenger banks and fintechs. All of these institutions also have to serve a huge number of people – the US population topped 331 million in 2021 (Duffin, 2022). The industry has to remain competitive in order to retain customers, and innovation is the key here – the banking industry can ill afford to stand still.

According to Statista Research Department (2022), there were 4,236 FDIC-insured commercial banks in the US in 2021. FDIC stands for Federal Deposit Insurance Corporation, which Statista defines as 'an agency that insures the banking system in the US'. That figure has declined since the year 2000, though, when there were more than 8,300 FDIC-insured banks in the country, with the decline largely due to consolidation and in the aftermath of the Financial Crisis of 2008–09.

There are three major banks that dominate US market share, however: JPMorgan Chase, Bank of America and Citigroup, as of December 2022. Of these, JPMorgan Chase is the largest, ranking first not only in terms of market share of total assets, but also with 'the largest market capitalization and value of total and domestic deposits' (Statista, 2023). Interestingly, between 2013 and 2020, JPMorgan Chase generated the majority of its global net revenue from the consumer and community banking sector (Statista, 2023). This was overtaken by the bank's corporate and investment banking division in 2021 (Statista, 2023).

Statista reports that the value of assets of JPMorgan Chase was equivalent to 8.26 per cent of the total value of assets of all FDIC-insured institutions in the United States. By comparison, Bank of America and Citigroup accounted for 6.24 per cent and 4.56 per cent of total US banking assets, respectively (Statista, 2023).

To get a sense of the scale of the US banking system, let's introduce some perspective. As of 2021, official International Monetary Fund figures put the number of banks in Canada at 81, while the UK had 311 (Fitzpatrick and Hollerith, 2023).

Regulation-led open banking

In the immediate aftermath of the financial crisis of 2008–09, the banking sector came under close scrutiny from regulators, particularly in the UK. The UK's open banking implementation is covered in much more detail in Chapter 5 but, in short, the decision to mandate open banking came out of a retail banking market investigation in the UK. In stark contrast to the US banking sector, the Competition and Markets Authority's (CMA) investigation concluded there was a lack of competition in UK retail banking. To remedy this, the CMA ordered the UK's major banks – among them HSBC, Barclays, NatWest, Lloyds Bank and Santander, which became known as the CMA9 – to adopt open banking.

The regulator saw the introduction of an open banking regime as an opportunity to stimulate competition by mandating the nine largest current account holders to open up their data. It is a very different approach from the market-led implementation, but certainly one more suited to the banking environment in the UK at the time. This regulatory-led approach relies on a 'roadmap' of deadlines for financial institutions to meet and a set of industry standards to work towards. Another key feature that differentiates the UK's approach is oversight and accountability – the CMA set up the Open Banking Implementation Entity, or OBIE, to establish the roadmap for UK banks to comply with and to act as 'overseer'.

Australia opted for a similar approach, although it is important to note that open banking in Australia is one part of a much wider data-sharing regime, called the Consumer Data Right, or CDR. While the CDR has other Australian sectors and industries in its sights, including insurance and energy, the initial implementation is focused on banking. The Australian Competition and Consumer Commission is the lead regulator of the CDR, which means that if Australians choose to share their data, they can only do so with ACCC-accredited third parties (Australian Banking Association, 2023).

Australia's open banking regime officially kicked off on 1 July 2020, with the major banks required prior to that to meet deadlines relating to the provision of data under the labels 'Phase 1' and 'Phase 2' products. Phase 1 essentially covers product reference data from current accounts, savings accounts, transaction accounts, and credit and charge cards, while Phase 2 expanded to include home loan, personal loan and mortgage offset accounts. So, when 1 July 2020 came round, the incumbents were ready to provide product reference for 'Phase 3' products, such as business finance, investment loans, retirement savings accounts, asset finance and foreign currency accounts.

This section on implementations is really an overview of how the two main approaches can look in different countries. Their effectiveness in terms of promoting financial inclusion will be explored in Chapter 3.

All in it together – banks and fintechs in partnership

One key aspect of open banking, if it is to work effectively, is collaboration between banks and fintechs. This is regardless of whether a country decides to implement consumer-directed finance through its regulators or adopt open banking through market-driven standards.

It is obvious, really: incumbent banks have the distribution and reach, as well as the existing clients, while fintechs have the agility, meaning they can bring new products and services to market faster. In many countries, the existing banks also have the trust and loyalty of individuals, which fintechs are yet to win.

Banks can provide what we might call 'mass market' banking products and services, while fintechs have the ability to serve perhaps a single demographic or consumer niche. In many instances then, the larger banks stand to benefit from fintechs' nimbleness and technology, and in turn, fintechs might need any number of resources that an established banking group can provide – investment, compliance or distribution network.

Actually, though, that distribution need works both ways, as fintechs can serve parts of the retail market that banks cannot. After all, banks need to be profitable for their shareholders – if a customer base is not profitable, then the likelihood is they won't serve it. Many unbanked individuals might not make a good business case, as such. To get them into the banking system and keep them there might require levels of investment from banks that mean they are not profitable customers. This could be because those who are unbanked typically do not earn enough money and what they do earn they may withdraw as cash, to spend that way. If unbanked individuals have no credit history, then they are usually not eligible to take out credit, a loan or use some other services offered by banks. Huw Davies, co-founder and co-chief executive officer of Ozone API (Davies and Michael, 2023), which helped to create a blueprint for open banking in the UK, says:

> Historically, it's [been] a relatively small number of big organizations that control the banking market and they have very big cost bases, because they have huge portfolios of branches and big compliance costs, which creates a sufficient cost base that there's always a line where [below it], profitability per customer is really hard. But also, universal banks serve so many different types of customers, it's hard to be an expert in one particular segment. One of the things open banking/open finance allows [is] it removes the barrier to access for some of the financial institutions and fintechs that might have greater expertise in certain pockets.

What has been something of a vicious cycle in financial services is finally being disrupted. The fintechs spawned by open banking have demonstrated they have – through their expertise and agility – the power to intercept and disrupt that cycle.

Tiago Aguiar, who is head of new platforms at TecBan in Brazil, identifies collaboration as one of open banking's three fundamental pillars – the other two are regulation and standardization (Aguiar, 2022). He says that open banking 'presents a new context for the financial market, in which people are no longer clients of one bank, but instead they are clients of the entire financial system'. On this basis, he explains, in order to expand the distribution of financial products, 'banks will need fintechs to reach audiences that are currently outside the financial system and, in turn, fintechs need banks to lend their balance sheets and their ability to offer and guarantee credit'.

The great debate: do consumers need to know what open banking is?

I've called this 'the great debate' because across the open banking industry there is a firm split between those who believe a huge part of the success of open banking lies in educating individuals about what it is and how it works. On the other side of the argument, there are those who believe that, rather than explaining what open banking is, consumers simply need to see it in action and trust that it works – in doing so, this will generate further demand and the market will grow.

I've often heard it likened to plumbing – most of the time, we want to be able to turn on a tap and fresh water will come out of it, but we don't need to actually 'know' how that happens. That's why we rely on a plumber to come and fix a tap when our knowledge of the most basic mechanism doesn't do what we understand it should. Yes, there might be the odd person who wants to get to grips with the inner workings of a tap – maybe they read up about it and teach themselves how to fix a tap in the future. But even then, in all likelihood their comprehension is limited to their domestic plumbing and doesn't span the local or national plumbing network.

Where open banking differs somewhat is that it involves people's hard-earned money or life savings. In which case, don't they deserve to be informed about how open banking might affect their finances?

I put this question of consumer education to Chris Michael, co-founder and co-chief executive of Ozone API, who has worked not only on the blueprint for UK open banking, but also on Brazil's implementation, along with his co-founders and colleagues Huw Davies and Freddi Gyara. He believes the 'evidence to suggest that people need to know about open banking per se' is lacking:

> I think what people need to know and be better informed about are the dangers of credential sharing, or using insecure methods of authenticating, or giving usernames and passwords to a bad actor. People need to understand which firms are regulated... [they] should be able to trust a regulated financial institution, whether it's a bank or a fintech. People need to know where to go to understand the validity of those firms, so they know whether it's a genuine firm or a scammer.
>
> There is definitely an education job but I'm not sure the education job is about the concept of open banking, or data sharing in general. Because what we're talking about now in terms of open banking is extending into open finance and smart data – or open data – all over the world, we're seeing this gradual progression. So, it might be just a banking issue now in the UK, for example, but over time, who's to say it doesn't stop at healthcare, or social media, or data that you've got as a citizen, or a business. You need to know how to share it securely, who you're sharing it [with] and how not to be conned into sharing access to the wrong person. But I don't think that's necessarily just open banking.
>
> So, there is definitely a role to educate and inform people and to have better signposting around who the good guys are and what to do if something goes wrong. That's what we should be focusing on.

Australia's view on awareness among consumers

In Australia, where open banking is better known by the term 'Consumer Data Right' and where it encompasses more than just the banking sector – see Chapter 9 – the government has agreed on a slightly different approach to consumer awareness. An independent Statutory Review of the Consumer Data Right (CDR), which was undertaken to inform the future direction of the CDR, found that stakeholders observed there is 'very little consumer awareness' of it (Australian Government, 2023). The review suggested that education and a 'technical understanding' are not likely to drive adoption; what will is the availability of new products and services that can 'remove frictions' from consumers' lives or 'benefit them in other ways' (Australian Government, 2023).

Interestingly, the review recommended establishing a CDR 'brand', which it defined as 'a trust mark of sorts'. In its response, the Australian Government agreed that developing such a brand will help consumers choose 'a safer alternative' for sharing their data (Australian Government, 2023).

This aligns with Ozone API's Chris Michael's view on 'signposting'. To me, it looks akin to a labelling system like the one used on certain food products to reassure consumers of the origin and quality of their purchase, which would be equally effective for open banking and open data ecosystems.

Calls to action

I'm in agreement with Chris Michael that the banking sector does not need to tell consumers, or business customers, what open banking is. The phrase itself is potentially misleading – people often associate the word 'open' with the idea that their data is open or accessible to anyone or any entity, rather than retaining ownership of their own data. Or they assume 'open' is in relation to bank branches being open or reopened.

There is an opportunity to showcase the myriad benefits of open banking far more effectively than giving banking customers a definition of open banking, and that is by showing them. Here's what organizations and those working in the ecosystem should be asking themselves:

- Rather than bombarding consumers with more financial jargon, can you demonstrate open banking's real-life uses instead?
- Which use cases are likely to resonate most with individuals and how can you best illustrate these? Typically, infographics, video and bullet points are a concise way to provide clarity and brief explanations.
- Is it clear that the financial institution or provider you work at is regulated and who by? Do you signpost customers to the regulator

or a financial ombudsman in the event they need to report poor practice?

In (open) banking we trust?

Certainly, there is an argument that the financial services industry needs to establish trust among consumers – this is of particular importance when asking consumers to share their data.

Banks will argue that they are trusted, of course, and that they work hard to win new customers. Without this trust at the heart of customer relationships, banks are aware that the unbanked will remain unreachable, while existing customers will be harder to retain and may disengage from financial services altogether (see Chapter 1 on un- and under-banked). Despite their best efforts, in the UK in 2023, 25 per cent of adults 'feel that banks are not there for them' – and this sentiment is rising, up from 18 per cent the previous year (Plend, 2023).

'When customer trust is strong, financial services firms reap financial, competitive, and reputational benefits, enabling them to expand and extend customer relationships' and 'when it is weak, they lose those benefits and have to fight harder to win business' (Clarke, 2022).

A study by global market research company Forrester discovered a 'unique blueprint for customers' trust in financial services firms' in the US and Canada (Clarke, 2022). According to the findings, 'dependability' is the most important factor to earn trust for US and Canadian banks, while 'empathy' is the second. However, the Forrester Financial Services Customer Trust Index reveals that, in 2022, only 54 per cent of US customers and 50 per cent of Canadian customers believe that their 'primary bank' – that's their main banking provider – 'exhibits empathy'.

Establishing trust in financial services is quite crucial to open banking's success, then, especially if the measure is how many people it enables to go from being un- or under-banked, to fully banked. Another way of looking at it is that open banking, given that it explicitly asks consumers for permission to share their data, will naturally establish more confidence among consumers. According to the authors of an article published by the *Harvard Business Review*, companies that are transparent about the information they gather, give customers control of their personal data, and offer fair value in return for it will be trusted and will earn ongoing and even expanded access (Morey et al, 2015). However, the authors also warn that those organizations that 'conceal how they use personal data and fail to provide value for it stand to lose customers' goodwill – and their business'.

This is where the hyper-personalization that open banking can enable is also playing a huge part. If financial institutions can deliver products and services that seem bespoke or designed specifically for their customers, this helps to instil trust because it makes consumers feel that they are 'seen' and understood – this, in turn, engenders trust. This has become increasingly important given the widespread closures of bank branches in developed economies, and the lack of a bank branch network in emerging economies, certainly in rural areas.

Individuals in developed countries can tend to hark back to a period when they could visit their local branch to be met by familiar faces and a branch manager who knew their name and, perhaps, even their occupation. Of course, there is something to be said for banking in this way and many community banks or credit unions in the US and Canada continue to offer this type of in-person service. A consumer survey conducted by EY (Lele et al, 2021) found that although 24 per cent of respondents expected to visit a bank branch 'less often' in the future, 82 per cent consider the presence of a local branch as 'extremely or very important'.

Certainly, the Covid-19 pandemic demonstrated to many individuals what could be lost and gained from a future where banking is entirely online. No doubt the pandemic hastened the demise of many branches, but it also created a surge in demand for hyper-personalized banking. As the authors of an article published by EY put it: 'The pandemic has accelerated the movement from selling and servicing products to providing integrated, personalized customer experiences' (Lele et al, 2021).

They go on to write that Covid-19 has 'shaken consumers' sense of financial wellbeing' and that this in turn has presented opportunities to financial institutions that can provide 'convenient access to tailored advice and solutions traditionally reserved for high-net-worth (HNW) customers'. They coin it 'private banking for the masses', which is enabled by technology and customer-centric operating models.

In the UK, Allica Bank specializes in lending to businesses and is built around the idea of local relationships, or what its website calls 'modern relationship banking'. The relationship banking part of its offering is 'having feet on the ground in our local communities', so a local relationship manager, while what makes it modern is the technology – the delivery of loans via digital banking. On the 'About Us' section of Allica Bank's website, it argues that businesses with between 10 and 250 employees 'have been left behind by the big banks, who have stripped away their local relationship managers and tailored support'.

Let's face it, for the large banking groups, there is also a business case for building trust among consumers. As Forrester's Financial Services Customer Trust Index reveals, 90 per cent of US banking customers will open another account with their primary bank if they place high levels of trust in it, while only 34 per cent of customers with low levels of trust are likely to do the same.

Trust in the wake of Silicon Valley Bank's collapse

Trust in the banking sector in the US was seriously tested in March 2023, when a run on Silicon Valley Bank – a US and UK institution specializing in serving science and technology firms – resulted in its rapid demise in the US. SVB's assets were put into receivership by the Federal Deposit Insurance Corporation (FDIC). The UK arm of the bank was ultimately saved after the government and the Bank of England, along with leaders from across the fintech sector, coordinated a rescue deal. SVB's UK arm was bought by HSBC for £1, meaning that it lives on – crucially, the sale was facilitated without the need to use British taxpayers' money. At the time of its collapse, SVB was the 16th-largest commercial bank in the US, with operations as far afield as Canada, China, Denmark, Germany, Ireland, Israel, Sweden and, of course, the UK (Ziady, 2023).

A brief history of what triggered the SVB run

SVB's US customers began pulling their money in response to social media reports of the institution's poor investment decisions that called into question its risk management approach. The bank had invested in longer-dated bonds but, as the US Federal Reserve began raising interest rates far more rapidly in 2022 and 2023 in an attempt to counteract higher inflation, the value of the US Treasury papers fell (Duncan, 2023b).

The SVB collapse was the first sign of vulnerability in the US banking system since the financial crisis of 2008–09. Naturally, it did not take long before media outlets began posing the question: is this the start of another banking crisis? The speed of the collapse triggered concerns about contagion and laid bare the realities of an online banking system that allows both retail and business customers to quickly and easily withdraw money from any account. This was in stark contrast to images of customers queuing outside bank branches in 2007 and 2008 in a bid to withdraw their savings – at that time, banks could simply stem outflows by closing branches. A flaw in digital banking had been exposed.

SVB was not the only US bank to collapse – Signature Bank also folded on 12 March, 2023. Then, on 1 May, JPMorgan Chase acquired the 'substantial majority' of assets and assumed all the deposits, both insured and uninsured, of First Republic Bank (JPMorgan Chase & Co, 2023). The deal was the result of a 'competitive bidding process' brokered by FDIC, after customers pulled $100 billion of deposits in March.

So, how did consumer trust fare in the immediate aftermath? Not as badly as you might think, according to one survey by Morning Consult, conducted among approximately 2,200 US adults (Jacobson Snyder, 2023). It found that 70 per cent of all adults trust banks, while 23 per cent don't and 7 per cent had no opinion or 'didn't know'.

More interesting, though, are the varying levels of trust among different customer types. When the findings are broken down by income level, adults whose income is below $50,000 demonstrated less trust than those with an income of more than $100,000 – see Table 2.1. The type of institution those adults banked with also had a bearing on trust, as Table 2.2 shows.

Table 2.1   Trust in banks based on income

Income	Level of trust
<$50,000	67%
>$100,000	77%

SOURCE Jacobson Snyder, 2023

Table 2.2   Trust in banks based on type of institution

Type of institution	Level of trust
Regional banks	81%
National banks	78%
Community banks	71%
Digital banks	57%

SOURCE Jacobson Snyder, 2023

When asked, most US consumers were also still largely confident that their bank could return all their money to them if need be, and that their deposits were secure. Morning Consult found that 19 per cent are 'very confident' and 39 per cent 'somewhat confident' that the government would support their bank if it were to experience 'extreme financial hardship, including failing'. However, at the time of the survey, prior to the collapse of First Republic, the majority of US adults, at 65 per cent, said they thought more banks would be put into receivership by FDIC. One aspect of the research that is concerning – or at least should be to those who believe open banking has the potential to ensure more individuals are banked – is that one in five US adults with primary bank accounts moved some or all of their money from their account to 'somewhere else, such as their home or a safe' in response to SVB's demise.

Maintaining consumer trust in the banking system is vital – as research quoted earlier in this chapter revealed, the more trust people have in their bank, the more services they will use (Clarke, 2022).

If consumers start to feel that their savings or deposits are more valuable and safer to them in the form of cash, then open banking is never going to be able to reach its full potential as an enabler of financial inclusion. The onus, then, is on government, regulators and financial institutions to ensure they do everything possible to build on the trust that already exists between banks and consumers. More than 10 years on from the Great Financial Crisis, is it possible that institutions have become complacent?

The fintech threat – and the threat to fintechs

The advent of open banking has heralded a new era in which finance and technology go hand in hand, giving rise to fintechs. Subsequently, the Covid-19 pandemic accelerated the global adoption of fintech and digital financial services, with the growth in transaction value of retail-facing fintech platforms increasing by 47 per cent between 2019 and 2020 (CCAF, 2022).

The growth of the fintech sector has introduced more competition and innovation into financial services and enabled an expansion of services to the financially excluded. In the words of Bryan Zhang, co-founder and executive director of CCAF, or the Cambridge Centre for Alternative Finance, 'By providing new and innovative channels and instruments, fintechs can make financial services more accessible, convenient and affordable for consumers and small and medium-sized enterprises.'

However, as the events of early 2023 in the US banking industry showed, fintechs – particularly those operating as digital lenders – are not immune to the systemic risks that have often plagued longstanding institutions. In fact, increased access to digital financial services has brought new risks – to financial stability and integrity and to consumers, according to CCAF (2022).

As the collapse of SVB in the US, its UK arm's rescue by HSBC, and JPMorgan Chase's purchase of First Republic Bank's assets prove, one of the biggest threats to fintech lenders is being swallowed up by much larger corporates. This in turn damages consumer trust in these smaller banks and lenders, but reinforces their trust in the traditional banks, on the basis they are 'too big to fail'.

Consolidation in the banking industry is not new – it is one of the reasons the number of financial institutions in the US, for example, has declined more recently, as referred to earlier in this chapter. But it does raise questions about the willingness of governments, central banks and regulators to bail out smaller institutions – the fintechs that most likely are serving more specialized communities of banking customers. Being swallowed up by a much larger institution – as SVB UK was by HSBC, for instance – does mean those customers continue to be served. It can help the incumbent bank to onboard a demographic they have not previously been able to, due to profit margins or expertise, as touched upon before. On the other hand, those same large banks and institutions come with history – a history of predominantly serving those individuals with higher incomes, of charging customers for certain services and products, and of failing to provide the type of service and personalized offerings that customers of fintechs require or prefer.

Fintech and financial inclusion

The survival of fintechs is critical in the pursuit of financial inclusion. As the CCAF 3rd Global Fintech Regulator Survey reveals, fintechs and financial inclusion go hand in hand (CCAF, 2022). The survey asked respondents – 128 financial authorities from 106 jurisdictions – whether fintech was 'supportive or harmful' in their efforts to achieve their policy objectives during the Covid-19 pandemic. It found that financial inclusion was one of the top three objectives, cited by 87 per cent, where fintech has had a positive impact – only the adoption of digital financial services came higher (88 per cent), which it could be argued is a form of inclusion. Where market development had been a policy objective, 85 per cent reported fintech as having been supportive of achieving this.

In its report, CCAF states: 'Far fewer respondents consider that fintech has negatively affected their ability to achieve their objectives, but it is notable that 29 per cent of respondents reported possible negative impacts in consumer protection, followed by financial stability (18 per cent), and market integrity (18 per cent).'

The recognition of fintechs, then, as a type of financial institution in their own right, quite aside from banks and credit unions, should endure.

Summary

Open banking regimes are being rolled out worldwide, from the US to Australia and from the UK to the Kingdom of Saudi Arabia, taking in Nigeria, Brazil, Mexico, Singapore and Europe – and many other jurisdictions. Open banking might rely on technology, but at its heart it is all about the consumers – or, at least, it should be. Individuals consent to their account and transaction data being shared with third parties, in return for improved access to credit, a comprehensive view of their spending and saving habits, and the ability to move to bank with another institution, perhaps a newer challenger or digital bank.

For this to happen, banks and other financial institutions need to either be mandated by a regulatory body to implement data sharing, or adopt a market-driven approach, in recognition of the competitive benefits and innovation opportunities at stake. In either approach, to stimulate widespread adoption there needs to be a commercial incentive. Where a regulatory body is driving implementation, the onus is on them to provide a commercial model – especially in those jurisdictions where the incumbents have had to bear the cost of implementation, such as in the UK (see Chapter 5).

There is little doubt of the importance of the longstanding financial institutions in making open banking a success – the large banks, credit unions and lenders need to have buy-in to enable the successful rollout of open banking in any country, given they already serve huge swathes of populations. But just as vital a part of the ecosystem are fintechs. Their agility, tech stacks and understanding of their customers – which often stems from the founders' own experiences of financial exclusion, as we'll come onto – make them able to target niche customer groups. Those might be individuals who have little to no credit history, without which larger institutions are unable to serve them, or it could be that the cost-to-serve per customer does not justify onboarding them.

This chapter has considered how much consumers' trust in the banking system and the institutions themselves has been tested over time, but also how critical it is to establish confidence among consumers – without this, individuals will continue to remain unbanked or underserved on the basis that cash is more trusted. Open banking ecosystem participants, both those that have existed for decades and those with a track record of just a few years, need to restore trust among those consumers who remain sceptical. Telling individuals that open banking gives them ownership of their data is not enough – but using their data to deliver personalized services can make individuals feel valued which, in turn, restores confidence in financial institutions. In other words, the benefits of open banking need to be tangible, particularly when many people will not even be aware that screen-scraping is already accessing their account information and other financial data, and in a way that is detrimental to their security.

In this chapter, much of the explanation of open banking has been describing it in the abstract – for case studies and use cases that really bring the technology to life, go to Chapters 4 and 5.

References

Aguiar, T (2022) How Brazil opens everything – TecBan interview. The Paypers, 07 February, https://thepaypers.com/interviews/how-brazil-opens-everything-tecban-interview--1254399 (archived at https://perma.cc/5VTG-SXNM)

Allica Bank (2023) About Us, www.allica.bank/about-us (archived at https://perma.cc/9KNF-96WU)

Australian Banking Association (2023) Priorities: Open banking, www.ausbanking.org.au/priorities/open-banking/ (archived at https://perma.cc/36D2-QW5F)

Australian Government (2023) Government Statement in response to the Statutory Review of the Consumer Data Right, https://treasury.gov.au/sites/default/files/2023-06/p2023-404730-gs.pdf (archived at https://perma.cc/5PQX-V8H3)

Cambridge Centre for Alternative Finance (2022) The 3rd Global Fintech Regulator Survey, www.jbs.cam.ac.uk/faculty-research/centres/alternative-finance/publications/3rd-global-fintech-regulator-survey/ (archived at https://perma.cc/7554-X78Q)

Clarke, A (2022) Financial services firms need to learn how to earn customers' trust [Blog] Forrester, 08 November, www.forrester.com/blogs/financial-services-firms-need-to-learn-how-to-earn-customers-trust/ (archived at https://perma.cc/S9AG-5AFZ)

Consultative Group to Assist the Poor (2020) Open APIs in Digital Finance, www.cgap.org/sites/default/files/2020-11/11-2020-Open-APIs-in-Digital-Finance-Infographic.pdf (archived at https://perma.cc/9EZV-M8TN)

Costello, B (2021) AISP and PISP Explained, Envestnet Yodlee, 25 March, www.yodlee.com/europe/open-banking/pisp-aisp-open-banking (archived at https://perma.cc/KA4J-EM2N)

Davies, H and Michael, C (2023) Interview with Ellie Duncan, 12 April

Duffin, E (2022) U.S. population by sex and age 2021, www.statista.com/statistics/241488/population-of-the-us-by-sex-and-age/ (archived at https://perma.cc/XC33-SAJ4)

Duncan, E (2023a) Feature: How Saudi Arabia is taking Open Banking from 'vision' to reality, Open Banking Expo, 21 February, www.openbankingexpo.com/features/feature-how-saudi-arabia-is-taking-open-banking-from-vision-to-reality/ (archived at https://perma.cc/S3SD-KJEN)

Duncan, E (2023b) Silicon Valley Bank: 'Rapid demise' accelerated by having single client type, Open Banking Expo, 14 March, www.openbankingexpo.com/news/silicon-valley-bank-rapid-demise-accelerated-by-having-single-client-type/ (archived at https://perma.cc/77DQ-L6VZ)

Fitzpatrick, D and Hollerith, D (2023) Why does the US have so many banks? Thank Thomas Jefferson, Yahoo! Finance, 08 April, https://uk.finance.yahoo.com/news/why-does-the-us-have-so-many-banks-thank-thomas-jefferson-140029962.html?guce_referrer=aHR0cHM6Ly93d3cuZ29vZ2xlLmNvbS5VrLw&guce_referrer_sig=AQA (archived at https://perma.cc/76DA-KTFX)

Hallas, D, Mercer, C and Kosky, L (2023) The Great Open Banking Crossroads: Grasping the opportunity, https://coadec.com/wp-content/uploads/2023/03/Open-Banking-March-2023-For-Release.pdf (archived at https://perma.cc/ZXA5-MTW2)

Jacobson Snyder, A (2023) Consumer trust in banks remains high despite recent bank collapses, Morning Consult, 15 March, https://morningconsult.com/2023/03/15/silicon-valley-bank-collapse-consumer-trust/ (archived at https://perma.cc/UG82-PBB6)

JPMorgan Chase & Co (2023) JPMorgan Chase acquires substantial majority of assets and assumes certain liabilities of First Republic Bank, JPMorgan Chase, 1 May, www.jpmorganchase.com/ir/news/2023/jpmc-acquires-substantial-majority-of-assets-and-assumes-certain-liabilities-of-first-republic-bank (archived at https://perma.cc/3JTE-VBLS)

Lele, N, Udiavar, A and Mannamkery, R (2021) How financial institutions can win the battle for trust, EY, www.ey.com/en_us/nextwave-financial-services/how-financial-institutions-can-win-the-battle-for-trust (archived at https://perma.cc/AZ73-HYTK)

Mallick, A, McIntyre, A and Scott, E (2021) Catching the Open Banking wave: Super apps and the open data economy, Accenture, www.accenture.com/content/dam/accenture/final/industry/banking/document/Accenture-Catching-Open-Banking-Wave.pdf (archived at https://perma.cc/F4K8-TQZP)

Morey, T, Forbath, T and Schoop, A (2015) Customer data: designing for transparency and trust, *Harvard Business Review*, May, https://hbr.org/2015/05/customer-data-designing-for-transparency-and-trust (archived at https://perma.cc/4LFR-RTFU)

Plend (2023) Financial Inclusion Report 2023 – The impact of a cost of living credit crunch, https://plend.co.uk/blog/plend-financial-inclusion-report-2023/ (archived at https://perma.cc/XPX3-GRHT)

Statista Research Department (2022) Market share of leading banks in the United States as of December 2022, by total assets, www.statista.com/statistics/727548/market-share-top-banks-thrifts-usa-by-assets/ (archived at https://perma.cc/E9EU-HM6C)

Statista Research Department (2023) Net revenue of JPMorgan Chase 2013-21, by segment, www.statista.com/statistics/680566/jpmorgan-chase-net-revenue-by-segment/ (archived at https://perma.cc/ENT6-NEAD)

Van Putten, J, Eerdsmans, A, Meijburg, T and Maser, C (2022) Screen scraping: A balancing act for banks, Capgemini, 3 March, www.capgemini.com/insights/expert-perspectives/screen-scraping-a-balancing-act-for-banks/ (archived at https://perma.cc/CK96-CC7T)

Ziady, H (2023) Why Silicon Valley Bank collapsed and what it could mean, CNN, 13 March, https://edition.cnn.com/2023/03/13/investing/silicon-valley-bank-collapse-explained/index.html (archived at https://perma.cc/3W72-M9DX)

How to design an open banking framework that promotes a financially inclusive society

03

Introduction

As established in Chapter 2, there is no one way for a country to implement open banking. This chapter will explore whether there is an optimal implementation approach to promote and enable financial inclusion.

CHAPTER OBJECTIVES

The main questions to be answered in this chapter are:

- What are the key features or attributes of an open banking ecosystem?
- Within the two main implementation approaches – market-driven and regulation-driven – does one better serve the financially excluded? Or is there an alternative third way?
- Has any country fully addressed financial exclusion in the design and implementation of its open banking regime?
- If financial inclusion isn't the ultimate goal of open banking, then what is?

It is difficult to put an exact number on just how many countries have open banking in operation, as figures differ slightly from report to report. As of 2023, nearly 100 countries have adopted or are considering adopting open banking, according to the Open Bank Project (Thiam, 2023). Konsentus, which has been tracking global open banking developments since Autumn 2021, puts the number closer to 70 (Duncan, 2023). Back in 2021, Konsentus reported that around 25 jurisdictions were establishing open ecosystem frameworks outside of the European Economic Area. By early 2023, it counted around 40 jurisdictions – rising to 70 countries including the individual EEA markets – going through 'the various phases of setting up and implementing trusted open ecosystems' (Duncan, 2023).

Among those jurisdictions still considering the implementation of an open banking regime, or where standards are still in development, it is worth understanding what we know about which implementation directly tackles the issue of financial exclusion – or even if one exists. And if it doesn't, then what that framework might look like to deliver a financial services regime that works by not just ensuring that more individuals are banked, but that once they are, they are increasingly well served. If there is no definitive answer then, as always, there are lessons to be learned from other markets, governments and regulators.

Open banking models – a deeper dive

As set out in Chapter 2, those countries that have embedded open banking already have done so in what is considered one of two ways: either it has been mandated by government and/or the relevant regulatory body, or the market has driven open banking based on commercial incentives.

But within those two broader categories, there are nuances depending on a number of factors, including a country's existing banking system, the ultimate end goal of open banking, and many others, such as the role of the jurisdiction's financial regulator – whether it is reactionary or more proactive in applying rulemaking. The approaches adopted by jurisdictions can further be broken down, according to the Open Bank Project report (Thiam, 2023). The organization supposes there are four approaches to open banking at the country level, with two dimensions: mandatory versus voluntary and standardization versus non-standardization.

It places mandatory and voluntary at either end of a horizontal axis, with voluntary on the far left, and standardized interfaces and non-standardized interfaces at either end of a vertical axis, with the former at the top. This creates four sections, which the Open Bank Project categorizes from top right moving clockwise as 'Commander', 'Architect', 'Diplomat' and 'Advocate', providing a definition of each.

- **The Commander** approach to open banking implementation is regulated, top-down, hands-on standardization, where 'the regulator provides the legal and security framework and the technical interfaces, which are standardized across banks'. Among the countries identified by the Open Bank Project as having followed this approach are Brazil, the UK, Saudi Arabia, Australia, India, Canada, Mexico and Nigeria.

- **The Architect** approach is similar, the only difference being that standardization is 'hands free'. So, the regulator still provides the legal and security framework for the regime, but not the technical interfaces. Canada and India also fall into this category, according to the report, as do Ukraine, Turkey and the European Union (EU).

- **The Diplomat** is a market-driven approach, defined as bottom-up and hands-free standardization, which means the regulator provides 'information and guidelines for banks wanting to voluntarily adopt open banking'. Among the countries that have chosen this route to open banking adoption are New Zealand, Singapore, Switzerland, China and Colombia.

- **The Advocate** approach is differentiated from the Diplomat by coming under the definition of hands-on standardized, although it is still market-driven and bottom-up. According to the Open Bank Project, the industry provides a standard offered for voluntary adoption – it is no surprise, then, that the US falls under this approach, as do Hong Kong, Malaysia, Russia, Japan and Thailand.

Based on a review of 12 open banking regimes conducted by the Consultative Group to Assist the Poor (CGAP), there are three countries with 'explicit financial inclusion objectives in their open banking regimes' – Brazil, Mexico and Indonesia (Plaitakis and Staschen, 2020). In the same report, the authors also established that in the UK and Australia, considered among the early adopters of open banking, 'vulnerable populations have been identified as a specific subset of the population with needs that can be met with open banking-enabled products', citing HM Government in the UK and in Australia, the Consumer Data Standards 2019.

Even in countries which might be said to have chosen the 'Commander' approach outlined above, companies and organizations within those jurisdictions can still adapt open banking to suit their business models – Banking as a Service (BaaS) or Banking as a Platform (BaaP) – and their existing customers.

In a paper published by Altitude Consulting, specifically written to explain how a challenger bank might enter 'the ecosystem economy', the authors describe open banking as 'not a one-size-fits-all implementation', despite regional guidelines (Piryatinsky and Akbari, 2023). Large financial incumbent institutions and challenger banks will have to, and should, take considered and differing approaches. The authors write that among the considerations for large financial institutions are 'access to new data, providing enhanced competitive offerings to meet the evolving needs of consumers and businesses, preserving market share, creating new revenue streams and an enhanced customer experience'. While there will be some commonalities, challenger banks will have different priorities. According to the Altitude Consulting paper, their main objectives will be gaining market share, diversifying offerings to reach new customer segments, increasing net promoter score, creating an improved customer experience and creating new products that drive increased revenue.

Accenture, a global consulting firm, has identified what it argues is a way to better understand some of the regional nuances in open banking – that is, to measure 'readiness' across four 'dimensions'. Accenture states that using these measures will reveal more about the capabilities that banks 'will need to develop if they are to compete in different territories'. Those four dimensions are consumer readiness, regulatory approach, technology and competition (Mallick et al, 2021).

In Accenture's research, consumer readiness is defined as consumers' digital maturity and 'their openness to new digital and integrated banking services'. On a sliding scale, the research found North American consumers are more digitally pioneering than those in other regions, just ahead of Asia-Pacific consumers. Firmly in the middle of the scale, at the other end of which is 'traditionalists', are European and Latin American consumers.

In countries where financial institutions must comply with open banking regulation, it can become a tick-box exercise, in particular for long-established financial institutions. There is a risk, though, that those institutions will fail to address the need for more personalized financial services that appeal to a wider range of customers or potential customers. This short-sighted approach is also costly – complying with open banking requires a substantial amount of investment that incumbents, typically, bear the brunt of. However, if they take the opportunity to improve their existing offerings and also partner with fintechs to come to market with new services and products, there is clearly an opportunity for value creation and the chance to not simply recoup their initial outlay, but to develop new and lasting revenue streams.

Investing in open banking – worth it in the long run?

Open banking costs money for financial institutions to implement. It inevitably requires more investment from some institutions than others – in particular, banking groups that have legacy technology to upgrade and are much bigger in size and scale than challengers or digital banks.

Back in 2018, Brian Hartzer, the chief executive officer of Westpac, an Australian bank, estimated that it would cost between AUS$150 million and AUS$250 million to implement, 'because of the complexity of our systems environment' (Barbaschow, 2018). He made the prediction while addressing the House of Representatives Standing Committee on Economics, telling them that a smaller bank 'with less capability to offer its customers and fewer products' will find it easier than a larger bank 'with a complexity of products and systems like Westpac'.

European financial institutions across all segments of finance spent an average €32.1 million on 'their open banking objectives' in 2020, according to a survey by Tink (2022). Retail banks spent the most of any institution, at €84.1 million, followed by wealth management firms at €78.7 million. Mortgage providers, challenger banks, whole-sale banks, credit providers and payment service providers all typically invested below the mean.

Open banking is a nascent industry in many respects and that means it requires vision and commitment from all ecosystem players for it to succeed and to fulfil its potential. Financial institutions investing heavily in the technology now are doing so in the expectation that this will pay off in the long term. Head of exploratory banking and strategic partnerships at Nordic financial services group SEB, Stefan Stignäs, said the bank estimates that by 2030, up to 50 per cent of the profits it generates will come from new or not-yet-invented products and services (Tink, 2022). It seems likely that many of those will be aimed at currently underserved parts of the market.

Market + regulation = hybrid

Having established the key features of an open banking regime and explored some of the nuances in approaches within the two main implementations – market-driven and regulatory-driven – in Chapter 2, perhaps what stands out is that neither one approach nor the other provides the key to democratizing financial services. Rather, there are some features and elements of both implementations that, applied in certain countries, will help to reduce the numbers excluded from the banking system. This 'best of both' model is increasingly being considered as an optimal way to implement open banking for the benefit of consumers.

Reuben Piryatinsky, chief executive officer of Altitude Consulting, sets out his argument for why, ultimately, a hybrid approach, combining top-down regulation and market forces, lends itself to best serving the unbanked and underbanked:

> My personal hypothesis and point of view is that market-driven implementations are going to promote financial inclusion a lot more, simply because of the way they are structured. Organizations such as FDX [Financial Data Exchange] in North America are focused on the needs of the market, first and foremost: where industry participants from financial institutions both large and small are teaming up to define the industry standard, what it means for data sharing and for money movement, what use cases will be defined, and so on.
>
> Certainly, a regulatory approach does encourage competition. However, in some cases, financial institutions may treat it primarily as a compliance exercise. When open banking is regulatory-driven, financial institutions are required to comply; they're required to build open banking connectivity, they're required to build APIs, [and] to satisfy a specific set of requirements – which is a plus because you know that they are going to do things in a uniform, standard(ized) way.
>
> However, the downside of that is that if the financial institution is not bought into the vision and what open banking is going to unlock for it, it might just treat it simply as a compliance exercise [and] invest as little money into it as possible [to] build an API, build a connection capability and focus on the regular, business-as-usual activities. So, with top-down, regulatory-driven environments, it's really important to make sure that the market itself understands the value and that market participants are actively involved in shaping what their organization will look like – the use cases, the customer types they are going to service and how they're going to service them.
>
> I believe that the hybrid approach we have here in North America, in both Canada and the US, has the potential of overtaking the top-down regulatory-driven jurisdictions in some ways.

Why hybrid?

Chris Michael, co-founder and co-chief executive officer of Ozone API, which is based in the UK, agrees that if financial inclusion is the desired outcome, then a combination of market-driven open banking and regulation-led open APIs is required. He suggests that an entirely market-driven regime lacks consumer protection regulations and is less likely to have requirements that stipulate which organizations can and can't play in the space. There is also the risk that without a mandate, incumbent financial institutions will either move slowly to adopt open APIs, given that this stimulates competition and poses a threat to their business model, or will not move towards open banking adoption at all. He believes that a strong regulatory mandate is important because of the overall protection framework it puts in place.

However, if there's no skin in the game and no obvious benefit for financial institutions – and it is on the regulators and governments to ensure there is – then it becomes purely about compliance, Michael says, noting that this is what has happened in Europe.

His colleague, Ozone API co-founder and co-chief executive officer Huw Davies, is in agreement. Davies says:

> In the market where regulation is the catalyst, the market will only thrive longer term if there is then a commercial build on top of that and more value-adding services made available through APIs that drive more use cases and value for all parts of the ecosystem.
>
> Equally, where you have a market-led approach, inevitably it will need some sort of regulatory oversight and control to make sure the participants are sufficiently robust and can be trusted; that it's being done in a way that is open to all and based on standards and [is] interoperable, rather than a series of islands around the biggest players.

Regulation begins outpacing market-driven

Despite some concerns about the regulatory approach, there is evidence that more countries are now opting to mandate open banking, rather than rely on the market to roll it out. Konsentus' World of Open Banking Map indicates that, at the end of February 2023, the number of countries with regulatory-driven open banking frameworks (33) far outnumbers those that are market-driven (6) – and it only counts one example of a hybrid approach, in Colombia (Konsentus, 2023).

According to Konsentus, the US, Switzerland, South Korea, Qatar, Singapore and South Africa are the only countries where market-led open banking is underway. Brendan Jones, chief commercial officer at Konsentus, observes that when they first began recording open banking implementations in 2021, there was 'a more even split' between the regulatory-driven versus market-driven approaches (Duncan, 2023).

Why this shift is happening is not entirely clear. With slightly differing definitions of what constitutes regulation versus market versus hybrid implementations, there is more nuance than Konsentus' map suggests. However, there does appear to be a preference for regulators to take the lead on open banking – not such a surprise in what is, generally, a highly regulated industry. Given that some of the countries that come under the market-led approach are considering some form of oversight – the US being one (see next section) – I think it likely we will end up seeing an increasing number of countries' open banking frameworks defined as 'hybrid'.

Indeed, the Government of Canada's Advisory Committee on Open Banking coined the term 'a hybrid, made-in-Canada' approach to implementation in its final recommendations issued in 2021. In the report, the advisory panel defined this hybrid as neither 'exclusively' government-led nor industry-led, but as an approach that is based on collaboration between the government and industry (Duncan, 2021). That seems like a definition that could apply to several countries – and in fact, while Canada was still waiting on an open banking timeline from the Department of Finance (see Chapter 7 for further reading on Canada's open banking progress and why it has stalled), many in its fintech and banking industries believe the US has already implemented the 'made-in-Canada' hybrid approach.

The Consumer Financial Protection Bureau sets out its regulatory stall

As alluded to earlier in this chapter, while the US approach to open banking has relied on market forces to get underway, government agency the Consumer Financial Protection Bureau (CFPB) had promised there would be some regulatory intervention in 2023. In October that year, the CFPB proposed what it called the Personal Financial Data Rights rule which, rather than establishing technical standards for open banking, seeks to provide industry standards that it deems 'fair, open and inclusive' (CFPB, 2023). The proposed rule intends to offer consumers protection from what it calls 'bad' services and products by giving them the option to 'walk away' with their data and to prevent 'unchecked surveillance and misuse of data'. The CFPB stated in a press release outlining the proposed rule that it would mark 'a move away' from 'risky' data collection practices – in other words, screen scraping.

It is worth noting that, as of October 2023, the CFPB was inviting comments and feedback on its proposed rule up until 29 December 2023, so the final rule could end up looking slightly different. What is known is that it will be the first proposal to implement Section 1033 of the Consumer Financial Protection Act which, as the CFPB states, charged it with 'implementing personal financial data sharing standards and protections'. The government agency makes it clear that any implementation of the Data Rights rule will be 'phased', with larger providers subject to the requirements 'much sooner' than smaller providers. Also, credit unions and community banks that do not have a digital interface will be entirely exempt.

The CFPB's press release is strongly worded, stating that it will stimulate competition by 'forbidding' financial institutions from 'hoarding' someone's personal data. Another aspect of the rulemaking to note is that banks and other providers will have to make consumers' personal financial data available to the individuals or their 'agents' free of charge – or, as the CFPB puts it, to 'get their data free of junk fees' (CFPB, 2023).

The CFPB has put US consumers at the heart of its open banking rulemaking and it will be interesting to observe whether this approach instils Americans with enough confidence and trust to lead to more widespread adoption of financial data sharing. By making it clear to consumers that they own their data and, ultimately, they control which financial institutions and third parties they can share it with, the CFPB is placing the onus on the industry to provide more competitively priced and designed products and services.

Will it stimulate financial inclusion? The intention is there, given that one of the main aims of the Data Rights rule is for financial institutions to offer a wider range of products and services, including 'cash flow-based underwriting' which would 'improve pricing' and access to credit markets (CFPB, 2023). What the rule does well, seemingly, is to explain to consumers what open banking is but without telling them that's what it is doing. The CFPB's explanation is couched in language around data and ownership of that data that consumers can understand. Not only that, but when this rule comes into effect in the US, it should help assuage any fears consumers have about their data being shared or held without their knowledge and for the financial benefit of the institution holding it.

The scope of the rule is also potentially quite wide-ranging, given that the CFPB states it 'intends to cover additional products and services' in future rulemaking. Nevertheless, the rule as it stands in October 2023 has its limitations. Tom Noyes, who has a background in banking and payments, having worked at banks including Citi, wrote a blog post detailing his initial reaction to the CFPB's proposed rule (Noyes, 2023). In it, he flagged some data ownership 'gaps' in the proposal, particularly around the responsibilities of a 'data requestor' and any penalties that may be incurred by 'fraudulent actors' in the data requestor space. Interestingly, Noyes observes that the CFPB's 'goals' to enable competition and 'bank switching' align the US with the UK, EU and Australia. However, changing longstanding and deeply entrenched consumer behaviours is going to be the real challenge, especially given that the average US consumer keeps their bank account for 14 years, according to Noyes (2023). He also writes that another behavioural difference between UK and US consumers is that 'bank customers will instantly switch if savings rates differ by 0.05% in the UK', but that this is not the case among US consumers, who 'won't switch for 5%'.

Let's come back to the cost of open banking, as covered earlier in this chapter. Some US financial institutions that have not already supported open banking will soon be required to. So, what will be the cost for them to comply with the CFPB's proposed rule? Will this require additional investment? In his blog post, Noyes writes that banks will have to provide developer API access, but that they are 'likely' to be able to charge developers 'connection fees to cover the costs of building and maintaining' the developer interface (Noyes, 2023). According to Noyes, the reported costs of developing and maintaining such an interface are estimated to run to anywhere between $2 million and $47 million per year – or a median investment of $21 million annually. The financial pressures are likely to be felt widely. Smaller data providers will find the ban on fees 'particularly burdensome' because of their 'limited resources', while larger institutions will need to 'reserve resources', financial or otherwise, to comply with the Data Rights rule in as little as six months of the effective date (Steinberg Barrage et al, 2023).

However, smaller banks and credit unions are said to be 'voicing concerns' about the possible cost of compliance (Steinberg Barrage et al, 2023). This is worrying, given that many of these smaller players, such as credit unions and community banks, serve or appeal to individuals who do not want to bank with a much larger institution. So, this could prove to be a real test of their staying power – Canadian credit unions may also be watching closely to understand the implications for them.

Open finance in Mexico – tackling financial inclusion head on

It is, perhaps, no coincidence that some of the countries with the highest proportion of unbanked – those individuals who lack access to formal financial services – have made financial inclusion an explicit aim and outcome of their open banking or open finance implementation, namely Mexico, Brazil and Indonesia. For an in-depth look at open finance in Brazil, go to Chapter 4.

In Mexico, more than 50 per cent of the population does not have a bank account (Belvo, 2022). The open banking opportunity, then, is vast, particularly when you consider that smartphone penetration is high across Latin America, at 80 per cent, and around 72 per cent of the entire region's population have access to, and use, the internet (Belvo, 2022).

Mexico published its Law to Regulate Financial Technology Institutions, known simply as the 'Fintech Law' or 'Ley Fintech' locally, in March 2018 – marking the country out as an early adopter. At this time, many Mexicans – in fact, the majority – had access to credit by informal means, according to BBVA Research (2018). It reported back in 2018 that 70.2 per cent of borrowers in Mexico obtained financing wholly or partly through informal channels, defined as money borrowed from 'a savings group at work or run by acquaintances, a pawnbroker, friends or acquaintances, relatives, or others'.

So, which approach did Mexico choose to take?

In this law, Article 76 applies to open banking, establishing that all financial institutions are obliged to share information using Application Programming Interfaces (APIs) in a standardized manner, enabling the exchange of data between banks and authorized third parties (Belvo, 2022).

Mexico is one of the countries that can be said to have opted for a hybrid that straddles a regulation-led implementation and the approach that relies on market forces to adopt open banking and, ultimately, is on a path to open finance. It sits somewhere on the 'unregulated spectrum', according to Belvo (2022).

The promotion of financial inclusion is one of the explicit objectives of Mexico's Fintech Law. When asked what impact the measures enacted in Mexico are expected to have, Dorian Loyo, a regulatory specialist, told Belvo's Isabel Cabrero in an interview that end users will have a choice of financial products that suit their needs, while companies will be able to create new business models (Cabrero, 2023). In doing so, they will be able to appeal to individuals who have previously been unable to access financial products, thereby promoting financial inclusion.

However, despite the early promise of Mexico and its ambition to provide financial services to larger swathes, and eventually all, of its population, thereby reducing the numbers of unbanked and those relying on informal finance, progress has been slow. Official data appears to show that the Fintech Law has, it seems, not lived up to expectations in this regard, with 40 million Mexicans remaining unbanked (PYMNTS.com, 2022).

The lack of movement is best illustrated by Mexico's National Inclusion Report (ENIF) given that it published one in 2018, when open banking was first introduced, and then followed up in 2021, when it took the temperature of financial inclusion three years later, amid Covid-19. In 2021, cash remained the preferred way to pay for goods and services among Mexicans, with cash used for 90.1 per cent of payments of 500 pesos or less, and 78.7 per cent of payments of 501 pesos or more (BBVA Research, 2022). Meanwhile, the percentage of Mexico's population that claimed to have at least one financial product was down 0.5 per cent to 67.8 per cent compared with 2018 (Woodford, 2022). Between 2018 and 2021, the percentage of adults who did not save actually increased. Among those who did save, the percentage who did so through informal services fell, which is positive, while those who saved exclusively formally increased slightly, by 1.6 percentage points (BBVA Research, 2022).

Maelis Carraro, managing director at consulting firm BFA Global, told Reuters that 'fintech innovators have not yet delivered on their potential to build solutions that are centred on underserved communities' (Woodford, 2022). She noted that despite attracting millions of users, 'startups are struggling to move the needle around Mexico's informal economy'. According to the same Reuters article, Mexico lags India, Kenya and Brazil in terms of financial inclusion and its reliance on cash.

This belies the fact that Mexico is home to many hundreds of fintechs – in that sense, the country's Fintech Law has been effective. Statista puts the number of fintech startups worldwide at more than 26,000 at the end of 2021, of which 40 per cent were located in the Americas (Statista, 2023). Come 2022, Mexico had 650 fintechs and the number of Mexicans using fintech services is growing each year. Statista reports that by 2027, more than 90 million are expected to be a customer of a fintech. Which begs the question, why is financial exclusion still stubbornly high among Mexico's population?

The answer seems to lie in the types of services offered by the fintechs that Mexicans are using. A closer look at official data showed that where Mexico has made progress is in card and digital payments. Mexico's National Institute of Statistics and Geography reported that the segment of the country's population making card payments increased from 12 per cent prior to the pandemic, to 52 per cent at the end of 2021 (Ozone API, 2023). Statista backs this up by pointing out that, of those 90 million forecast to be fintech customers by 2027, 'practically all of those users are expected to take advantage of specifically the digital payment segment of fintech' rather than alternative lending and personal finance services being offered.

While this represents a breakthrough of sorts in Mexico, for the country's financial inclusion levels to make more sustained progress, the population needs to access credit and make use of personal financial management tools by formal means. The tide might be turning though, as there are plenty of signs that formal lending services are in demand. Kueski, which offers instant loans to Mexicans via its platform, reported granting nearly 10 million loans at the start of 2023, up from 5 million in 2021 (Statista, 2023). Kueski recorded 2 million visits to its website in January 2023 – a clear indicator of not just a growing interest in applying for formal loans, but also an awareness of fintechs such as Kueski in providing them.

In Mexico, it seems digital payments are acting as a gateway to inclusion for those who are financially excluded. The real-time payments data being gathered enables lenders to build up a better picture of those who are underserved and offer them other types of financial service, such as personal loans or savings accounts.

What lessons can be learned from Mexico?

One of the first lessons to take from Mexico's open finance implementation is that, if financial inclusion is the end goal, then do not expect it to be reached overnight. The road to widespread financial inclusion is a long one, even in countries such as Mexico, where use of smartphones and internet access is the norm. It is not as straightforward as simply dismantling informal financial services and replacing them with shiny, new formal ones – and then expecting people to use them.

Mexico's fintechs have shown that one way to change the mindset of a population that is reliant on an informal economy is via payments. The digitalization of payments has been widely adopted in Mexico – non-bank payments appeal to individuals and to a country that is used to sitting outside the formal banking system. Using the services of a fintech is akin, perhaps, to some of the informal means by which Mexicans have 'banked' for years.

The increasing use of digital payments in countries such as Mexico means that individuals begin to leave a digital footprint. In many ways, how are banks able to customize products and services when they have little to no prior knowledge or insight into the banking habits and needs of potential customers?

Pablo Viguera, co-chief executive and co-founder of Belvo, calls the need for new data sources a 'defining issue' in Mexico (Viguera, 2023). He points to the information that can be gathered from utility bills as an example, because this provides a 'view of recurring consumption' and helps to build up a picture of an individual's 'capacity to pay'. He suggests, though, that data can also be extracted from Mexico's social security systems to establish an individual's job status, or to provide information on an individual's pensions and savings.

Open banking in Indonesia – an opportunity to increase financial access?

Indonesia is on its own open banking journey to help improve levels of financial inclusion among its large and majority young population. Indonesia has the fourth-largest unbanked population in the world (ADB, 2022). More than 273.5 million people populate the islands that make up Indonesia and approximately 66 per cent of the population is unbanked, even though there is an internet penetration rate of 56 per cent (Arvinci Ngabut, 2022). This latter figure can be explained by the fact that more than half of Indonesia's population is under the age of 30.

Indonesia suffers not only from a lack of access to financial products by both consumers and businesses, but also little financial education and inadequate financial supervision and consumer protection, according to the Asian Development Bank, or ADB (2022).

In Indonesia, open banking is part of a much wider drive by the central bank. It is, in fact, the first of five initiatives outlined by Bank Indonesia under its Payment System Blueprint 2025, or BSPI 2025, the main aim of which is to bring Indonesia's unbanked into the 'formal economy' (BRI API, 2022). In the central bank's own words:

> Authorities need to identify integrated solutions to bring in 91.3 million unbanked people and 62.9 million Micro, Small and Medium Enterprises (MSMEs) into formal economics and finance by taking advantage of digitalization. The financial inclusion program needs to be expanded from being limited to ownership of payment instruments or bank accounts to sustainably accessing financial markets and the goods market as a whole (Bank Indonesia, 2019).

The country's central bank is impressively ambitious in its scope. But then, when a country has that much of its population outside of the financial system and potentially exposed to harm through the risks of informal financial services, it needs to be.

The central bank, BI, has created an open API framework to implement open banking. BI states that the scope of its open API standardization includes data, technical aspects of API, security and governance, including contractual standards, to enable the 'disclosure of financial information and interlinks between banks and fintech' (Bank Indonesia, 2019). Standardization is vital for open banking's success in Indonesia. After all, the central bank stated back in 2019 that open banking implementation has 'not yet run in an ideal footing', citing varied applications of open APIs that had not been standardized, either contractually or technically, and constraints when it came to the high cost of implementation, dependence on legacy systems and 'limited talent'.

Given that Indonesia's open banking implementation has a roadmap that takes it up to 2025, it is hard to assess the impact so far on levels of financial inclusion. On the face of it, the country's five-pronged approach appears to leave no stone unturned – all aspects of

Indonesia's retail payments, banking and data infrastructure are covered. There are indications that Indonesia's financial sector is embracing open banking, which would suggest it is heading in the direction of bringing more of its population into the financial system. In an interview published in March 2022, Gavin Tan, the chief executive officer and co-founder of Brick – which is an Indonesian fintech developing an API layer that connects fintechs to third parties, including banks – revealed that 'there are now hundreds of fintechs, not just in Indonesia, but in other SouthEast Asian markets too' (DigFin Group, 2022). Tan observed that banks and regulators are 'starting to follow the open banking movement that began in the West' and that the major banks now have API portals. However, he also comments that banks prefer data to flow 'towards themselves' and even suggests it might require regulation to change banks' mindsets. But Tan insists that banks want to engage with open banking technology to reach those individuals who remain unbanked and to serve 'poorer customer segments', as long as they can accept that 'the customer will belong to a partner organization'.

There is also evidence, though, that Indonesians are beginning to stray from the incumbent financial institutions to use products and services offered by fintechs, or neobanks. Traditional banks remain what is called the 'preferred primary financial relationship', given that 56 per cent of Indonesians have a financial services product with one of the incumbent banks, according to EY (Karunia Wiradharma, 2022). However, the findings from the same survey also showed that 42 per cent of Indonesians have a product or service with a neobank. Interestingly, their perceptions are that technology brands provide better products and services, and 'were more innovative than traditional banks'. So far, Indonesia's open banking initiative is working in several ways: it is meeting demand for digital financial services, traditional banks are gradually buying into the opportunity, and it is also establishing trust in newer fintechs among consumers.

EY's Evan Karunia Wiradharma also reports that banks are being 'urged to embrace the open banking era by making more application programming interfaces (APIs) available to e-payment companies', as well as fintechs and other types of digital platforms and that, in turn, open APIs are enabling institutions to work with 'multiple digital ecosystems' in order to reach a wider audience. So, the industry is still familiarizing itself with collaboration, but it is heading firmly in the right direction. What the Indonesian banks have in their favour is high levels of consumer trust, but they must build on this through innovation, and this means opening up their APIs in line with the central bank's framework.

Perhaps the most interesting statistic that supports the argument that banks in Indonesia should adopt open banking is that 90 per cent of Indonesian respondents to the EY 2021 NextWave Global Consumer Banking Survey said they would value trusted financial brands more if they partnered with other financial services providers or tech companies to offer an expanded range of products and services that better meet their financial and lifestyle needs – a much higher percentage than the 74 per cent global average (Karunia Wiradharma, 2022).

What lessons can be learned from Indonesia?

The aspects of Indonesia's implementation that stand out are its ambition and its comprehensive roadmap, as well as the central bank's role in open banking. Having signposted where open banking is going and by when, the industry is better able to prepare, to set aside investment and to work to a deadline.

Indonesia's incumbent banks clearly have reservations when it comes to open banking. Naturally they, like many other longstanding institutions around the world, are having to weigh up the cost of open banking with the prospect of facing increased competition for their customers and clients from newcomers. One of the lessons this offers is the need for regulators, central banks and governments to ensure they bring these institutions on the open banking 'journey', as it were, with them. Why is this as much an opportunity for existing banks as it is for fintechs and challenger banks? The answer is particularly obvious in countries like Indonesia, where the majority of its population is unbanked. With research showing that for the majority of Indonesians, banks are still their primary financial services provider, this indicates that consumers are not fleeing banks in their droves and banks should capitalize on this. Firstly, they should adopt open banking to attract more of the unbanked population to use their services in the first place. They have the track record and distribution base to appeal to a broad spread of the population. Secondly, they should view partnering with fintechs as an opportunity and not a threat – moreover, partnerships can be a more cost-effective way to upgrade legacy technology than attempting to upgrade systems entirely in-house at huge cost and requiring more resources.

Education is vital – and I don't mean explaining to individuals what open banking is. In countries where vast swathes of the population are not regularly banking, or perhaps do not trust the industry, it is necessary to start with the basics of opening a current account, saving into a simple savings product and applying for a loan, or being able to manage household finances. Governments in countries where being unbanked is the norm need to lead on this, with support from the financial services industry. See Chapter 6 for a case study on this – a startup called Sequin, based in the US, has taken an educational approach to encourage more women to become financially independent.

Summary

In setting out to write this chapter, I had – perhaps naively – assumed that a clear route to financial inclusion would emerge. Instead, it gradually became clear that given the pros and cons of each implementation type, somewhere in the middle is a hybridized version that might offer the best of both and provide countries with the most likely way to tackle financial exclusion effectively.

Yet, even in jurisdictions where financial inclusion has been established from the outset as a key outcome of open banking implementation, this is by no means a guarantee of outcome. As this chapter has outlined, in some countries – Mexico being one of them – open banking has been slow to take off, meaning that significant numbers of its population continue to access informal, rather than formal, banking services. In such countries, there has to be acknowledgement that use of cash and informal financial services is so ingrained in people's everyday lives that changing mindsets and gaining their trust will take time and investment. At the industry level, there has to be vision and a concerted effort to adopt open banking and then provide individuals with a reason to become banked – that means appealing to their needs but also being ready to educate. Low financial literacy levels in places like Indonesia go hand in hand with a reliance on more risky and unregulated forms of finance.

One question that does need answering: could a lack of ambition at industry level be stymying efforts to promote financial inclusion? Financial institutions – in particular the incumbent banks – remain gatekeepers of financial access in many respects. These organizations have to want to serve individuals who have previously been excluded. They need to recognize that so often these same individuals have been excluded by banks' own measures of creditworthiness and ability to repay, or due to their reliance on historic, as opposed to real-time, credit bureau data. This too requires a change of mindset and a recognition that there are limitations to the services traditional financial institutions can provide as long as they fail to embrace open APIs and initiate collaboration with third parties such as fintechs. In Indonesia there are signs of change in both consumers and among financial institutions. More importantly, Indonesians are telling banks they want the types of services that rely on investment in open banking. Institutions can only stick their heads in the sand for so long – eventually, if they choose not to embrace open banking – and truly embrace it, as a long-term and ongoing model, rather than a one-off project – they risk becoming irrelevant.

Finally, individuals have a right to be able to access financial services in a safe and regulated environment. We know that in many parts of the world individuals may be using informal finance, but they also regularly have access to and use the internet. Here is a direct route for banks to communicate with new customers – fintechs are already doing this. As people become more aware, not of open banking as such, but of the digital transformation that is taking place globally in financial services, they will demand more from traditional institutions. The opportunity is here – the industry needs to grasp it.

References

Asian Development Bank (2022) ADB's $500 million loan to support financial inclusion reforms in Indonesia, ADB.org, 15 November, www.adb.org/news/adb-500-million-loan-support-financial-inclusion-reforms-indonesia (archived at https://perma.cc/BBY5-UGYE)

Avinci Ngabut, R (2022) Open Finance Global Progress Ebook: Indonesia, Open Future World, 17 May, https://openfuture.world/open-finance-global-progress-ebook-indonesia/

Bank Indonesia (2019) Indonesia Payment Systems Blueprint 2025, Bank Indonesia: Navigating the national payment systems in digital era, www.bi.go.id/en/publikasi/kajian/Documents/Indonesia-Payment-Systems-Blueprint-2025.pdf (archived at https://permacc/4MHW-GT4R)

Barbaschow, A (2018) Westpac predicts Open Banking to cost AU$200m to implement. ZDNet, 11 October, www.zdnet.com/finance/westpac-predicts-open-banking-to-cost-au200m-to-implement/ (archived at https://perma.cc/7HXT-TWQS)

BBVA Research (2022) Mexico I ENIF 2021: Financial inclusion declines and gender gap reaches 13.8pp, BBVA Research, 23 May, www.bbvaresearch.com/en/publicaciones/mexico-enif-2021-financial-inclusion-declines-and-gender-gap-reaches-138pp/ (archived at https://perma.cc/5UPR-VT7N)

Belvo (2022) The state of open banking in Latin America: The main trends and regulation steps to expect in 2022, https://go.belvo.com/hubfs/ENG-Belvo-The_state_of_open_banking_in_Latin_America-V2.pdf (archived at https://perma.cc/N7VA-EAM8)

BRI API Team (2022) Understanding Open API Framework in Indonesia's Open Banking Initiatives, 24 May, https://developers.bri.co.id/en/news/understanding-open-api-framework-indonesias-open-banking-initiatives (archived at https://perma.cc/C4R3-NF4H)

Cabrero, I (2023) The State of Open Banking regulation in Mexico, Belvo, 6 February, https://belvo.com/es/blog/estado-regulacion-open-banking-mexico/ (archived at https://perma.cc/FFC9-2RAU)

Consumer Financial Protection Bureau (2023) CFPB proposes rule to jumpstart competition and accelerate shift to open banking, www.consumerfinance.gov/about-us/newsroom/cfpb-proposes-rule-to-jumpstart-competition-and-accelerate-shift-to-open-banking/ (archived at https://perma.cc/Z8F6-HUAD)

DigFin Group (2022) Open banking in Indonesia: brick by Brick, DigFin, 15 March, www.digfingroup.com/indonesia-brick/ (archived at https://perma.cc/6GPY-7VG6)

Duncan, E (2023) Konsentus Open Banking map indicates growing preference for regulatory-driven approach, Open Banking Expo, 15 March, www.openbankingexpo.com/news/konsentus-open-banking-map-indicates-growing-preference-for-regulatory-driven-approach/ (archived at https://perma.cc/QSE4-K9V6)

Duncan, E (2021) Final report on Open Banking in Canada sets 2023 deadline, Open Banking Expo, 5 August, www.openbankingexpo.com/news/final-report-on-open-banking-in-canada-sets-2023-deadline/ (archived at https://perma.cc/S3YL-XBJX)

Karunia Wiradharma, E (2022) Riding the wave of Indonesia's financial services growth, EY, 2 December, www.ey.com/en_id/banking-capital-markets/riding-the-wave-of-indonesias-financial-services-growth (archived at https://perma.cc/3WJE-UW9K)

Konsentus (2023) The World of Open Banking Map, Feb 2023, 7 March, www.konsentus.com/open-banking-world-map-feb-2023/ (archived at https://perma.cc/FQ6D-E59P)

Mallick, A, McIntyre, A and Scott, E (2021) Catching the Open Banking wave: Super apps and the open data economy, Accenture, www.accenture.com/content/dam/accenture/final/industry/banking/document/Accenture-Catching-Open-Banking-Wave.pdf (archived at https://perma.cc/F4K8-TQZP)

Michael, C and Davies, H (2023) Interview, Ozone API, 12 April

Noyes, T (2023) Open Banking in US – quick take CFPB proposed rule, Noyes Payments Blog, 21 October, https://blog.starpointllpcom/?p=6395 (archived at https://perma.cc/XZ6F-8ZZB)

Ozone API (2023) Innovation Atlas: Mexico Open Banking, https://ozoneapi.com/the-global-open-data-tracker/atlas/mexico/ (archived at https://perma.cc/6ME6-8RP4)

Piryatinsky, R (2023) Interview with Ellie Duncan, 28 February

Piryatinsky, R and Akbari, H (2023) Winning the open banking race: a challenger's path to entering the ecosystem economy, Altitude Consulting, www.achievealtitude.com/winning-the-open-banking-race (archived at https://perma.cc/TL2X-D4VK)

Plaitakis, A and Staschen, S (2020) Open banking: how to design for financial inclusion, CGAP, www.cgap.org/research/publication/open-banking-how-to-design-for-financial-inclusion (archived at https://perma.cc/WG35-2WLY)

PYMNTS.com (2022) Digitizing payments in Latin America playbook, www.pymnts.com/wp-content/uploads/2022/02/PYMNTS-Digitizing-Payments-In-Latin-America-February-2022.pdf (archived at https://perma.cc/7D3T-6ZVR)

Statista Research Department (2023) Fintech in Mexico – statistics and facts, Statista, 16 February, www.statista.com/topics/5277/fintech-in-mexico/#topicOverview (archived at https://perma.cc/94NH-4XSD)

Steinberg Barrage, A, Borgia, M T, Hurh, B J, Schuerman, W and Aulakh, A S (2023) First impressions on CFPB's proposed open banking rule: considerations for key stakeholders, Davis Wright Tremaine LLP, 25 October, www.dwt.com/blogs/financial-services-law-advisor/2023/10/cfpb-consumer-data-access-third-parties-fintechs (archived at https://perma.cc/CB4P-ZFVS)

Thiam, D (2023) Regulating Open Banking 2023: A snapshot of global progress, Open Banking Project, www.openbankproject.com/reports/regulating-open-banking-2023-global-progress/ (archived at https://perma.cc/YV8B-P9UA)

Tink (2022) 2021 Survey Report: Open banking investments and use cases: Following the money, https://tink.com/survey-reports/investments-use-cases/ (archived at https://perma.cc/WK66-XY5V)

Viguera, P (2023) Open finance in Mexico: what awaits in 2023, *Mexico Business News*, 11 January, https://mexicobusiness.news/entrepreneurs/news/open-finance-mexico-what-awaits-2023 (archived at https://perma.cc/E9J9-4Z6Y)

Woodford, I (2022) Fintechs fail to make a dent in Mexico as cash remains king, Reuters, 26 May, www.reuters.com/business/finance/fintechs-fail-make-dent-mexico-cash-remains-king-2022-05-26/ (archived at https://perma.cc/89J2-Y7FZ)

Open banking in an emerging market – Brazil: a case study

04

Introduction

Brazil has been an early adopter of open banking, not only in Latin America but globally. Its phased, regulated approach to what is, essentially, open finance – more on which later – has progressed rapidly, overseen by the country's central bank. Nevertheless, as we'll discover, there is still a long way for Brazil's financial services industry to go on its open finance journey.

CHAPTER OBJECTIVES

As this is a case study, this chapter will take a deeper dive into the following aspects of open banking, or open finance, in Brazil:

- How has the history of financial services in Brazil failed to truly address financial exclusion and how has this shaped its open finance implementation?
- What are the stages or phases that Brazil has gone through to see open banking and, ultimately, open finance come to life?
- How is open finance in Brazil changing people's lives for the better?
- What are the successes and failures so far of open finance in the country? What are the lessons other emerging markets can learn from Brazil?

- What is Pix, and how have payments been transformed by it?
- Is open finance a panacea to Brazilians' financial woes?

A history of Brazil's unbanked

In 2022, the population of Brazil was 213.91 million and forecasts suggest this will keep rising through to 2028, when Statista estimates the country's population will have reached 227.55 million (Statista, 2023a). There are 34 million unbanked adults in Brazil at the last count, defined as those who do not have a bank account or who use it infrequently. Of those, 10 per cent of the population, or 16.3 million inhabitants, do not have a bank account, while another 17.7 million, approximately 11 per cent, have not used their bank account for a month (Carneiro, 2021).

It is no surprise then that there are high levels of underbanked Brazilians – as much as 79 per cent of the population is considered to be underserved by the financial services sector. Among this group are people who do have access to a bank account and who use it, but for whom other services remain inaccessible, such as investments, savings, credit or loans, and insurance. Typically, those who fall outside of the financial system are women and those aged 18 to 29, as well as the less well educated and individuals who live in remote areas (Carneiro, 2021).

These are people for whom cash is still very much an everyday part of their lives – they are paid in cash, if they work at all, and then keep any savings they do have in cash. Historically, cash has been a dominant form of payment for Brazilians. This is, however, changing as digital banking and digital payments become more widely available to lower-income households and individuals.

Hyperinflation in Brazil

No history of Brazil's economy would be complete without reference to its decades-long battle with high inflation – or hyperinflation, as it is more accurately known. This was most prevalent during the 1980s and into the early 1990s, according to Fabio Caldeira, LatAm general manager at Ozone API (Caldeira, 2023).

In April 1990, Brazil's annual rate of inflation reached a record 6,821.31 per cent and averaged 2,947.7 per cent that year. Data shows that between 1980 and September 2022, the country's inflation rate was 318.68 per cent on average (Wulandari, 2023). One particular period of hyperinflation ran from 1990 to 1994, when prices increased by 50 per cent per month. According to accounts from the country's central bank, Banco Central do Brasil, hyperinflation in the late 1980s and early 1990s saw people 'run to supermarkets as soon as they received their wages and spend their cash before the currency lost purchase power'. It also reports instances where supermarkets would change the price tags on products up to three times a day – each time, the cost of goods increased. The central bank states it was also not unusual to witness families buying more than a month's worth of supplies at a time. The introduction of the Brazilian currency, the Real, in 1994 did help bring to an end this prolonged period of economic uncertainty and instability (Banco Central do Brasil, nd:a).

More recently, Brazil's single-digit inflation rate has looked more in line with its developed market counterparts. By May 2023, the inflation rate had fallen to 3.94 per cent – the lowest rate since October 2020 (Trading Economics, 2023). In fact, it marks an era of ultra-low interest rates which could hit banks' balance sheets. In an interview, the chief executive officer of Brazilian bank Bradesco, Octavio de Lazari Junior, remarked that the era of 'stratospheric gains' for the large banks are over. He also said, 'We have never had such low interest rates in Brazil in all my life' and that 'we don't really know what that means' (Bnamericas, 2020).

So, who is banked in Brazil?

Brazil is one of what is commonly referred to as the BRIC countries – Brazil, Russia, India and China – with an 'S' sometimes added to include South Africa. The term was coined in 2001 by the economist Jim O'Neill in a paper he wrote while working at Goldman Sachs as its head of global economic research (Goldman Sachs, nd). The four countries that form the acronym were posited as the coming decade's drivers of global economic growth. Certainly, this has been true of India and China – Brazil might be considered in some respects to have fallen short of its global economic expectations, due to successive government failures and a possible lack of global ambition when compared to its Asia-Pacific counterparts.

Although there are many millions of individuals in Brazil who do not have access, or at least regular access, to a bank account and other types of financial products, there are plenty who do. So who are they?

On the surface, it looks like a case of the haves and have nots. Ozone API's Caldeira says Brazil has been struggling with financial inclusion for decades, with a 'huge distance between the poor people and the rich people', creating an 'uneven balance of money around the country' (Caldeira, 2023).

The wealth disparity in Brazil is fairly typical of an emerging market economy. What is unusual is just how profitable its banks are – thanks to a business model that largely serves the wealthiest members of society and is replicated throughout Latin America. In Brazil, 80 per cent of deposits are held by just five banks (Bnamericas, 2020):

- Banco do Brasil
- Caixa Economica Federal
- Itau Unibanco
- Santander Brasil
- Bradesco

As a consequence, the banks of both Brazil and Mexico generate a return on equity (RoE) – a measure of profitability – of around 18 per cent, which is five times the RoE of French banks and twice that of US banks (Strange and Hafemeister, 2021). Chapter 2 established that the US has a huge number of banks and credit unions, running into the thousands, which serve an enormous population. Well, by comparison, Brazil has just 174 banks – and that is high compared to Mexico's 51 and Colombia's 25 banks in operation (Strange and Hafemeister, 2021).

With the dawn of open finance, incoming fintechs and challenger banks have the opportunity to shake up this financial system, which has historically been designed to exclude the less affluent through its product and service offerings, and underwriting processes.

Caldeira believes it is because of this volatile economic environment that Brazil's financial services have grown to be so quick to adapt and to adopt technological innovations. The combination of this willingness to embrace innovation in financial services alongside such a reliance on cash among so much of the population, has created what appears to be the perfect environment to implement open finance and promote widespread financial inclusion.

Playing catch-up during Covid-19

Levels of financial inclusion in Brazil have been steadily improving, with some of the biggest gains made during the pandemic. In part, this was due to the government handouts that large swathes of the population received, particularly aimed at low-income individuals or informal workers – around 66 million were recipients of the emergency aid, called coronavouchers (Martins, 2021). The first payments of these into people's bank accounts did not change financial behaviours in any way, as many individuals simply withdrew the full amount in cash. Thereafter, however, the state aid was deposited into free digital accounts created by state-owned bank Caixa Economica Federal (CEF) with the stipulation that they could not be withdrawn in cash or transferred to another account for around 30 days (Martins, 2021). Funds were distributed to vast numbers of unbanked individuals via a mobile-based savings account, from which they could go on to make digital payments – for many Brazilians, for the first time.

The impact of CEF's emergency aid was nothing short of astounding. Reports revealed that 24 hours after the CEF launched the emergency aid registration website and app, it had processed applications from more than 25.1 million Brazilians – 39.3 per cent of whom went on to open the digital account offered by CEF to receive their monthly coronavouchers (Mari, 2020).

The digital distribution of state aid proved – if proof were needed – that financial institutions could reach unbanked citizens of Brazil en masse via digital means. In addition, it showed that among Brazil's underserved population, not only is there a demand for such services, but these groups can and will use them. However, let's be under no illusion: it did not change behaviours overnight. According to Statista, cash is still preferred by a segment of the population. By August 2020, a breakdown of how distributed coronavoucher funds had been used showed that 36 per cent were used in processing virtual debit card payments. Yet 15 per cent of transactions were logged as withdrawals (cash), while Boleto payments – 'a popular Brazilian cash-based payment method' – accounted for 19 per cent. The rest was made up of transfers within CEF (13 per cent), transfers to another bank (9 per cent), while as little as 8 per cent were used to make bill payments (de Best, 2022).

Generally, though, cash usage in Brazil in the years before the pandemic had been in decline. Official figures show that between 2010 and 2020 across Latin American countries, use of cash fell, with Brazil leading the way. Over the period, Brazil recorded a 12 percentage points decrease in cash usage (Statista, 2023b). Banks and fintechs simply capitalized on this trend as Covid-19 swept the region – after all, Brazilians have so much to gain from making the move to a cashless society, as this chapter will go on to explore.

Open finance: the democratization of data

Brazil's central bank, Banco Central do Brasil (BCB), and National Monetary Council (CMN) opted for a regulatory-driven, phased implementation of open banking in the country. Broadly, the first phase covers data on the participating institutions, the second phase is all about customer data, the third phase focuses on services and the final phase is about 'other' data. Phase four is really the point at which open banking morphs into open finance in Brazil (Banco Central do Brasil, nd:b).

Open finance extends, as the name suggests, beyond purely banking services or products offered by banks, to encompass all other areas of finance, from pensions to investments, mortgages, household bills – energy, water, telecoms – and insurance.

Brazil is not the only country to have a vision that extends beyond open banking, as earlier chapters point out. Australia, with its Consumer Data Right, has its sights firmly set on this 'open everything' approach. Even in the UK, where open banking was initially mandated, other types of financial data are gradually being incorporated and examples of open finance are cropping up – as Chapter 5 explores.

According to BCB, the 'ultimate goal of the implementation of the Open Finance environment is to enhance the efficiency in credit and payments markets by promoting a more inclusive and competitive business environment'. However, the central bank is also clear in its intention that any competitive advantage is 'not based on the participants' scale or capital, but on the proper understanding… [of] the demands of customers' which it recognizes have been changing at pace. Financial inclusion is at the heart of open finance in Brazil.

Data ownership and consent

For open banking, and indeed open finance, to be adopted successfully, the regulator or government needs to communicate to citizens that it is all about being the owners of their own data and having the ability to port that data to other financial institutions for their own benefit. This is important, especially because the name 'open banking' can be, and often is, misinterpreted. It requires a change in mindset, given that the incumbent banks have never before had to give up this data if requested by a customer – in fact, looked at the other way, individuals have never before felt any ownership of their personal data.

BCB stipulates that data sharing must take place through 'open and integrated platforms' and in a 'safe, swift and convenient way'. It goes on to state that participants of an open finance ecosystem are responsible for ensuring the 'transparency, data quality (reliability, integrity and availability), security and privacy of data and services shared', as well as 'non-discriminatory treatment, reciprocity and interoperability'.

The way I see it, open finance is almost like hitting 'reset' or going back to factory settings on Brazil's decades-old financial services industry. Where previously financial institutions could essentially choose who they served by creating the rules around lending and borrowing, and by retaining data held on customers' transactions and their personal data for their own use, now with open finance, BCB is taking the opportunity to reshape the financial system. In doing so, it is levelling the playing field and paving the way for fintechs and challenger banks to enter the market. These new entrants will be able, by way of customer-consented data sharing, to create more specialized offerings that appeal to different and underserved segments of the population. And, crucially, open finance stimulates the provision of cheap or free financial services, with much broader appeal.

Perhaps the most significant wording in the central bank's outline of open finance is that the consent by individuals for sharing their data must be given via a 'dedicated electronic interface' or 'exclusively through electronic channels'. In stating this, Brazil's central bank is hailing the digitalization of financial services throughout the country and, in doing so, normalizing it.

BCB also states clearly and with intent that open finance 'puts the customer at the centre of the financial industries' strategies' and that it does so by giving customers full control of the use of their data within the ecosystem. The central bank sets out that greater transparency, in turn, strengthens trust in open finance and 'supports better decision-making processes for the client'. This is a crucial aspect of open banking and open finance – with more information at their fingertips about their own financial situation, individuals can access financial services knowing they are fully informed, and that their bank or fintech is too.

Positioning open finance as a two-way exchange

The central bank has established 'reciprocity' as one of the main principles of open finance in Brazil, stating clearly that 'all institutions receiving data must share data and services as well'. The wording makes it clear that open banking, or open finance, is not a one-way street. In other words, while there may be an onus on the incumbent banks to give up their customers' data, should they consent, the open finance initiative is not about taking away banks' business or denting their revenues. In fact, it would be counterintuitive for a central bank to actively want a hugely profitable industry to suffer financially and to lose market share.

Rather, the reciprocity that the BCB defines is more about existing banks and financial institutions recognizing that they can benefit from open finance, too – it can be commercially viable for them, should they use the opportunity to receive data to inform new services for their existing retail and commercial banking customers.

The stipulation also ensures that fintechs and newer digital banks realize their role in this new ecosystem too. It can't be all take, take, take – they are required and expected to share their data, should customers request it, with other larger account providers or payment initiation service providers. This could be a learning from the UK's implementation, where the largest current account providers were required to give up their data but at a significant cost – the nine biggest banks, as Chapter 5 explains, bore the cost of open banking being implemented. What was not, perhaps, immediately made clear in the UK was how the banks could also benefit from open banking – what was the financial incentive?

In Brazil, the central bank's wording and approach to implementation appears to recognize, it seems to me, that the largest banks will continue to serve more affluent individuals. In that sense, there is no immediate threat to their business model from open banking/finance. But it also indicates that the BCB is not being complacent – open finance will stimulate new entrants to the financial services market and these institutions will be potentially more nimble and technologically advanced than the incumbent banks. It is also apparent, however, from witnessing other open banking implementations around the world, that these fintechs and newcomers will, naturally, target underserved segments of the population. In other words, they should fill the gaps – and there are a lot of 'gaps' in Brazil. These are, typically, the groups or demographics that make little or no economic sense for large institutions with vast distribution networks to serve.

Opinion

Tiago Aguiar, head of new platforms, digital innovation at TecBan, a Brazilian company that helps institutions comply with open finance requirements in the region, believes that open banking provides a 'new context' for the financial market (Aguiar, 2022). This is because, as he sees it, under open banking and open finance, people are no longer clients of one bank, but 'of the entire financial system'.

He suggests that, in this new ecosystem, banks and fintechs need each other in slightly different ways. Given that fintechs are able to 'reach audiences' that are outside the financial system, banks will be able to use that to their advantage to expand the distribution of financial products. In turn, Aguiar explains that fintechs need banks to 'lend their balance sheets and their ability to offer and guarantee credit'.

It is a balancing act though – getting buy-in from existing institutions with decades of history and so much to lose from digitalization at pace, at least on the surface, and encouraging challengers into an established market which many individuals are used to and trust with their money and savings, to a degree. The question is, has Brazil managed it?

The phases of open banking into open finance

Open banking launched in Brazil in February 2021, in the form of basic data sharing between banks. At the time, banks had to 'move fast, or miss out' (Hayes, 2023). Since then, the BCB and National Monetary Council (CMN) have, together, moved at pace to roll out open banking and, subsequently, open finance.

Several other timelines came and went throughout 2021 – 13 August marked the commencement of the second phase, in which individuals were able to share their registration data and, by the end of September the same year, they were able to share information about financial transactions with any financial institution participating in the ecosystem (Aguiar, 2022). Another key date was 30 August 2021, when open banking's third phase came into force, enabling Brazilians to initiate payments from different devices, according to TecBan's Aguiar (2022).

Then, in 2022, came the open finance part of the implementation, which comprises three phases. In May of that year, the financial and insurance market's regulatory and supervisory bodies published joint resolution No. 5/2022, establishing the rules for 'interoperability in open finance' in Brazil. The standard was defined by the Super-intendence of Private Insurance, or Susep, and the central bank, and was approved and issued by the central bank, CMN and the National Council of Private Insurance (Susep, 2022). The joint resolution is intended to 'allow the standardized sharing of data, with the consent of the client, in a secure, agile and precise way, between banks, pay-ment institutions, credit unions, insurance companies, open entities of supplementary pension… and other institutions authorized to operate by the Central Bank and Susep', the organization states (Susep, 2022).

No longer did the data being shared cover only traditional bank-ing products and services, but it began encompassing data on other types of financial services, including insurance, investments, pensions and foreign exchange (Open Banking Expo, 2022). This next step marks a widening of the initiative. The first phase of open finance saw the sharing of 'public data on service channels and insurance products, open pension plans' and had been completed by February 2023 (Susep, 2023).

From 1 March 2023, the second phase of open insurance com-menced, with the sharing of insurance customers' personal data, and ran until 1 July 2023. Thiago Barata, general project coordinator of Susep, said: 'With phase II, the possibility of sharing, with proper consent, of personal data of customers, begins. Initially, registration data and home insurance data will be shared' (Susep, 2023).

Thereafter, the third and final phase of Brazil's open insurance implementation took effect in September 2023, providing for the 'initiation of services through the ecosystem' (Susep, 2023).

Altogether, it will have taken Brazil two years to go from implementing open banking to open finance. The speed at which the country's central bank and its regulators have rolled out their open ecosystem is impressive, particularly for a country of its size, both in economic and population terms. Certainly, it has outpaced many other Latin American countries and those beyond the region. In that sense, the initiative can be deemed a success. But time to market is only one way to measure it – how do the numbers stack up in terms of adoption? And is open finance encouraging wider uptake of financial services, even at society's margins?

Open finance in numbers

Official data from Brazil's central bank indicates that financial inequality is being reduced, thanks to banks' embrace of digitalization and open banking. According to the Financial Citizenship Series, advances have been made in increasing access to and use of financial services by Brazilians, in particular among those on lower incomes (Febraban, 2023). Digital payments has been an area of immense progress, where the gap between rich and poor has closed significantly. The central bank reported that, in 2017, 43 per cent of the lowest income group in Brazil made use of digital payments, compared to 68 per cent of the wealthiest – a 25 percentage point difference. However, by 2021, this gap was revealed to have narrowed considerably, to just seven percentage points, with 72 per cent of the poorest people in Brazil making digital payments.

The same Financial Citizenship Series also revealed that between 2017 and 2021, the number of adult account holders in financial institutions in Brazil rose by 14 percentage points, given that 84 per cent of respondents reported having a bank account in 2021. Diogo Nogueira Cruz from the Department for the Promotion of Financial Citizenship of the Central Bank says that this rapid adoption of digital financial services can be attributed to several factors: an increased number of service providers in the market, the expansion of fintechs – particularly payment institutions – as well as the creation of Pix (see section on Pix payments) and growing and more widespread access to the internet and smartphones among Brazil's population (Febraban, 2023).

Two years on from its launch, Banco Central do Brasil reports that Brazil has reached 15 million 'unique clients' and 22 million 'active consents in the system' and asserts that the reforms to the financial system in the country have been 'far-reaching' (Banco Central do Brasil, 2023). João André Pereira, head of the Financial System Regulation Department at the BCB, says: 'The major effects of Open Finance, such as reducing information asymmetry and promoting competition, will be perceived over time, gradually.' He adds that the first two years were 'necessary' to structure the ecosystem and develop the 'evolutionary agenda'.

Opinion

Isaac Sidney, president of Febraban, Brazil's Federation of Banks, says that Febraban's ability to engage the banks has enabled Brazil to implement open finance in record time and 'with a greater scope than that observed in other countries'.

There are 12 different working groups at the organization that are dedicated to implementing the country's open finance infrastructure, he notes (Finextra, 2023).

Yet, it is not just what open banking and open finance has already achieved in Brazil that is impressive, but what is still to come. Market intelligence firm Serasa Experian estimates that open banking has the potential to include 4.6 million more Brazilians in the financial system. In addition, it has forecast that, by 2026, open banking will have created 94 billion reais – Brazil's local currency – in retail loans or new credit, the equivalent of $20 billion, for individuals (Feliba, 2022). Furthermore, over the next decade, Serasa Experian expects that to grow to 760 billion reais, or $150 billion, of new credit into Brazil's economy, equal to approximately 15 per cent of Brazil's total $1 trillion loan market (Feliba, 2022).

Fintechs – finding their feet

There are a huge number of fintechs now in Brazil and, really, the fintech landscape has changed in a short time. The International Trade Administration puts the number of financial startups in Brazil at an estimated 1,289, making Brazil the largest fintech market in

Latin America and the fifth largest globally (International Trade Administration, 2023).

Unsurprisingly, then, investment in Brazil's fintechs has ballooned. In 2015, fintechs secured $52 million of investment, but by 2022 that had reached $4.5 billion. Certainly, a move by the central bank to allow fintechs to 'grant credit without the intermediation of a bank' under resolution 4,656/18 gave fintechs a boost. According to the International Trade Administration, the regulation passed by the central bank enabled credit fintechs to be controlled by investment funds, having previously been prohibited from doing so (International Trade Administration, 2023).

The Administration also reports that the central bank issued further rules for the regulatory framework covering fintechs 'which aim to foster competition and ease market entry for new competitors in the payments industry'. The rules came into effect in January 2023 and are expected to be fully implemented by January 2025.

Pix: heralding a new era of payments

In an interview with the European Payments Council, when asked the main reasons behind the development and launch of Pix, the Brazilian Central Bank's Carlos Eduardo Brandt and Breno Lobo alluded to the prevalence of cash as Brazilians' main method of payment (Brandt and Lobo, 2022). Brandt, a deputy head in the central bank's Department of Competition and Financial Market Structure, and Lobo, a senior adviser, referred to a survey in 2019 which revealed that 77 per cent of retail transactions in Brazil were cash based. As a result, they say, the retail payments market in Brazil was inefficient, given the 'high social costs associated with cash'.

Before the introduction of Pix, there was no interbank direct debit scheme in Brazil, according to Brandt and Lobo, who explain in the interview that debit and credit cards were not widely accepted by merchants due to a combination of high fees and the length of time it took for payments to reach the recipient – for credit cards, as much as 30 days, on average, for the funds to become available (2022). Card interchange fees – those charged by the likes of Visa and

Mastercard – can be significant for merchants and, as such, have come under increasing scrutiny in developed and emerging economies.

In other words, the conditions presented Banco Central do Brasil with an opportunity to create and install a nationwide instant payments system that enables transactions to take place at a much lower cost to all players – merchants and consumers alike. And so, the central bank launched Pix, its instant payment ecosystem, in November 2020. Without a doubt, Pix has been a success and, by early 2023, was being used by in excess of 700 financial institutions and was available to more than 120 million users (Sarkisyan, 2023).

Sergey Sarkisyan of the Wharton School, University of Pennsylvania, wrote: 'Since PIX is more convenient than cash and cheaper than debit or credit cards, it creates an incentive for the unbanked population to open accounts.' He also notes that instant payment systems created by central banks are especially beneficial for small banks, 'as large banks currently dominate deposit markets – partly because they offer payment convenience' (Sarkisyan, 2023).

Pix relies on the open ecosystem that is also operated by the country's central bank. On its website, BCB states that 'as an open payment scheme, Pix transactions can be performed between any payment institutions or financial institutions that comply with the Scheme's access rules' (Banco Central do Brasil, nd:c). Individuals who need to transfer money to one another can do so using Pix; the system also allows business-to-business and business-to-government, and individuals can also use it to make payments to businesses and government. In August 2022, 407 million transactions were initiated by individuals to businesses, accounting for 18 per cent of the total Pix payments (Bell, 2022).

The instantaneousness of Pix payments has helped to reduce the likelihood of an individual facing a shortfall of funds in their account and having to turn to other means of credit, and Pix has stimulated competition in the market.

Brazil's Pix has, without a doubt, been game changing. As such, other countries are looking to replicate the instant payments scheme, including the US with FedNow, and in Latin America, Colombia is developing 'a system of immediate digital transfers', or SPI (Bell, 2022). See Chapter 9 for more on Colombia's approach to open finance and its payments system.

Who is already benefitting from open banking?

Open banking in Brazil is still only three years in, while open finance – the expansion of the initiative's scope to cover non-banking data – is in its infancy. However, the transition to digital banking and payments was well underway before the Banco Central do Brasil implemented an open ecosystem through regulation. The rollout of an open ecosystem is likely to build on the already positive impact that digitalization has had on the lives of some Brazilians. After all, this spurred the creation of many fintechs in the country, specializing in serving niche demographic groups and segments of the population.

One such group is truck drivers. There are now a range of digital banking services available to those men and women whose profession means they are constantly on the move, often driving through or staying in remote areas and away from home for long periods of time. These digital accounts provide much more than a way for truck drivers to receive and store money, though. They also offer those in the profession financial security for themselves and their families, particularly those who are self-employed.

According to the 2019 Trucker Profile, published by the Confederacao Nacional do Transporte, 98 per cent of truckers access the internet daily, while the average working day is 12 hours and they are typically away from home 16 to 20 days of each month (Frotabank, 2023).

Truck drivers are not the only profession to benefit from Brazil's digital banking journey. Ozone API's Fabio Caldeira says that other digital account offerings are available for workers in hairdressing, construction and the gig economy, to name a few examples.

'This is how digital transformation is being implemented on the Brazilian streets, to financially include those millions of non/under-banked people', Caldeira says, acknowledging that while this is 'not yet a direct benefit from open finance, it will certainly help to accelerate that in the next few years'.

CASE STUDY
Target Bank

Target Bank is one of a number of truck driver-focused digital account offerings in Brazil. On its website, the company lists the features of its digital accounts for freight drivers. Unlike opening an account at a traditional bank in Brazil, Target Bank and others, such as Frotabank, do not charge a monthly fee or an initial fee to open an account with them. As explored in Chapter 1, current account and other bank fees have kept so many people out of the banking system in so many countries.

According to Target Bank's website, translated from Portuguese, the process of applying for an account is 100 per cent online and requires an individual to take a selfie to verify their identity, with an account opened within three days. Truck drivers who refuel with the Target digital account in TMPay, using a QR code, can receive cashback. Banking with Target provides several 'logistics solutions'. With the Target Visa Cargo debit card, carriers and shippers can 'carry mandatory freight and toll values, replacing the old "freight letter"'. Target Bank lists a number of benefits of this debit card, including 'a way to reduce operating costs' and comply with government, and that it 'drives the financial inclusion of truck drivers and their families'. By giving drivers 'transparency' of receipts for tolls and other logistics costs, they are less likely to face fines and unexpected charges.

In addition to banking services, Target provides its customers with insurance and investments. Through a partnership with Tibi Seguros Digitais, customers can take out auto insurance and 'trucker protection insurance'. A partnership with broker Orama enables Target to offer a white-label solution, with drivers able to access investment funds and government bonds, as well as receive investment advice. Finally, the online bank has teamed up with MParts so that its digital account customers can order parts, tyres and lubricants for their truck and pay for these online.

These are savings, insurance and current account products and services that many people might take for granted. However, for those Brazilians who have never been served by a financial institution in this way, this type of digital account is potentially life changing.

Summary

With such a vast number of unbanked people in Brazil, the country has little to lose and everything to gain from implementing open finance. The incumbent banks don't have much to lose in the way of customers either, given that their business model relies on serving middle- and higher-income individuals.

Indeed, since 2022, more challenging trading conditions have reinforced some banks' longstanding business models, meaning that they continue to prioritize wealthy consumers over those on lower incomes, who might typically be categorized as underserved. Bradesco's chief executive officer Octavio de Lazari Junior gave an interview at the end of 2022 in which he said the bank had become even more 'selective in issuing credit cards and is preferring to expose itself to clients with a medium- and high-income profile, assessed as lower risk' (Ripardo and Critchley, 2022).

Nevertheless, Brazil's largest banks would do well to embrace the digital transformation that is sweeping the country. Santander Brasil appears to have made the shift to digital banking in Latin America, investing approximately $6 billion between 2022 and 2024 to promote the digital transformation of its operations in the region. One might have expected the banking group to make that investment in digitalization a little sooner, given that 40 per cent of Santander's profits come from Latin America, with Brazil its largest market. The fact that it has 80 million customers throughout Latin America suggests the banking group's position in the market is well established – the bank is secure in its dominance, having consolidated its market share many years ago.

It is still early days for Brazil and open finance – while significant progress has been made in terms of financial inclusion, there is no time to be complacent. Brazil's central bank needs to ensure that it maintains pressure on the financial services sector to keep the momentum that has made the country one of the leading and early adopters of this groundbreaking and life-changing technology: open banking.

References

Aguiar, T (2022) How Brazil opens everything – TecBan interview, The Paypers, 7 February, https://thepaypers.com/interviews/how-brazil-opens-everything-tecban-interview--1254399 (archived at https://perma.cc/5VTG-SXNM)

Banco Central do Brasil (nd:a) The Brazilian Currency, www.bcb.gov.br/en/banknotesandcoins (archived at https://perma.cc/W54Z-CY77)

Banco Central do Brasil (nd:b) Open Finance, www.bcb.gov.br/en/financialstability/open_finance (archived at https://perma.cc/5P7L-T2V4)

Banco Central do Brasil (nd:c) Pix, www.bcb.gov.br/en/financialstability/pix_en (archived at https://perma.cc/35J7-KE5X)

Banco Central do Brasil (2023) Open Finance in Brazil completes two years with 15 million customers and defined evolutionary agenda, 1 February, https://cdn-www.bcb.gov.br/en/pressdetail/2462/nota (archived at https://perma.cc/3H7E-ME84)

Bell, JG (2022) What are the benefits of replicating PIX in Colombia? Sensedia, 7 October, www.sensedia.com/post/what-are-the-benefits-of-replicating-pix-in-colombia (archived at https://perma.cc/T6DD-6N9F)

Bnamericas (2020) Brazil banks to see stronger loan demand, competition in 2020, Bnamericas, 1 January, www.bnamericas.com/en/analysis/brazil-banks-set-to-see-stronger-loan-demand-competition-in-2020 (archived at https://perma.cc/5MDJ-HTA4)

Brandt, C E and Lobo, B (2022) Pix: the rapid development of instant payments in Brazil, European Payments Council, 14 April, www.europeanpaymentscouncil.eu/news-insights/insight/pix-rapid-development-instant-payments-brazil (archived at https://perma.cc/L2LG-YJJQ)

Caldeira, F (2023) Interview with Ellie Duncan, 19 April

Carneiro, L (2021) 34 million Brazilians still do not have access to banks in the country, Valor Investe, 27 April, https://valorinveste.globo.com/produtos/servicos-financeiros/noticia/2021/04/27/34-milhoes-de-brasileiros-ainda-nao-tem-acesso-a-bancos-no-pais.ghtml (archived at https://perma.cc/PK9P-LR7M)

De Best, R (2022) Distribution of coronavoucher funds granted in Brazil as of August 2020, by use, Statista, 30 March, www.statista.com/statistics/1228059/coronavoucher-funds-brazil-use/ (archived at https://perma.cc/CT9R-B7WD)

Febraban (2023) Digital payments expand financial inclusion in Brazil, says BC study, Febraban Tech, 16 February, https://febrabantech. febraban.org.br/blog/pagamentos-digitais-ampliam-inclusao-financeira-no-brasil-diz-estudo-do-bc (archived at https://perma.cc/8SRN-46LR)

Feliba, D (2022) Open finance unravels new opportunities in Brazil's $1 trillion credit market, Fintech Nexus, 30 September, https://news. fintechnexus.com/open-finance-unravels-new-opportunities-in-brazils-1-trillion-credit-market/ (archived at https://perma.cc/6CQ5-ESGW)

Finextra (2023) Brazil celebrates 2 years of open finance, Finextra, 2 February, www.finextra.com/newsarticle/41721/brazil-celebrates-2-years-of-open-finance (archived at https://perma.cc/8CGY-7P3Z)

Frotabank (2023) Digital account for the truck driver: with agency at the station! See advantages, 21 April, www.frotabank.com.br/conta-digital-caminhoneiro-agencia-posto-vantagens/ (archived at https://perma.cc/P7J5-T677)

Goldman Sachs (nd) With GS Research Report, 'BRICs' are born, www.goldmansachs.com/our-firm/history/moments/2001-brics.html (archived at https://perma.cc/LF9Q-DY83)

Hayes, K (2023) Enabling Open Finance with TecBan in Brazil, Ozone API, 18 January, https://ozoneapi.com/enabling-open-finance-with-tecban-in-brazil/ (archived at https://perma.cc/E8CE-K8XY)

International Trade Administration (2023) Brazil – Country Commercial Guide: Finance, 28 March, www.trade.gov/country-commercial-guides/brazil-finance (archived at https://perma.cc/76VQ-G9EK)

Mari, A (2020) Brazil undertakes massive tech-enabled financial inclusion exercise with 'coronavoucher', ZDNET, 9 April, www.zdnet.com/article/brazil-undertakes-massive-tech-enabled-financial-inclusion-exercise-with-coronavoucher/ (archived at https://perma.cc/CQQ4-UTHP)

Martins, P (2021) Brazil has 34 million unbanked adults, PagBrasil, 11 June, www.pagbrasil.com/news/brazil-34-million-unbanked/ (archived at https://perma.cc/RG9L-GWAY)

Open Banking Expo (2022) Central Bank of Brazil launches Open Finance, 25 March, www.openbankingexpo.com/news/central-bank-of-brazil-launches-open-finance/ (archived at https://perma.cc/NBP3-KYVY)

Ripardo, S and Critchley, A (2022) 'We're in a perfect storm, but it will pass' Bradesco's CEO Says, Bloomberg Linea, 9 November, www. bloomberglinea.com/english/were-in-a-perfect-storm-but-it-will-pass-bradescos-ceo-says/ (archived at https://perma.cc/F3MK-U6K7)

Sarkisyan, S (2023) Brazil's PIX payment system teaches us a valuable lesson, The Banker, 24 February, www.thebanker.com/

Brazil-s-PIX-payment-system-teaches-us-a-valuable-lesson-1677229744 (archived at https://perma.cc/CB48-AL46)

Statista (2023a) Brazil: Total population from 2018 to 2028, 20 April, www.statista.com/statistics/263763/total-population-of-brazil/ (archived at https://perma.cc/3JLH-84ZY)

Statista (2023b) Share of cash used in total payment transactions in selected countries in Latin America in 2010 and 2020, 13 June, www.statista.com/statistics/1229696/latin-america-cash-usage-payment-country/ (archived at https://perma.cc/3PLJ-KEB8)

Strange, A and Hafemeister, M (2021) Latin America's Fintech Boom, Andreessen Horowitz, 13 April, https://a16z.com/2021/04/13/latin-america-fintech/ (archived at https://perma.cc/UHQ2-PWHQ)

Susep (2022) Financial system regulators publish joint resolution on interoperability in Open Finance, Ministry of Finance, 21 July, www.gov.br/susep/pt-br/central-de-conteudos/noticias/2022/maio/reguladores-do-sistema-financeiro-publicam-resolucao-conjunta-sobre-a-interoperabilidade-no-open-finance (archived at https://perma.cc/EV9U-WAU3)

Susep (2023) Implementation of Open Insurance Phase II Initiated, Ministry of Finance, 28 February, www.gov.br/susep/pt-br/central-de-conteudos/noticias/2023/fevereiro/iniciada-a-implementacao-da-fase-ii-do-open-insurance (archived at https://perma.cc/7UXN-S4C6)

Target Bank (2023) Digital Account for Truckers, https://targetbank.com.br/solucoes-para-caminhoneiros/ (archived at https://permacc/4HLH-YS7B)

Trading Economics (2023) Brazil Inflation Rate, 7 June, https://tradingeconomics.com/brazil/inflation-cpi (archived at https://perma.cc/JFD6-S7T4)

Wulandari, F (2023) Brazil inflation rate: Will the Lula administration bring inflation down to BCB's target? Capital.com, 11 January, https://capital.com/brazil-inflation-rate-single-digits (archived at https://perma.cc/ZGU6-KLBU)

Open banking in a developed market – the UK: a case study

05

Introduction

The UK was one of the first countries in the world to adopt an open banking regime and, as a consequence, its implementation is considered a blueprint by many other jurisdictions, including Brazil (see Chapter 4). As a first mover, the UK not only provides a model for others to follow, but it also offers up some vital lessons.

CHAPTER OBJECTIVES

As this is a case study, this chapter will take a closer look at the following aspects of open banking in the UK:

- The reasons behind the implementation of open banking in the UK – why open banking was mandated.
- The role of the Open Banking Implementation Entity and what's next for this body.
- Has the UK's regulatory-driven approach tackled financial exclusion and, if so, how? A case study of financial inclusion will explore this.
- How have credit reference agencies historically generated credit scores, and have these been a help or a hindrance in individuals getting access to credit?

- How is the UK transitioning from open banking to open finance, thereby incorporating other data into the initiative?
- Does the UK need to adopt a nationwide digital identity scheme?

Where did it all begin?

The origins of open banking in the UK are twofold. The first aspect to consider is that the European Union's Payment Services Directive (PSD), which later became the second Payment Services Directive, commonly known as PSD2 – followed by the latest iteration, PSD3, published in 2023 – provided a template for the UK to follow. The first version of this EU Directive was introduced in 2015, but, it was PSD2 that had a much wider impact when it took effect on 13 January 2018 across the entire EU and European Economic Area.

The UK's Financial Conduct Authority (FCA) stated that the EU Directive, PSD2, 'sets requirements for firms that provide payment services, and will affect banks and building societies, payment institutions, e-money institutions and their customers' (Financial Conduct Authority, 2017). It noted at the time that 'as well as promoting innovation, PSD2 aims to improve consumer protection, make payments safer and more secure, and drive down the costs of payment services'.

Importantly, the FCA brought more services within the scope of PSD2 – notably, account aggregation services, which 'aim to help consumers manage their finances by bringing all of their bank account data together in one place'.

The second aspect to consider in the UK at the time all this was happening was a drive at government and regulatory level to increase competition in the banking sector. The Competition and Markets Authority (CMA) conducted an investigation into the retail banking sector and found it lacking when it came to two aspects – namely, competition and innovation. In 2016, it published the findings of its investigation into retail banking, having come to the following conclusions: 'The older and larger banks, which still account for the large majority of the retail banking market, do not have to work hard enough to win and retain customers and it is difficult for new and smaller providers to attract customers' (Competition and Markets Authority, 2016). Areas of particular concern flagged by the organization at the time were the charging structures applied to current accounts, both for personal and business customers, and the charges levied on overdraft users by banks.

The CMA sought to remedy this by 'requiring banks to allow their customers to share their own bank data securely with third parties using an open banking standard' (Competition and Markets Authority, 2016).

It was by no means all bad news for the retail banking industry, though. The CMA also reported that new entrants – among them digital banks – had adopted new business models and begun offering specialist products and services. It also observed that non-banks were making new types of payment services, lending and financial management services available.

Next came the Retail Banking Market Investigation Order 2017. Released in February of that year, it put into action the reforms outlined in the earlier report, including open banking. But also it enacted the introduction of a monthly maximum unarranged overdraft charge, standardized business current account opening procedures, and a requirement for banks to publish 'service quality statistics' (Competition and Markets Authority, 2017).

Where does financial inclusion come into play?

You'll notice that there is no explicit mention of financial exclusion or inclusion in the wording around open banking in the UK, unlike in other countries. The main reason the UK adopted open banking was to stimulate competition among its nine largest personal and small business current account providers, or the CMA9, as they are more commonly known. The banks and building societies included in this grouping are Allied Irish Bank Group, Bank of Ireland, Barclays, Danske Bank, HSBC, Lloyds Banking Group, Nationwide Building Society, NatWest Group and Santander.

The closest the CMA came to referring to a more financially inclusive retail banking system was in the following wording when it outlined the 'remedies' it had come up with to address the issues raised in its investigation: 'help customers to find and access better value services and enable them to take more control of their finances' (Competition and Markets Authority, 2016).

However, Pat Phelan, managing director, UK and Ireland, and chief customer officer at GoCardless, views it another way:

> The sense I get is, despite the fact that inclusion was, in theory, secondary [to encouraging competition between the banks] I do think, in terms of an output it definitely was a fairly big component of the entire purpose in the first place. The reality is, the more competitive the landscape and the market gets, the more access and benefit it's going to have for consumers. And it's clear that inclusion was going to be one of those benefits (Phelan, 2023).

Likewise, the term 'open finance' does not feature either – this initiative is firmly focused on the banking sector; it was only later that the UK's authorities broadened the scope and ambition to other industries. However, in initiating the open banking movement, if you will, in the UK, the CMA, the FCA and government were visionary, bold and ambitious. They recognized the way in which an open standard could transform banking and, crucially, ensure that consumers and businesses are better served by the incumbent banks.

The role of the Open Banking Implementation Entity

The Open Banking Implementation Entity, or OBIE, was created in 2016 to implement open banking standards in the UK in light of the CMA's investigation and its findings. The CMA9 funded the establishment of the OBIE, and determined its governance, composition and budget (Competition and Markets Authority, 2018). The OBIE was overseen by the CMA, the Financial Conduct Authority and HM Treasury.

According to Ozone API, the OBIE 'publishes and maintains the UK's Open Banking standard, supervises the UK's Open Banking ecosystem, and provides assistance in the form of information-sharing platforms, certification, as well as managing disputes and complaints' (Standards Library, 2023).

In January 2018, the rollout of open banking officially got underway in the UK. The OBIE had six weeks to 'bring the UK's largest account providers and regulated third parties online and fully test the system using selected testing accounts only', so that all parties could be 'absolutely certain that the system is stable, fully secure and ready for UK consumers and small businesses' (Competition and Markets Authority, 2018).

The OBIE played a prominent role in the delivery of open banking, convening fintechs, the CMA9, policymakers and regulators to get the initiative over the line. By January 2023, the CMA's 'Roadmap' had been completed, following confirmation from the OBIE that open banking standards in the UK had been fully implemented by six of the largest banking groups – HSBC, Barclays, NatWest, Nationwide, Lloyds and Santander. The end of the roadmap also coincided with the fifth anniversary of the second Payment Services Directive, which made open banking a regulatory requirement in the UK (Duncan, 2023a).

Looking back over the previous five years, Charlotte Crosswell, who was chair and trustee of the OBIE at the point of completion of the CMA's Roadmap in 2023, said that the UK's 'thriving ecosystem' should take a certain amount of pride in 'the financial innovation and benefits delivered to consumers and businesses' (Duncan, 2023a).

However, the work does not end there. Sarah Cardell, chief executive officer of the CMA, committed to ensuring the standard is 'maintained' during the next phase of open banking and open finance in the UK, continuing to hold providers to their obligations under the CMA's Order, including making sure that the 'remaining banks reach the same data-sharing standard' (Duncan, 2023a).

CASE STUDY
Navigating the UK's financial system – from credit 'invisible' to credit 'impaired'

Rob Pasco is the chief executive officer and co-founder of Plend, a UK-based lender that specializes in offering affordable loans to those with a 'thin' credit history. The idea to start Plend came after Pasco tried to navigate his own way through the UK's financial system and ended up in debt, with very little improvement in his credit score to show for it. He had moved to the country from New Zealand and, as he explains, had a steady career in London. However, Rob firmly believes that the way the system is set up – particularly the credit scoring system – is rooted in bias and outdated modes of borrowing. As he puts it, 'you essentially have to build up credit by taking out bad credit first'.

But let's start at the beginning, with Rob having made his home in the UK, only to realize that, just because he had a 'good' job, this was to have no bearing on his ability to access even the most basic financial services:

> I moved from New Zealand about 11 years ago now and, like anyone who's new to the country or new to credit, you essentially don't have enough data on you held by the large credit reference agencies. That data is a very tried-and-tested central depository of information which lots of [financial] providers contribute to. And if there's no data on you, then it's very difficult for you not just to access credit, but also get a rental contract, or a reference for some jobs. For example, you need to have a credit check done to get a phone contract.
>
> There are several points in your life where you need to have your credit history reviewed, so there were lots of restrictions. I had moved to London and was working in the city at a good job and progressing along a very good career path. But the best product I could access given my credit history, regardless of my income, was a credit card with a 40 per cent APR. The irony of this is you have to take out a product that's the least aligned with what you're trying to do. What I mean by that is, a £500 credit limit on a credit card is not going to do much for me really. If you have a big life event or a large purchase, you're moving country, or city, you're paying for a wedding or a funeral, or even a rental deposit – whatever it might be, £500 pounds on a credit card isn't going to cut it.
>
> Also, the way you pay it back isn't going to cut it either because if you don't pay the full balance, then it becomes a loan, and a 40 per cent APR loan was very, very expensive at the time. So, I fell into that trap pretty early on. And even though my career was progressing, my income was progressing, my credit score never did. It got to the point where I had two expensive credit cards, both of which were maxed out, but I couldn't afford to pay back more than the monthly repayments. I went onto a debt management plan with StepChange Debt Charity, and that really changed my life, for many reasons. Essentially, I have an impaired file now.

So, by making that decision, it's pretty much a nuclear option with your life, your credit score. The way the debt management plan works is you pay off all your loans, pay everything off over a long period of time, and your creditors will default you and put these black marks on your file, which lasts for six years. I went from being invisible and trying to build credit history, to the opposite where I had a credit history that is very negative.

The legacy of that still affects me today – I cannot access any form of credit now. And even though I run a regulated lender and we've lent over £107 million of loans, I cannot access a single cent of credit, which is the irony of the situation (Pasco, 2023).

How relevant are credit scores and do they help or hinder financial inclusion?

Companies – whether those are lenders, mortgage providers or letting agents – have long relied on credit scores as a means of finding out whether an individual will be able to repay a loan, keep up with mortgage repayments, or take on a rental property. They can even be requested by employers during the job application process.

Plend's Rob Pasco explains that the data held by credit bureaus is, typically, 90 days 'out of date' and is fed into a credit score via 'a very manual process'. He also emphasizes that 'credit bureau data is not your data – you, as an individual, don't legally own that data; the owner of that data is the contributor'. He cites Plend customers as an example where, if someone has a loan, the data Plend puts into the credit bureau is owned by Plend, so only they are 'legally allowed to change it and control that data'. According to Pasco, there are 'many people who have an inaccurate credit score, so 8 million [people] or so experience inaccurate credit scores, but those consumers cannot change that data point because it's owned by the contributor'. And for a provider like Plend, Pasco explains, it costs them £12 to change information on an individual's credit file, meaning there is little incentive to do so.

Some of those inaccuracies that Pasco refers to may actually stem from historical discrimination and bias. In the US, for example, the Equal Credit Opportunity Act of 1974 disallowed the use of information related to gender, marital status, race and religion from being used in credit scores (Campisi, 2021). A credit reference agency like FICO will now draw on a range of data, including payment history, length of credit history, amounts owed and new credit, to generate credit scores. However, as Frederick Wherry, professor of sociology and director of the Dignity and Debt Network at Princeton University points out, this data is likely to be 'influenced by generational wealth that many Black and Hispanic borrowers did not have equal access to' (Campisi, 2021).

Likewise in the UK, where an individual's credit score, despite the industry's best efforts, is still rooted in historical discrimination and inequality. Steve Elliot, managing director at LexisNexis® Risk Solutions UK and Ireland, writes that individuals from poorer households, rural areas and ethnic minorities are still 'disproportionately' underserved by financial services. He explains:

> At the heart of the issue is the way in which lenders traditionally determine risk, using credit checks which only consider a very narrow aspect of an individual's propensity to manage their finances. Given that a poor credit history or a lack of credit history (a so-called 'thin file') can significantly limit a person's ability to access financial services, lenders should look at a much broader range of data elements when deciding whether to approve a credit application (Elliot, 2022).

In the UK in 2021, around 7.15 million people fell into the definition of being financially excluded – that equates to one in seven adults who found it difficult to access 'affordable and fair' credit, or financial services of any kind (Elliot, 2022). The same report found that among this total are 637,000 individuals, or 1.1 per cent of the UK's population, who are considered 'credit invisible', in other words 'effectively un-scorable in credit risk terms'.

People who have a poor credit score to their name are made to pay for it – literally, as research has shown. Calculations made by Moneycomms.co.uk, commissioned by personal finance app TotallyMoney, found that for the average credit card balance of £2,472, those individuals with a 'poor' credit score may pay an additional £58 a month, or £693 a year, in interest, compared to people with a 'good' score (McCaffrey, 2022). The analysis also showed that a credit score increase of just 75 points could move a sub-prime borrower's credit score into 'prime score band', which would result in an average monthly saving of £55.

Ask anyone 'what is your credit score?' and not many people will know it as a figure, if indeed they know whether they have one at all. It is likely that they might know their credit score is 'good enough', as it were, to be able to take out a loan or rent a room, but nothing beyond that. I've often heard people say that one way to improve your credit score, should you need to, is to take out a credit card and then make the repayments. But what if I don't need or want a credit card? Why is the rest of my financial history not proof enough of my credentials?

GoCardless's Pat Phelan recalls leaving Ireland in the late 1990s to come to the UK to live and the process of trying to open a current account. 'I'll still never forget the day I got a bank account, and I think it was probably about nine months after I started the process,' he says. He describes being able to demonstrate maybe two or three aspects of his life at that point in time: 'Did I have an address? Did I have utility bills?' Neither of which he could have had without a current account in the first place – a vicious cycle.

'Nobody cared about the fact that I had a master's degree. Nobody cared that I'd paid my rent for the previous seven or eight years [in Ireland].' Unlike a credit score, Phelan suggests that open banking data offers a 'fuller picture' of the 'nuances' of people's lives (Phelan, 2023).

Unfortunately, Phelan is not alone in his experience of accessing financial services in the UK as an immigrant. Research commissioned by cross-border credit bureau Nova Credit discovered that 66 per cent of working immigrants who live in the UK have found that the process they have to go through to receive credit products takes longer than it should 'on account of a lack of UK credit history' (Nova Credit, 2023a). The research, conducted among 1,000 working-age individuals who had moved to the UK in the past 10 years, further revealed that they received different treatment from lenders and financial institutions simply because they do not have a UK-based credit history – 55 per cent 'feel' they have been treated differently on account of this and 59 per cent have been told by lenders and financial services providers that they would have to be treated differently.

Immigrants to the UK pay the price in many ways, not least mentally and emotionally, with 39 per cent reporting feeling isolated and having difficulty making friends as a consequence. However, they also felt a significant impact on their living standards, with 37 per cent saying they had been unable to afford 'a good enough standard of accommodation' for themselves and their families (Nova Credit, 2023a).

It may come as a surprise that an individual's credit history does not move with them when they decide to move to another country to live and work – the research by Nova Credit revealed that 63 per cent of immigrants are not aware that their past credit history will not transfer overseas.

In its report, Nova Credit argues that 'this archaic system of siloed credit systems that do not speak to one another' across borders is, in fact, a vast market opportunity.

One UK bank has seized this opportunity by partnering with Nova Credit and using its technology. In September 2023, HSBC announced that 'newcomers' to the UK would be able to include their international credit history free of charge when applying online for an HSBC UK credit card (HSBC, 2023). New and existing HSBC customers can choose to share their credit history from an initial list of 12 countries:

- Australia
- Brazil
- Canada
- Dominican Republic
- India
- Kenya
- Mexico
- Nigeria
- Philippines

- Spain
- Switzerland
- United States

One of the features of the partnership between HSBC and Nova Credit is that immigrants can open a new account even before they arrive in the UK and without having to step foot in a branch of the bank.

According to its website, Nova Credit's 'Credit Passport' translates international credit data from approximately 2 billion credit profiles in real time into a standardized credit report (Nova Credit, 2023b). By providing access to consumer-permissioned credit data, it is helping lenders to serve this historically underserved market.

Open banking – a silver bullet?

Rob Pasco acknowledges that, on the one hand, the information held by credit reference agencies on individuals is 'the most reliable dataset out there, because it is the most prolific in the UK'. And on the other hand, 'You're still stuck in this archaic system which relies on third-party data'.

He sees open banking as an exciting opportunity, but admits it's not 'a silver bullet'. 'It's not like, overnight, every lender is now adopting it and using this for their risk modelling,' he says. 'The reality is every major bank has very complex risk controls and modelling, based on historical data points, and they used credit bureau data to underwrite. So, to go and completely change these assumptions overnight is pretty much impossible.'

He says, rather, it is the new players in the market, fintechs and digital banks, which can afford to underwrite every loan based on open banking data. He insists that Plend 'can take that risk and we're going to change the assumptions – we're not going to use, for example, postcode data, which is one of the biggest parts of your credit score, where you live.'

Pasco explains that Plend will continue to use both credit bureau and open banking data, because there are still some important information points that credit reference agencies gather, including bankruptcies and court information.

CASE STUDY
Plend and GoCardless – using Open Banking data to build a financial picture

Plend, the affordable credit lender that Rob Pasco co-founded alongside Jamie Pursaill, Plend's chief technology officer, uses Open Banking data to make lending decisions. But it has also found another use for open banking.
Pursaill says:

> Open banking creates an incredibly important opportunity to level the playing field for access to financial services through better uses of data. Typically, when requesting loans, data from credit bureaus offer a very poor picture of what people can actually afford right now and in the future, and yet are the key deciding factor in determining access to borrowing. Using open banking has enabled us to gather a clearer, more accurate view of recent financial activity from which a truly individualized assessment can be made (Pursaill, 2023).

He also makes an important observation about more vulnerable customers, or those people who are 'overwhelmed by their finances'. Pursaill adds that they can 'find it hard to collect the comprehensive information financial experts need in order to help them restructure things', whereas open banking data 'can do it for them: comprehensively, neutrally and automatically'. Pasco notes that individuals now being able to connect their own information, which is 'real', in the sense it 'isn't out of date, isn't inaccurate', he believes marks a 'massive shift in the data dynamic and how you access products'.

Plend is also working with GoCardless, which is an online payment processing provider that enables the collection of instant one-off payments and automated recurring payments via open banking, as its website states. Through GoCardless, Plend is able to offer variable recurring payments (VRPs) to its customers, so that they can make changes to their repayment plans, such as payment holidays and interest rate freezes (Duncan, 2023b). At the time the partnership was announced in March 2023, Pursaill said that, additionally, VRPs can be used by its own team to be 'more responsive' to those of its customers in financial difficulty, or who have missed payments, and can therefore come to 'a resolution even sooner'.

GoCardless's Phelan says that working with Plend is helping 'accelerate their current mission, which is very explicitly around financial inclusion' (Phelan, 2023). Through open banking-enabled VRPs, Plend's customers can make loan repayments and, importantly, make changes to those repayment plans at any time. Phelan says that this is opposed to what has been, up until now, 'a relatively clunky, admin-heavy exercise'. Instead, the process is being made 'as streamlined as possible'.

'My hope is, that's going to evolve over time, as open banking use cases continue to evolve. We'll be able to work with them [Plend] to trial and test, and be at the cutting edge of that [evolution],' Phelan adds.

'We've now been able to lend to nearly new immigrants to the country, which is unheard of. If you have three months of bank history, we can make a decision there and then,' says Pasco of the open banking use cases Plend is using:

> The average rate we write loans at is 12 per cent and the average loan is £10,000. What we're trying to provide is a bank-level product for customers who can't get a bank loan. Buy now, pay later is very prolific. But it's very hard to borrow large amounts of money for a life goal and to repay over four or five years. Most loans now are short-term or have a tight repayment profile, which can also restrict customers, and they're more expensive too – banks have to charge more money to make it profitable.
>
> Our most popular product is a solar panel product for homeowners recently on the property ladder. Those are larger loans, around £15,000 on average and it's about 6 per cent. Generally, these customers own properties but still don't have enough data to get additional funding. It takes eight weeks to close the product. The average loan in the UK is written within less than a minute. It's a completely different dynamic because it's a five-year loan product. Someone has to go into a house and install the item. There is so much friction on the journey, but we like that because we can say yes to more people. We convert 65 per cent of those loans, compared to our website, where we accept only 10 per cent to 15 per cent. So, it's these types of use cases that we're seeing pop up (Pasco, 2023).

The role of digital identity and the lessons learned from India

A nationwide digital identity scheme has been discussed for a while in the UK, and also in Australia, by the respective governments of those jurisdictions. Chapter 1 detailed the Government of India's biometric digital identity scheme, Aadhaar, and assessed its effectiveness as a financial inclusion tool. However, where the UK and Australia differ from India's approach is that the onus is very much on protecting consumers' sensitive data, given that cyber attacks in both countries have previously put this personal data at risk.

A report jointly published by UK-based bank NatWest and National Australia Bank (Carr et al, 2023) concluded that both Australia and the UK would need digital identity schemes in place for open banking – or the Consumer Data Right (CDR) as it is known in Australia – to achieve its full potential. The banks referred to it as 'of vital importance to have an economy-wide mechanism to identify and authenticate individuals and businesses reliably and safely across the digital ecosystem'. Among the features identified by the banks as necessary for a digital identity solution to work effectively are interoperability, strong privacy protections, consumer empowerment and choice of authentication party, and to 'integrate in a manner that provides a seamless customer experience'.

The joint report indicates a pressing need in Australia for a digital identity solution, given 'recent cyber incidents'. So, where has Australia got to with its digital identity plans? The Australian Government began developing the Trusted Digital Identity Framework, or 'TDIF', in 2015 and consultation on Phase 3 of the Trusted Digital Identity Bill took place in late 2021 (Carr et al, 2023). Then, in September 2023, there was a flurry of activity. The government released a draft Digital ID Bill alongside draft Digital ID Rules and Digital ID Accreditation Rules, which builds on the TDIF developed by the Digital Transformation Agency (McGovern et al, 2023). The timeline established by Finance Minister Katy Gallagher was fairly tight, with stakeholders given until various dates in October 2023 to feed back on the draft legislation. That is because the Minister intends to have introduced the Bill by the end of 2023 and wants to 'ensure we stay on track'. She had already announced in July 2023 that the Australian Competition and Consumer Commission (ACCC) will be the interim regulator for Digital ID, citing its experience in dealing with 'consumer issues'.

All of this followed the release in June 2023 of the National Strategy for Identity Resilience in Australia, which was developed by the government in 'close collaboration' with Commonwealth, state and territory agencies (Australian Government, 2023). The idea behind this initiative is to 'strengthen identity infrastructure' and make it harder to steal people's identities – and easier to 'restore' them if they are stolen. So, Australia is marching ahead with its plans for a nationwide digital identity system as part of efforts to tackle cybersecurity and identity theft concerns.

Where is the UK on its digital identity journey? In their joint white paper, NAB and NatWest point to 'limited success in rolling out a digital identity framework' to date. This is largely because the UK's 'Verify' digital identity programme was to be phased out in 2023, citing lack of take-up and cost overruns (Carr et al, 2023).

However, in early 2023, Matt Warman MP, Minister for Digital Infrastructure, provided an update, following the publication of version two of the UK digital identity and attributes trust framework alpha in June 2022 (Department for Digital, Culture, Media and Sport, 2023). He wrote that organizations will be able to express their interest in taking part in the first live tests of this framework. The UK digital identity and attributes trust framework will 'let people use and reuse their digital identities'.

Speaking at a conference in February 2023, chair of the trade association UK Finance, Bob Wigley, said 2023 'will be the year that we finally persuade the banking system that we need an economic digital identity system, just like the NHS app' (Aldane, 2023).

Banks' foray into digital ID

In March 2023, Lloyds Banking Group made an investment of £10 million in a digital identity company called Yoti, with the proceeds funding the development of a 'reusable' digital identity proposition (Trotman, 2023). That proposition came to fruition just seven months later, with the release of the Lloyds Bank Smart ID app in October (Prendergast, 2023). It has been made available as a free app in the UK and works by allowing individuals to share specific information with businesses that request it – including name, date of birth, proof of age – from their phone. In other words, it removes the need for people to produce physical identity documents which, in turn, ensures their personal data is not compromised. In a statement announcing the app's launch, Yoti chief executive Robin Tombs explained that digital IDs can 'reduce identity theft, increase the security of our personal data, and create more trust between people and businesses (Prendergast, 2023).

It is not only Lloyds Banking Group that Yoti has worked with to create digital IDs – in fact, the company is behind a few digital identity apps. However, the most significant are Yoti ID and Post Office EasyID, which can be used as proof of identity when collecting parcels, and as proof of age at cinemas and convenience stores. Both these apps have also been certified by the UK government as proof of identity for right to work, right to rent and criminal record checks. Along with the Lloyds Bank Smart ID, the three digital ID apps can be accepted by the same businesses and are interoperable. Together, they form the UK's largest network of reusable digital ID apps, having been downloaded more than 4 million times, according to Yoti (Prendergast, 2023). The company also reveals that, by 2026, the reusable digital identity market is forecast to be worth $266 billion.

Perhaps unsurprisingly, NatWest has jumped on the digital identity bandwagon, partnering with digital identity services provider OneID, also announcing its foray into digital ID in March 2023 (Duncan, 2023c). The bank signed a deal with OneID to make its 'Customer Attribute Sharing' service available to businesses as an embedded digital ID solution. The service is powered by NatWest's Bank of APIs and is being used in e-document signing and also for digital onboarding. Much like Lloyds Bank and Yoti's offering, NatWest and OneID emphasized the safety and security aspect of enabling people to verify their identity online. Speed and convenience are another selling point – one e-signature provider testified that the new service had reduced its document signing process from five minutes, down to just 45 seconds. Customers are also able to give permission for businesses to be instantly notified when they update their details, such as address, which reduces manual processes, including scanning and uploading documentation (Duncan, 2023c).

Not to be left out, on the other side of the world, Australia's banks are also making strides when it comes to digital identity solutions. Australian Payments Plus, which brings together Australia's domestic payment providers, BPAY Group, eftpos and the New Payments

Platform, launched its digital identity offering, called ConnectID (Australian Payments Plus, 2023). At the time of its release in October 2023, ConnectID was available to customers of two of the country's largest banks, NAB and Commonwealth Bank, on a number of use cases. Two other major banks, Westpac and ANZ, are also strategic partners of the initiative.

Andrew Black, the managing director of ConnectID, explained in a press release that the solution is intended to prevent individuals from 'oversharing' their personal data to verify their identity, and to give them more choice about the data they are sharing and with which organizations (Australian Payments Plus, 2023). It also reduces the risk for businesses, Black noted, given that they only end up collecting the data that is required. He also emphasized that ConnectID does not work by creating new 'pots of data', but rather it acts as the 'bridge' between the entity wanting to verify an individual's identity and the entity providing the verification. This means that Connect ID never actually sees or stores people's data. Much like open banking, the service only works once the customer has authorized it. ConnectID became the first non-government operator of a digital identity exchange to be accredited, in 2021, under TDIF (Australian Payments Plus, 2023).

Does Sweden's BankID offer the UK a digital ID blueprint?

Closer to home, Sweden has a digital identity scheme in operation that might provide the UK with a model to replicate. Paula Sussex, chief executive of OneID, has written that Sweden's BankID has 'played a leading role in building the foundations of a digital society' and that, moreover, banks are 'ideally positioned as the base' for a digital ID scheme (Sussex, 2023). She reasons that this is because not only are they highly regulated entities, but they also tend to 'invest heavily' in security to protect customers' data.

BankID is the digital identity service provider in Sweden, which is essentially owned by the banks. The statistics are very impressive indeed. Most Swedes have it – 99.2 per cent of registered Swedish citizens between the ages of 18 and 65 have BankID. Take-up has

Table 5.1   BankID sector coverage in 2022

Sector	Percentage connected to BankID
Banking and finance	54%
Mobile payments	18%
Other private sector	20%
Public sector	8%

SOURCE BankID

been high since 2019, when 96.9 per cent of the population in this age range had the form of digital ID. Not only does nearly everyone in Sweden have BankID, but they actually use it, with 8.4 million unique users reached in 2022, having grown from 7.6 million in 2019 (BankID, 2023a). In 2022, BankID was used 6.7 billion times, up from 6.3 billion the previous year and 4.1 billion back in 2019.

More than 6,000 organizations, businesses and authorities are 'connected', which means they offer BankID for identification and digital signatures.

To obtain this form of digital identity in Sweden requires the individual to have a Swedish Personal Identity Number, to be an existing customer of one of the banks that issue the identity and, finally, to be able to show a valid form of ID (BankID, 2023a). In all, 10 banks in Sweden are 'connected' to BankID, including Handelsbanken, Swedbank, Skandiabanken and Danske Bank in Sweden (BankID, 2023b). In April 2023, BankID announced it would be launching a digital ID card that will be stored in the BankID app. The new ID card will be used by Swedes to verify their identity in the same way as a physical alternative and will mainly be used by people who need to prove their age when purchasing alcohol, for example (Finextra, 2023).

For Paula Sussex, the benefits to banks are clear – in Sweden, she notes, it is an additional revenue stream. A bank-backed digital identity scheme also represents a 'shortcut' for governments, which are able to deliver e-services, but without the need to build and maintain the 'costly infrastructure', as that is already in place (Sussex, 2023). Finally, she argues that, with some parts of society in the UK seemingly averse to further government intrusion in their lives, banks are in 'a good position to play the role of the trusted party' in a nationwide digital identity ecosystem.

How successful has open banking been in the UK?

By all accounts, open banking in the UK is regarded as a success. Open Banking Limited (OBL) – the new name for what was previously the OBIE up until the CMA's Roadmap was completed – reported that during January 2023 alone, there were 7 million users (both consumers and SMEs) of open banking in the UK, which was considered a milestone (Open Banking Limited, 2023). This is based on combined data from the CMA9.

But it is hard to know from that figure alone where the UK sits in terms of global open banking standings. In 2021, the Yapily European Open Banking League Table was published, having taken into consideration several criteria, including regulatory oversight and enforcement, digital readiness of the population, domestic payments infrastructure, bank integrations, the presence of third-party providers, and API performance and standardization. It ranked 18 European countries on a scale, with 10 being the highest score. The League Table placed the UK firmly at the top, citing the country 'as the leading adopter of Open Banking, with its clear functionality and more widespread mandating of interesting features, such as Bulk Payments and VRP (variable recurring payments)' (Yapily, 2021). When the same League Table was published a year later, it revealed that the UK had maintained its ranking, stating that 'with significant political support and a pro-innovation regulatory environment, open banking adoption has continued to skyrocket in the UK' (Yapily, 2022). Yapily also noted that the UK has the highest number of registered third-party providers in Europe, which is 'helping to turbocharge the development of its open banking ecosystem'.

While the UK retained its top spot, Maria Palmieri, Yapily's director of public policy, suggested that 'other markets are fast catching up' and that, in order to stay there, the UK government 'must act quickly and decisively to encourage further growth and innovation' (Yapily, 2022). See Chapter 9 for an exploration of those countries, including the UK, that are making the move to open finance.

When it comes to financial inclusion, there are also promising signs. According to the OBIE's Open Banking Impact report published in 2021, of those using open banking products and services, 76 per cent said these had helped them 'save more and build a financial cushion'. Among those who were making use of personal financial management (PFM) apps, 75 per cent told the OBIE these were helping to 'keep on top of expenditure', 62 per cent to reduce 'unnecessary expenditure', 64 per cent reported using PFM apps to stick to a budget, and 55 per cent said these apps had reduced fees and costs for them.

Such has been their experience with open banking services that, when asked, 84 per cent of consumers told the OBIE they were interested in expanding their use, while 8 per cent would not (OBIE, 2021).

Most significantly, the OBIE profiled these 'early adopters of two core open banking-enabled propositions', and found that many of them were facing financial difficulties or hardship, in particular as a result of the pandemic. So, 27 per cent rated themselves 'low on financial confidence', while 43 per cent worried they did not have enough in savings, 31 per cent voiced worries about their debt levels, and 18 per cent admitted to struggling to pay monthly bills (OBIE, 2021). In other words, open banking in the UK is helping potentially financially underserved individuals.

Collecting tax with open banking

Another marker of open banking's success in the UK has been HM Revenue & Customs' (HMRC) adoption of open banking to make payments. It became the first tax authority in the world to implement open banking to collect taxes from UK citizens back in 2021, when Ecospend won a competitive tender to become HMRC's exclusive open banking provider (Open Banking Expo, 2021). HMRC's endorsement of open banking has provided a boost to payments, in particular. Even now, it can seem surprising to learn that a government tax department embraced open banking when no other government departments in the UK, let alone the world, were doing so. Unsurprisingly, it needed a cheerleader, of sorts, to get the ball rolling – and Nick Down, head of payments at HMRC, is that cheerleader.

Once the tender had been awarded to Ecospend, implementation took just 11 weeks, according to Down (Open Banking Expo, 2022). HMRC went live with self-assessment tax returns initially, because it is 'one of the largest areas of payments' within the department. Open banking payments were rolled out to Corporation Tax, PAYE for employers and VAT soon after. Down explained that part of the appeal of using open banking was that it 'made things simpler for the customer', because it meant they could 'reuse' data that they trusted, rather than 'having to key that data in again'. Human error is hugely costly in the world of tax – it can mean someone ends up overpaying, underpaying, or not receiving an amount they are owed. Prior to adopting open banking for payments, HMRC had to 'intervene and correct' over 2 million payments in instances where, as Down said, 'something has gone wrong' (Open Banking Expo, 2022).

Ecospend's role in this is to provide the account-to-account payment software to allow HMRC to process payments using open banking. Simon Lyons, who was then head of ecosystem engagement at the Open Banking Implementation Entity, anticipated that open banking would 'revolutionize the often time-consuming process' of completing a tax return and would, therefore, provide a 'tangible benefit' to consumers (Open Banking Expo, 2021). HMRC has acknowledged that the use of open banking does, indeed, 'significantly reduce the risk' of payments being misallocated and ending up in the wrong account (Abdullah, 2021). One of HMRC's digital product owners explains that it works by pre-populating the payment reference, which is what HMRC uses to 'match payments to the right person or business' and then passes it securely to the individual's bank (Abdullah, 2021). As well as easing concerns around human error by eliminating the need to input card details, instances of fraud are also greatly reduced.

For Down, who had to take into consideration the public purse, one of the main benefits was the low cost of implementation – or, rather, the rapid return on investment (Open Banking Expo, 2022). He noted that what HMRC cannot do is 'gamble with public money', but added that, as an IT project, open banking was neither 'big' nor 'expensive'.

Implementation by HMRC seemed to have had an almost immediate impact on adoption of open banking payments in the UK that year. Official figures released by what was the Open Banking Implementation Entity, now Open Banking Limited, showed that at the end of 2021, more than 26.6 million open banking payments had been made, equivalent to a 500 per cent increase in 12 months (Open Banking Limited, 2022).

Since then, HMRC has rolled out open banking payments beyond only self-assessment to other tax regimes. Between the start of 2022 and the end of August that year, HMRC added the 'pay by bank' option to 24 other regimes, having ended 2021 with 19 tax types using open banking (Hall, 2022). Gaming and bingo duty, the Climate Change Levy and Customs Declaration Service were among the regimes to take up open banking, it was reported at the time. By August 2022, the government department estimated it had saved UK taxpayers around £500,000 in bank charges since the initial implementation in early 2021 (Hall, 2022).

Statistics like that should prompt other government departments globally to make the leap to open banking. Down, when asked about the challenges of adoption and what other government institutions elsewhere can learn, should they want to follow HMRC's lead, has suggested that testing is important and so is avoiding 'building in complexity' (Open Banking Expo, 2022). HMRC designed a proof of concept early on, which would have flagged any major issues, particularly around security. Then, according to Down, they spent 'a bit of time designing the procurement' to make sure the right external partner was eventually selected (Open Banking Expo, 2022).

Another challenge posed was what to call it. Alfie Abdullah, a digital product owner within the online payments service team at HMRC, recalled that it was important to get the naming right, on the basis that people will not 'part' with their money 'if you felt like you didn't understand what was going to happen to it' (Abdullah, 2021). The department undertook rigorous research to establish this, ensuring that they conducted interviews with people across industries, as well as a mix of self-employed and employed individuals, those who pay HMRC regularly and those who only pay once a year, explained Abdullah. The outcome? Calling the open banking payment option 'Pay by bank account' resonated with people when it came to understanding and trust (Abdullah, 2021).

The UK government is not stopping at tax, though. In August 2023, in a blog post, Amanda Dahl, deputy director of digital service platforms at the Government Digital Service, wrote that it would start looking into how GOV.UK Pay might be able to offer open banking (Duncan, 2023d). She said it would give people the option to pay for services 'conveniently' using their banking app. Given that GOV.UK Pay already offers Google Pay and Apple Pay to central government digital services, it seems the next logical step. A recurring card payments functionality initially rolled out to Kent County Council will also go live with other public services, Dahl confirmed (Duncan, 2023d).

Summary

Competition and innovation may have been the watchwords in the UK, but open banking has also proved it can and is tackling financial inclusion. Encouraging more competition in the banking sector is really a byword for stimulating a wider range of products and services that serve those consumers who have historically been unable to access credit – or, at least, not credit at an affordable APR.

As Rob Pasco, co-founder and chief executive officer of Plend, found to his detriment, the data used to compile credit scores is archaic and, used alone, leaves individuals without the ability not only to improve their financial lives, but to make a life for themselves in a new country.

Yet, in combination with open banking data, lenders – whether those are incumbent banks or fintechs – are now able to capture far more recent, relevant and nuanced financial data. In turn, this gives them the ability to lend with more confidence to people who might otherwise have been denied credit. Equally important is that UK consumers are recognizing that, by using open banking, they are able to save more money, budget effectively, and lead financial lives that may previously not have been available to them. In that way, open banking is addressing financial inclusion in the UK in far more subtle ways than in an emerging market like Brazil.

References

Abdullah, A (2021) Open Banking Payments at HMRC, a team making history, Gov.uk, 19 November, https://lifeathmrc.blog.gov.uk/2021/11/19/open-banking-payments-at-hmrc-a-team-making-history/ (archived at https://perma.cc/E7B6-RXYJ)

Aldane, J (2023) UK government must create digital ID 'super app', says top financier, www.globalgovernmentforum.com/uk-government-must-create-digital-id-super-app-says-top-financier/ (archived at https://perma.cc/LR79-9XEV)

Australian Government (2023) National Strategy for Identity Resilience, Attorney-General's Department, 10 August, www.ag.gov.au/national-security/publications/national-strategy-identity-resilience (archived at https://perma.cc/3DZM-MYV8)

Australian Payments Plus (2023) Millions of verifications. No document sharing. ConnectID launches secure digital identity network for Australia, Auspayplus.com.au, 16 October, www.auspayplus.com.au/millions-of-verifications-no-document-sharing-connectid-launches-secure-digital-identity-network-for-australia (archived at https://perma.cc/49XQ-EWA5)

BankID (2023a) BankID in numbers, Bankid.com, www.bankid.com/en/om-oss/statistik (archived at https://perma.cc/5YDS-8GG3)

BankID (2023b) Get BankID, Bankid.com, www.bankid.com/en/privat/skaffa-bankid (archived at https://perma.cc/9B8U-ZH7W)

Campisi, N (2021) From inherent racial bias to incorrect data – the problems with current credit scoring models, Forbes Advisor, 26 February, www.forbes.com/advisor/credit-cards/from-inherent-racial-bias-to-incorrect-data-the-problems-with-current-credit-scoring-models/ (archived at https://perma.cc/7K3U-3FDT)

Carr, B, Abeyratne, A and Melling, C (2023) Lessons learned from Australia and the United Kingdom: The Consumer Data Right and open banking, https://openapi.ulsterbank.co.uk/bankofapis/v1.0/dynamic-content/content/assets/community-articles/NatWest_ebook_OpenBanking_Design.pdf (archived at https://perma.cc/VQJ7-T2VR)

Competition and Markets Authority (2016) Making banks work harder for you, https://assets.publishing.service.gov.uk/government/uploads/system/uploads/attachment_data/file/544942/overview-of-the-banking-retail-market.pdf (archived at https://perma.cc/5PGD-72RH)

Competition and Markets Authority (2017) Retail Banking Market Investigation Order 2017, Gov.uk, 2 February, www.gov.uk/government/publications/retail-banking-market-investigation-order-2017 (archived at https://perma.cc/9RRS-DK39)

Competition and Markets Authority (2018) Open Banking begins managed roll out, Open Banking Limited, 13 January, www.openbanking.org.uk/news/open-banking-begins-managed-roll/ (archived at https://perma.cc/Q4AG-TL84)

Department for Digital, Culture, Media and Sport (2023) UK digital identity & attributes trust framework alpha v2 (0.2), www.gov.uk/government/publications/uk-digital-identity-attributes-trust-framework-updated-version/uk-digital-identity-and-attributes-trust-framework-alpha-version-2 (archived at https://perma.cc/5LFM-AWHR)

Duncan, E (2023a) CMA announces completion of UK's Open Banking Roadmap, Open Banking Expo, 13 January, www.openbankingexpo.com/news/cma-announces-completion-of-uks-open-banking-roadmap/ (archived at https://perma.cc/NP58-XRXH)

Duncan, E (2023b) Plend selects GoCardless to introduce variable recurring payments, Open Banking Expo, 24 March, www.openbankingexpo.com/news/plend-selects-gocardless-to-introduce-variable-recurring-payments/ (archived at https://perma.cc/KJ6H-XSJ6)

Duncan, E (2023c) NatWest collaborates with OneID to launch new digital ID service, Open Banking Expo, 23 March, www.openbankingexpo.com/news/natwest-collaborates-with-oneid-to-launch-new-digital-id-service/ (archived at https://perma.cc/57P3-NHGR)

Duncan, E (2023d) UK Government to look into offering Open Banking through GOV.UK Pay, Open Banking Expo, 10 August, www.openbankingexpo.com/news/uk-government-to-look-into-offering-open-banking-through-gov-uk-pay/ (archived at https://permacc/7XV3-U93P)

Elliot, S (2022) Financial Inclusion in the UK – up to date analysis of access to affordable financial services across the UK, Lexis

Nexis, https://images.solutions.lexisnexis.com/Web/LexisNexis/ per
cent7B35c89fb9-7ac2-4c87-b58c-7d0a635734f2 per cent7D_financial-
inclusion-wp-uk.pdf

Financial Conduct Authority (2017) FCA finalises revised Payment Services
Directive (PSD2) requirements, 19 September, www.fca.org.uk/news/
press-releases/fca-finalises-revised-psd2-requirements (archived at
https://perma.cc/2Q2N-2NLX)

Finextra (2023) Sweden's BankID launches digital identity card, 28 April,
www.finextra.com/newsarticle/42228/swedens-bankid-launches-digital-
identity-card (archived at https://perma.cc/U79N-2WXU)

GoCardless (2023) Website homepage, https://gocardless.com/ (archived at
https://perma.cc/9JWV-HNNN)

Hall, I (2022) HMRC open banking rollout takes in 24 more tax types,
Global Government Fintech, 30 August, www.globalgovernmentfintech.
com/hmrc-open-banking-rollout-takes-in-24-more-tax-types/ (archived
at https://perma.cc/89XL-S47N)

HSBC UK (2023) HSBC UK partners with Nova Credit to offer
international credit decisioning, HSBC News and Media, 18 September,
www.about.hsbc.co.uk/news-and-media/hsbc-uk-partners-with-nova-
credit-to-offer-international-credit-decisioning (archived at
https://perma.cc/EC9N-9A8E)

McCaffrey, J (2022) Do you know how much a poor credit score will cost
you? TotallyMoney, www.totallymoney.com/press-centre/do-you-know-
how-much-a-poor-credit-score-will-cost-you/ (archived at https://perma.
cc/JK6Q-CJ7P)

McGovern, D, Farrall, L and Hamilton, P (2023) Digital Identity (Digital
ID) Consultation Process, Parliament of Australia, 26 September,
www.aph.gov.au/About_Parliament/Parliamentary_departments/
Parliamentary_Library/FlagPost/2023/September/Digital_ID_
Consultation (archived at https://perma.cc/M42U-DD9Q)

Nova Credit (2023a) 10 million UK immigrants: a market opportunity
hiding in plain sight, https://go.novacredit.com/ukmktresearch (archived
at https://perma.cc/9WPK-2EFV)

Nova Credit (2023b) Nova Passport: Extend credit to a world of new
customers, www.novacredit.com/uk/business (archived at
https://perma.cc/K3GE-2FFT)

OBIE (2021) Key consumer insights from the Open Banking Impact report.
Open Banking Limited, 17 November, www.openbanking.org.uk/
insights/key-consumer-insights-from-the-open-banking-impact-report/
(archived at https://perma.cc/4T7W-BAUU)

Open Banking Expo (2021) HMRC awards Open Banking contract to Ecospend, Open Banking Expo, 3 February, www.openbankingexpo.com/news/hmrc-awards-open-banking-contract-to-ecospend/ (archived at https://perma.cc/6A7J-6UG8)

Open Banking Expo (2022) Open Banking Expo Awards 2022: Winners' Supplement, https://assets.openbankingexpo.com/awards/2022/Open%20per%20cent%20Banking%20per%20cent%20Expo%20per%20cent%20Awards%20per%20cent%20Winners%20per%20cent%20Supplement.pdf

Open Banking Limited (2022) UK open banking marks fourth year milestone with over 4 million users, Press release, 13 January, www.openbanking.org.uk/news/uk-open-banking-marks-fourth-year-milestone-with-over-4-million-users/ (archived at https://perma.cc/68LP-H775)

Open Banking Limited (2023) UK reaches 7 million open banking users milestone, 20 February, www.openbanking.org.uk/news/ (archived at https://perma.cc/QPC2-2V6Z)

Pasco, R (2023) Interview with Ellie Duncan, 17 April

Phelan, P (2023) Interview with Ellie Duncan, 29 March

Prendergast, M (2023) Yoti releases a new Digital ID app with Lloyds Bank, Yoti, 2 October, www.yoti.com/blog/yoti-releases-a-new-digital-id-app-with-lloyds-bank/ (archived at https://perma.cc/4CHV-FDPT)

Pursaill, J (2023) Quote sent to Ellie Duncan via email, 1 March

Standards Library (2023) UK Open Banking Standard, Ozone API, https://ozoneapi.com/the-global-open-data-tracker-library/ (archived at https://perma.cc/Z7PZ-L7Y9)

Sussex, P (2023) Insight: Is bank ID a myth or reality for the UK? Open Banking Expo, 24 October, www.openbankingexpo.com/insights/insight-is-bank-id-a-myth-or-reality-for-the-uk/ (archived at https://perma.cc/RU6F-VX8W)

Trotman, R (2023) Lloyds Banking Group invests £10 million in digital identity company Yoti, Yoti, 2 March, www.yoti.com/blog/lloyds-banking-group-invests-10-million-in-digital-identity-company-yoti/ (archived at https://perma.cc/TQ2U-8GGR)

Yapily (2021) European Open Banking League Table, 11 June, www.yapily.com/blog/european-open-banking-league-table (archived at https://perma.cc/K5AM-U3FK)

Yapily (2022) Yapily's 2022 European Open Banking League Table, 6 July, www.yapily.com/blog/2022-european-open-banking-league-table (archived at https://perma.cc/K5AM-U3FK)

06

Women and financial inclusion: why are women more often financially excluded than men?

Introduction

In many countries, more women are excluded from the financial system than men. This chapter intends to explore what holds women back – such as being out of the workforce, living in poor rural areas and whether the pandemic has exacerbated their exclusion – and why the financial system has historically failed women.

CHAPTER OBJECTIVES

Some of the questions to be answered are:

- Is the financial system built to work for men and not for women? And if so, how is this being addressed?
- The role of trust in explaining women's exclusion – how is open banking helping restore trust in financial services?
- How are fintechs breaking new ground when it comes to serving female customers? And is it a case of women helping women?
- What are the opportunities for banks and fintechs to engage more female customers and continue to serve their changing needs?

Chapter 1 established the definitions of financial exclusion and inclusion, as well as the terms banked and underbanked, often referred to as underserved. So, this chapter will pick up where that one left off by revealing the statistics that expose the gender gap at the heart of financial exclusion. It will unpick what these tell us about how and why the financial system is not working for women, and identify some of the fintechs that have set out to provide education, products and services for women in an effort to address the issue.

Is there gender bias in the global financial system?

It is certainly too simplistic to say that the financial system as we know it today was designed by men, is still largely dominated by men in terms of their representation in the workforce and, therefore, works largely for men.

While this is partly true, such generalizations do a disservice to women. Let's face it, women are earning and spending more than ever before. Women control more than 32 per cent of total global wealth and 9 in 10 women are involved in spending and investing decisions in households. Moreover, by 2028, women are expected to own 75 per cent of discretionary spending, writes Kris Gopalakrishnan, chair of GFF 2022, chair of Axilor Venture and co-founder of Infosys (Financial Alliance for Women, 2022).

Should further proof be needed of women's spending power, then women are responsible for more than $31 trillion in yearly consumer spending (Cake Ventures, 2023). In short, women are increasingly wielding a huge amount of influence as more of them participate in the global workforce. In taking home more money, or their own earnings, women have an increased say in household spending and also in other financial decision making within the home.

There has undoubtedly been progress. While account ownership among women is lower than that of men, globally, the gender gap is narrowing (World Bank, 2022). Across developing economies where the gender gap in account ownership is most stark, this has fallen to 6 percentage points, from 9 percentage points where, the World Bank points out, it had 'hovered for many years'. It is a fact, still, that women are more likely than men to be unbanked (World Bank, 2022). The Covid-19 pandemic was widely reported to have set women back in terms of their careers and earning power. At the same time, as we'll see, the pandemic also spurred governments in emerging economies in particular to pay subsidies to women directly, often for the first time. This, in turn, encouraged many women to establish their own digital financial footprint.

The data tells a story

As ever, data can reveal the true extent of women's financial exclusion. The World Bank's Global Findex Database 2021 reported that an estimated 740 million women did not have a bank account globally, which equates to 13 per cent of all adults globally and 54 per cent of the world's unbanked. The Global Findex Database gives a sense of just how disproportionate financial exclusion is, noting that even in countries where the percentage of unbanked is small and where account ownership has been increasing, the majority of unbanked adults continue to be women. It cites Turkey as an example, where around a quarter of adults are unbanked, and 71 per cent of those are women. A similar pattern emerges in Brazil, Russia, Kenya, China and Thailand. In summary, women are so often excluded from formal banking services 'because they lack official forms of identification, do not own a mobile phone or other form of technology, and have lower financial capability' (World Bank, 2022).

The International Monetary Fund's Financial Access Survey (FAS) began collecting gender-disaggregated data on financial access in 2018. The latest data (IMF, 2022) revealed that the gender gap in financial access persisted in many economies in 2021, with women's account ownership, savings and outstanding loans consistently all lower than those of men.

Lack of financial capability and low confidence

Is it any wonder women so often lack the knowledge about managing their own finances when, in many cultures and throughout history, they have been denied jobs, and therefore their own incomes. It is still the case in some countries and cultures that if women do earn their own money, it is handed over to a male family member or their husband – without money or assets in their name, women are unable to build up a credit history. As Chapter 5 explored, being credit invisible can be hugely detrimental.

Over the years, being denied access to what they are owed or have earned has whittled away at confidence levels among women, and the longer women spend external to the financial system, the more this dents their confidence in, and familiarity with, the way it works.

In its Global Findex Database 2021, the World Bank points to a direct correlation between women who have a savings or current account in their name, and financial independence and economic empowerment. According to the report, in the Philippines, women's household decision-making power increased when they used 'commitment savings products' that encouraged them to make regular deposits into a personal bank account – it meant that, ultimately, they were able to make purchases for their household that directly benefitted them, such as a washing machine, for example (World Bank, 2022).

In India, a government programme that paid women their benefits directly into their own account – rather than to an account owned by the male head of the household – not only increased women's financial control, but also provided an incentive to find employment, particularly when compared to those who received the same benefits in cash (World Bank, 2022).

CASE STUDY
The story of Vrinda Gupta and Sequin

This is the experience of Vrinda Gupta, the co-founder and chief executive officer of US-based fintech startup Sequin and a first-generation immigrant to the US. She says:

> I was born in India, my family lived in India before we moved [to the US]. My parents – and especially my mother – really struggled to understand the US financial system, especially when it came to credit. But, for all things finances, my mum really relied on my dad because she was concerned that there were 'gotchas'.

These 'gotchas' that Gupta refers to are the idea that 'she could make a mistake in our family's finances and that could have pretty devastating effects – and she's not wrong'.

Growing up and seeing her own mother fear the system shaped Gupta's career trajectory. She recalls, as a young woman, her mother telling her the importance of being financially independent and of being 'financially empowered'. Gupta says it was 'one of the reasons I wanted to work in financial services in the first place'.

She began her career working at Visa, where she was a product manager, helping to design and develop credit cards. On her LinkedIn profile, Gupta details that she wrote industry standards for Visa Credit Card issuance and won first place in the 'Financial Inclusion' category of the 2016 Visa Hackathon.

However, when it came to applying for a credit card that she helped to build, Gupta was rejected and did not know why.

As she tells it:

> As I did more research, I realized I hadn't been building credit history effectively. The bulk of my credit history was actually tied into my dad's credit. He thought he was doing a great thing to get me credit visible. But, ultimately, especially after you're 18, it's really important to have a credit history in your own name so you're able to show your financial profile and your risk profile accurately. When I got rejected, I didn't have the requisite credit history, despite having a decent income, and despite working at Visa and building these products.

She explains that after this experience, it 'dawned' on her she had not been taught how to navigate the financial system:

In the US, women could be rejected for bank accounts, credit cards and business loans until 1974, which was not that long ago. The impact of that is this huge knowledge gap when it comes to finances, where women are much more likely to make avoidable financial mistakes – whether that is paying a late fee, paying interest, [or] paying the minimum on a credit card. Also, like me, having the bulk of our credit made of a partner or parent's accounts which, at best, leaves you credit invisible and, at worst, your credit can be negatively impacted by someone else. And it's a way of financial control as well, which is a huge problem.

In many instances, then, the first step to getting women banked is education. When it came to starting her own fintech business, Gupta put education at the heart of it, having observed that financial services companies provided the products, or 'financial tools', but did not teach women how to use them.

'If there was financial information, it was not approachable, it was very jargon-filled,' she says.

Gupta founded Sequin 'to help women step into their financial power', according to the Sequin website. She says:

What was really important for me with Sequin was being able to marry those two pieces: where you have a financial tool that is easier to monitor, to manage and more relevant to your lifestyle. But, also, you have the knowledge that's built in so you can take that knowledge and practise that with the tool (Gupta, 2023).

The pink tax

Another driver for Gupta in founding the business was what is known as the 'pink tax' – the term to describe gender-based price disparities. Several studies have been conducted which show just how much more women pay than men for the same everyday products in the US and UK.

The World Economic Forum's Spencer Feingold asserts that 'the pink tax has long imposed an economic burden on women around the world – especially since women continue to earn less than men' (Feingold, 2022).

A US government report focusing on New York found that women pay more throughout their lives for products ranging from toys through to personal care items. The price disparities are depressingly significant – the report reveals that girls' toys cost more 55 per cent of the time, while boys' toys cost more only 8 per cent of the time. Women's personal care products cost more 56 per cent of the time, compared to men's products, which cost more just 13 per cent of the time. The findings are based on analysis of 794 products 'with clear male and female versions from more than 90 brands sold at two dozen New York City retailers, both online and in stores' (New York City Department of Consumer Affairs, 2015).

A study in the UK revealed similar findings after comparing men's and women's toiletries across six retailers, and the price of children's clothing across four retailers (Rift Group, 2018). Women's deodorant is 8.9 per cent more expensive than men's, while a 50ml facial moisturizer for women was found to be 34.3 per cent more expensive than one designed for men. As in the US, the research found that the price disparities apply to women throughout their lives and begin when they are girls, with girls paying 2.73 per cent more for school shirts than boys are expected to pay. Meanwhile, girls' socks are 2.64 per cent more expensive than a pack of boys' socks.

How to appeal to female customers – and why it is important for fintechs to do so

There is a well-known saying – in fact, it is originally a quote from the 1989 film *Field of Dreams* – that is often applied in business: 'If you build it, they will come' (Fracica, 2013). As fintechs have begun to spring up in countries around the world, there has been an assumption that individuals will flock to open accounts and begin banking with these alternatives to the main banking groups. And, to an extent, this has proved to be true. However, a closer look at the demographics of fintech customers shows that not as many women as men have signed up to a fintech.

Globally, only 72 women use fintechs for every 100 men. Women are 26.6 per cent less likely than men to use the products and services being offered by fintechs – a bigger gender gap than in formal account ownership and smartphone ownership, respectively (Financial Alliance for Women, 2021). The Financial Alliance for

Women identifies several reasons for this, one of which is, it claims, that fintechs are adopting 'a gender-neutral approach to doing business' across areas including product development, sales and marketing. The report details that, among many fintechs, the 'user experience is not designed with women customers in mind' and that they fail to understand the behaviours and needs of potential female customers. It goes as far as to state that early-stage fintechs tend to 'target the young, urban male demographic' (Financial Alliance for Women, 2021). In an article for Forbes, Nicole Casperson points out that many financial services companies simply 'underestimate the power of female customers' and end up offering 'repackaged versions' of products and services that were originally designed for men (Casperson, 2023). Despite women accounting for roughly half the world's population, too often they are treated as a niche market, or are lumped together as one homogeneous group to be marketed to.

It is not only women who are losing out – fintechs are too. The Financial Alliance for Women has estimated that fintechs could see a revenue increase of up to 70 per cent should they grow their female customer conversion rates to levels equal to male conversion rates across what it calls 'the sales funnel'.

So, just what is behind this tendency among early-stage fintechs to neglect female customers? In its report, the Financial Alliance for Women (2021) suggests that the lack of female representation at the investor level may be a factor. It claims that 'mostly male' investors 'call the shots and unconscious bias may underpin their decisions'. The report also points to those same investors' focus on women's representation in company leadership and at staff levels within the fintechs they are funding, but explains that this does not extend to 'women's market offerings or the female customer base'. This is backed up by data which shows that only 12 per cent of global fintech founders and co-founders are women, while just 6 per cent have female chief executives (Lau, 2022). Moreover, female-founded startups received a paltry 2.1 per cent of the total capital invested in venture-backed startups in the US and at the 100 largest venture capital firms, women account for fewer than 10 per cent of partners (Lau, 2022).

Could it be that fintechs are falling into the age-old trap of designing products and services in their own image? It certainly seems so.

One obvious way to address the issue is to have more female investors, because they are likely to invest in female founders who, in turn, are likely to have a business that addresses the financial needs of women. However, this has proved to actually be detrimental in some cases, on the basis that female-led firms that raised their first round of venture capital funding solely from female VC partners are then half as likely to secure a second round of investment, compared to those whose first funding round included male partners (Solal and Snellman, 2023). It sounds rather like a Catch-22. Unsurprisingly, perhaps, the same study discovered that among male-led firms, the gender of their first-round investors had no discernible impact on their ability to raise further investment.

As Vrinda Gupta, founder of Sequin, found – and which has been to her fintech's advantage – once you have women customers, fintechs have to be prepared to offer them products and services specific to their needs, such as educational materials and programmes (Gupta, 2023). This is an approach that South Africa's Tyme Group has also adopted. Its banking arm, TymeBank, has 5.7 million customers, with women accounting for 53 per cent of these (Financial Alliance for Women, 2022). Women also make up 72 per cent of the bank's buy now, pay later customers and 64 per cent of its insurance customers. The Financial Alliance for Women reports that TymeBank, unlike other fintechs, has an 'inclusive sales funnel' and reaches 'new-to-banking customers' via kiosks in grocery and retail stores. Given that women are so often the members of their household, particularly in emerging economies, who are responsible for food shopping and purchasing clothing and other supplies for their children, this is a highly targeted way of appealing to them. Even more appealing is the fact that it takes five minutes to sign up to become a customer of the bank at one of these in-store kiosks, with the assistance of 'on-site ambassadors'.

According to the Financial Alliance for Women, TymeBank analyses sex-disaggregated data across its sales funnel, which means it has an understanding of how female customers improve its profitability and which also gives it the insight to be able to create offerings that directly appeal to them. Crucially, as the Financial Alliance for Women observes, while the co-founders are male, Rachel Freeman was the first woman to join the bank's C-suite as chief growth officer.

Access to banking through retailers – TymeBank

As mentioned, TymeBank's strategy has been to place its kiosks in stores and to make the signing-up process at these kiosks quick. But TymeBank is still a digital bank – it has simply found a way to offer an in-store service, if you like, but without the high costs and margins that come with running a network of branches. This has been made possible by the bank's efforts to forge distribution partnerships with several retailers in South Africa, including Pick n Pay, Boxer and The Foschini Group, or TFG. By January 2023, TymeBank had 1,450 kiosks and 15,000 retail points in stores around the country.

Of those 1,450 kiosks, 600 are located in TFG stores, so let's take a closer look at this partnership, which has seen the introduction of co-branded TymeBank-TFG Money financial products and services, not only in store but online as well (TymeBank, 2023). In a press release about the partnership, Coen Jonker, chief executive officer of TymeBank, referred to it as a 'new front door to banking'. It's an example, in my mind, of how true digital banking can be made available to the masses – unbanked, underserved and banked, alike. After all, Jonker states that the bank's mission is 'to bring accessible, affordable banking to all South Africans' (TymeBank, 2023). At a kiosk in a TFG store, someone can open a TymeBank TFG Money bank account without requiring paperwork and with no fees or charges applied.

Customers of the bank can use the kiosks and the app for other financial services, such as making electricity payments and initiating money transfers. This approach is undoubtedly working, with the bank reporting that it acquires 188,000 customers each month on average.

Women in fintech and financial services

Another reason women have been historically underserved by the financial services industry is that they have been underrepresented in the industry itself – certainly, at senior decision-making levels within organizations such as banks and lenders. How can financial services companies design and market products specifically aimed at women when there is a dearth of people represented within their organizations who truly understand this customer segment? That is, women themselves. As women increasingly make the financial decisions in households, and in some cases become the main breadwinner, and account for a larger share of global wealth, financial services companies that fail to address this growing customer base will see a hit to their bottom line. Aiming for better representation of women at all levels within organizations and ensuring they are remunerated in line with men in the same positions is one way to address this.

Unfortunately, while the number of women working in the industry has increased over the years, some parts of financial services are still lagging – namely, fintech. A joint report published by Ernst and Young (EY) and Innovate Finance, looking at the UK fintech sector, revealed that in the UK this sector is less gender diverse than the broader financial services sector, but more diverse than the tech sector in general (EY and Innovate Finance, 2023). The gender split in UK financial services is 56 per cent male and 44 per cent female, and is a much less even 73 per cent male versus 28 per cent female in the country's fintech sector. Within technology firms, EY reported that men make up 74 per cent of the workforce, with women accounting for just 26 per cent.

Does the picture look any better globally? Well, unfortunately not. The same EY and Innovate Finance report cites research from Findexable which found that only 16 of more than 1,000 fintechs globally were founded solely by women. It is also important to consider the roles that women sit in within fintechs, and it is no surprise to learn that they tend to work in marketing or human resources-type roles, rather than in the senior decision-making or product design jobs. Fewer than 6 per cent of fintech chief executives are women, and they make up fewer than 4 per cent of chief information officers and chief technology officers (EY and Innovate Finance, 2023).

The report's authors make an important point – in the context that men have been found to use fintech services more than women – which is that 'even if men make up the majority of the customer base, that's no excuse or justification for gender inequality'. Moreover, EY and Innovate Finance (2023) make the case that more women in the workforce generally, but also in more senior roles within fintechs, could help design products and services that appeal to a broader customer base.

It is a similar story in a report published by Deloitte (2022) – its own research revealed that globally, within financial services institutions, in 2021 women held just 21 per cent of board seats, 19 per cent of C-suite roles and a mere 5 per cent of chief executive positions.

However, there are also some positives to be found in the Deloitte report, which identifies that the US and Canada in particular are making progress when it comes to the share of women in senior industry roles. It reveals that, in Canada, women account for 22.5 per cent of C-suite roles, 21.2 per cent of senior leadership positions and 33.6 per cent of what it calls 'next generation' roles, defined as manager or equivalent titles below senior leadership.

Perhaps more importantly, according to Deloitte, that share is expected to grow. It predicts that by 2030, the share of women in C-suite positions will increase by 8.2 percentage points to reach 30.8 per cent. It is a similar picture in the US, with Deloitte forecasting a 7 percentage point rise in women at C-suite level, taking the proportion to nearly 30 per cent by the end of the decade.

It is hardly surprising that the largest percentage currently, or projected growth, in women's share of senior leadership roles is found in countries where the government or industry has adopted quotas or specific measures promoting gender equality. For example, Deloitte (2022) cites Canada's National Instrument 58-101, which requires transparency 'related to gender diversity policies', including explicit targets for females in executive positions.

Within Europe, Deloitte refers to France as 'a proponent of quotas to drive change' – an approach that seems to be working. The report states that women currently account for 21.4 per cent of C-suite jobs, and that this is expected to rise to 28 per cent by 2030. The implementation of a 40 per cent quota for women on supervisory boards nearly 10 years ago has accelerated this trend. In 2021, France introduced gender quotas for senior leadership and management committee seats that apply to those companies with more than 1,000 employees (Deloitte, 2022).

On the other side of the world, Australia has demonstrated real and measurable progress when it comes to women's representation in the higher echelons of financial services. According to Deloitte, it has the highest forecasted share of women in the C-suite by 2030, at 35.7 per cent. This has been made possible by the Workplace Gender Equality Act of 2012, which established the Workplace Gender Equality Agency. The Act requires Australian employers with 100 or more employees to disclose annually the gender composition of their workforce, as well as report each year against five other gender 'equality indicators' (WGEA, 2012). In 2023, Australia's government took proactive steps to address the gender pay gap, after the WGEA reported that women earn 22.8 per cent less than their male counterparts (Lee, 2022). Crucially, those working in finance companies saw the largest wage gaps between male and female workers, according to WGEA figures.

How did the government respond? It introduced new legislation in February 2023, requiring employers with more than 100 staff to publish their gender pay gaps on the WGEA website (Tilo, 2023). The idea is that this will encourage transparency and accountability.

Does reporting spur change? The UK's experience

This new Australian policy may sound familiar to those in the UK, where mandatory gender pay gap reporting was introduced in 2017. Employers with 250 employees or more are required to report their gender pay gap data on a specific date each year, known as the 'snapshot date' (Government Equalities Office, 2023). They must subsequently report and publish the gender pay gap data within a year of the snapshot date.

Now in its sixth year, has putting companies' remuneration data under the spotlight had a positive impact?

There is no doubt that, increasingly, companies are being held to account by the public, stakeholders and government for any gender disparities in pay, and other metrics too. Initiatives such as the one in the UK, which require full transparency, are becoming part of normal business operations. As PwC (2023) points out, the gender pay gap is a key metric within sustainability reporting frameworks, as part of the 'S' – which stands for 'social' – in ESG.

Evidence suggests, though, that in the UK companies consider this policy to be a reporting requirement and nothing more – with little incentive to take stock each year and consider what needs to be done to stimulate change and then act on it.

PwC's analysis showed that the building societies, banking and insurance sectors continued to have the highest mean hourly pay gaps in the 2022/23 reporting period, despite being one of the sectors with the largest decreases in mean gender pay gaps. In its report, PwC points out that organizations refer to 'social context and external challenges' as reasons for the lack of progress in closing the gender pay gap. The solution, as far as PwC is concerned, is for companies to see beyond 'reportable numbers' and to get to grips with understanding the 'underlying inequalities' that continue to affect remuneration.

Analysis of the UK's gender reporting gap found that at some of the largest companies the median hourly pay gap has, in fact, worsened. The FT reported that men are paid more than women at 79.5 per cent of companies, up from 77.2 per cent in 2017, when the mandatory pay gap reporting legislation took effect. Five years on, the median hourly pay for men is 12.2 per cent more than that of women, meaning it has increased from 11.9 per cent in 2017 (Murray, 2023).

Banks are some of the worst offenders, where the largest mean hourly pay gaps are to be found. Lloyds Bank has the widest median hourly pay gap at 40.9 per cent, although this has reduced by a slim 1.8 percentage points since 2017. Its parent company is not much better – Lloyds Banking Group pays its male employees 34.8 per cent more on average than their female colleagues. However, Lloyds has succeeded in reducing the bonus gap by a fifth over the past five years (Murray, 2023).

Addressing the lack of diversity in fintech

Hiring more women in senior positions within fintechs, as well as funding more female-founded fintechs, is all well and good. Yet, if the majority of those women are white, fintechs are still potentially failing to address certain demographic groups in their product design and marketing strategies. Within female representation, diversity is all-important. It is critical that, within those female-held roles, there

Table 6.1   Finance and tech professional demographics by race and gender in the US

% of workforce	Finance	Tech	Overall US workforce
Women	46%	25%	47%
Women in leadership (director, vice president, general manager and executive levels)	15%	11%	32%
Hispanic/Latinx	10%	8%	17%
Black/African American	6%	7%	13%
Asian	9%	20%	6%
American Indian/Alaskan Native	0.1%	0.005%	1%
Other/unknown	4%	No data	No data

SOURCE   Fintech is Femme and Array, 2023

is a cross-section of lived experiences represented. In this regard, there is still much work for fintechs to do. In fact, why stop there? Across the fintech workforce, diversity should be in evidence.

A US-focused report states that, in the tech and finance industries respectively, women and Black, Indigenous, and people of colour – referred to as BIPOC – are still 'significantly underrepresented' (Fintech is Femme and Array, 2023). In the US, the overall workforce is becoming more diverse – the same report cites the fact that women and people of colour account for a growing share of the entire workforce. However, within the finance industry in the US, only 26.4 per cent of finance professionals are women, with men accounting for 73.6 per cent (Zippia, 2023). The most common ethnicity among US finance professionals is white – see Table 6.1 for a full breakdown.

The statistics paint a stark picture of lack of diversity across the spectrum. So, what is the solution? Financial institutions, from the largest banks to the smallest fintechs, can effect change. In fact, early-stage fintechs may be in a better position to address the lack of diversity in the industry, given their nimbleness and the fact that, as they create new positions internally, they can fill senior roles in a way that creates a more diverse and inclusive workforce. Martin Toha, chief executive of Array, cautions that if fintechs do not start early 'when you're scaling', then it can become 'almost impossible' later on to rectify inequalities and underrepresentation (Fintech is Femme and Array, 2023). He also warns that it can be all too easy for 'sameness' to 'become normalized', particularly if it has proven to be successful.

- Establish a diversity, equity and inclusion policy, and disseminate among new and existing employees. Also, make it visible to clients and partners online – indeed, make it a core reason for them to work with you.

- Data is your friend – track progress. US-based fintech Array collects DEIB data to 'support ongoing action, transparency, thoughtful analysis and accountability' (Fintech is Femme and Array, 2023). That last point – accountability – is vital. Fintech founders and chief executives must be accountable for the progress, or lack thereof, in this area. Transparency is vital – make the data widely available internally.

- Recruitment – the language used in job descriptions matters because it has varying appeal to different demographic groups. Certain words are 'gendered' – that is, they typically appeal to either men or women. Take the word 'aggressive', which is generally considered a masculine 'trait' or descriptor and is, therefore, a turn-off for female applicants in a job description.

- It doesn't start and end with recruitment. If you already have a diverse workforce, then celebrate it. Array reports that it introduced monthly cultural and heritage celebrations as a way of learning, but also to increase awareness and empathy among its employees (Fintech is Femme and Array, 2023). This can be broadened to include a fintech's external community too – maybe the neighbourhood it is located in, or its clients and wider connections.

Is access to credit biased against women?

Is the system rigged to favour men, especially when it comes to accessing lines of credit? It is a loaded question and an emotive subject. As someone who identifies as female, it can tend to feel like the odds are stacked against us. But, as with so much in financial inclusion, there is nuance.

Let's take a look at the stats to answer this question and to build up a more accurate picture of the situation for women globally.

To begin with, we know that women earn less than men, typically, and that this applies worldwide. So, in some respects, women may have more reasons to apply for credit or a loan, given the shortfall in their income. However, there are times when higher earnings get individuals access to more banking and financial services than those on lower incomes.

In the US in 2022, women earned 82 per cent of the amount earned by men, on average, according to the Pew Research Center analysis (Aragao, 2023). Little has changed in the past two decades, it seems – back in 2002, women earned 80 per cent of what men earned.

Research conducted by the Federal Reserve Bank of Philadelphia among US men and women found there is a gender gap or difference in bank card borrowing limits, which it calls 'unexplained' (Konish, 2021). The research reveals the gap amounts to $1,323, with male borrowers having higher borrowing limits, even when controlling for credit score, as well as income and demographic characteristics. The gender borrowing limit gap was reported as varying 'by the size of consumers' credit limits', with women having more 'borrowing power' for smaller limits. Meanwhile, for higher limits of between $30,000 and $40,000, the research discovered men had access to more credit (Konish, 2021).

The way in which women use credit has also been found to differ.

The Equal Credit Opportunity Act

The introduction of the Equal Credit Opportunity Act of 1974 in the US has been a game changer for women – and, indeed, so many other demographic groups. It marked the point at which lenders were banned from discriminating against consumers based on their sex or marital status (McGurran, 2020).

In fact, it goes further than that, prohibiting discrimination on the basis of race, colour, religion, national origin and age, in addition to sex and marital status (Federal Trade Commission, nd). The Federal Trade Commission states that the Act brought in a requirement for creditors to provide an explanation to applicants any time a request for credit was turned down.

However, Geng Li, assistant director of the Federal Reserve Board, points out that data limitations as a result of the Act can make it difficult to ascertain gender-related discrepancies in the credit industry. This is because, as he writes, the Act prohibits the use of demographic information in the underwriting process, in pricing, reporting and scoring (Li, 2018). There is also another factor at play, which is that, as Li explains, married couples typically make financial decisions together, which adds to the 'complexity of identifying gender-specific credit market experiences and decisions'.

Despite the challenges of sourcing accurate and reliable data, Li's own study using a 'unique proprietary data set' to observe differences in the 'credit market experiences' between single men and women under the age of 40 is able to draw some valuable conclusions, namely that women in this age group tend to have lower credit scores than men in the same age bracket, reflecting the fact that 'single women have more intensive use of credit' and have experienced more difficulties paying off their debt in the past. Li suggests some of the factors at play include economic circumstances, labour market experiences, differing attitudes to borrowing between genders, levels of financial literacy, and the different ways in which men and women are treated by the credit market and institutions. Meanwhile, women's personal finances tend to be affected more than men's when marriages end in separation and divorce (Li, 2018).

The curious case of the Apple Card

One couple's experience of the credit lines available to them on their respective Apple Cards led to an investigation to determine whether the algorithm at the heart of the underwriting process could possibly be discriminating on the basis of gender. The discrepancies came to light via a series of tweets by one half of the couple in question, David Heinemeier Hansson, a software developer (Vigdor, 2019). The Apple Card is a partnership between Apple and Goldman Sachs, and was launched in August 2019. The tweets in November of that year were picked up by New York state regulators, who subsequently announced an investigation into the algorithm used by the Apple Card to make credit decisions (Vigdor, 2019).

Heinemeier Hansson's Twitter thread began with him explaining that he and his wife had 'filed joint tax returns, live in a community-property state, and have been married for a long time' but that 'Apple's black box algorithm thinks I deserve 20x the credit limit she does'. Both Hansson and his wife ended up checking their credit scores, at the suggestion of an Apple representative – as revealed in his Twitter thread – only to find that she had a higher credit score than him (Heinemeier Hansson, 2019).

Heinemeier Hansson and his wife were not the only ones who thought there was gender bias in Apple Card's algorithm. It turns out that one of the co-founders of Apple, Steve Wozniak, had the same experience when he and his wife applied for the card. He tweeted that he received '10x the credit limit' his wife was offered, adding that 'we have no separate bank or credit card accounts or any separate assets' (Wozniak, 2019).

However, the New York State Department of Financial Services investigation into the Apple Card, following consumer complaints, the findings of which were published in a report in March 2021, found no evidence of 'unlawful discrimination against applicants under fair lending law'. The investigation revealed that men and women applying for the Apple Card with 'similar credit characteristics' largely had the same outcomes. However, it did draw attention to what the superintendent of financial services Linda A Lacewell called the 'disparities in access to credit that continue nearly 50 years after the passage of the Equal Credit Opportunities Act' (New York State Department of Financial Services, 2021). The department's report stressed the need for the 'modernization' of credit scoring to 'improve access to credit'. It highlighted an important issue – and one that was raised by Heinemeier Hansson – that if an account owner shared their credit card with a spouse, even if they were added to the account as an 'authorized user', they were 'entitled to the same credit terms'. Whereas the department stated in its report that underwriters 'are not required to treat authorized users the same as account holders'.

Summary

Reading a story like the one recounted by Vrinda Gupta in this chapter, about her experience of being rejected for a financial product, and how she was able to overcome the financial fears that had dogged her mother to become financially independent, is hopeful. More inspiring still is that she uses these experiences to help other women through Sequin, the company she founded. But it also shows how far women still have to go to carve out a space for themselves in banking and the wider financial services industry.

Since founding Sequin at the end of 2019, Gupta says there has been 'more of a conversation around the necessity for gender-focused finances'. She also acknowledges, despite the work she is doing through Sequin, that 'we're very far from closing the [gender] gaps'. 'I think the issue is multi-faceted,' she explains. 'It's not enough to just say this is a problem. These are deep systemic issues that require time, but also they require a multi-faceted approach. Whether it is the knowledge, the tools, whether it's the way society talks to women about finances, whether it's the way women talk to one another about finances.'

Women have long been excluded from the financial system – they have repeatedly been denied access to financial services, and often to their own wealth and assets. Women are disadvantaged by the gender wage gap and, even earlier than that, before they are even able to earn money, girls are charged more for essential items than boys. Such setbacks are able to be overcome, particularly when women are allowed to design their own products and services – and, of course, when they are allowed to earn their own income.

One of the most effective ways for the financial services industry – that's banks and fintechs – to ensure they are specifically catering to female customers is to hire women to work within these organizations. That means also funding female-led startups and fintechs. Let's also move on from the unhelpful assumption that fewer women are customers of fintechs, therefore these companies do not need to target them as clients. As in the case of TymeBank, when the way women access and use credit is well understood and subsequently designed, both women and financial institutions benefit.

Holding companies to account and questioning their credit decisioning processes and algorithms is also proven to work. The Apple Card case is testament to that – although the subsequent investigation into Apple and Goldman Sachs may not have found evidence of gender discrimination, it did bring the issue to a wider audience via social media. It also put renewed pressure on financial institutions to move on from archaic credit scoring and decisioning processes, to a modern approach that reflects how men and women live today.

Most importantly of all, let's keep the conversation going about women's access to financial services and to credit. As Gupta puts it, the belief that it has been solved is the problem, 'because it stifles the conversation'.

References

Aragao, C (2023) Gender pay gap in U.S. hasn't changed much in two decades, Pew Research Center, 1 March, www.pewresearch.org/short-reads/2023/03/01/gender-pay-gap-facts/ (archived at https://perma.cc/T83T-8REM)

Cake Ventures (2023) Finding alpha: the trillion dollar female economy, www.cake.vc/whitepaper (archived at https://perma.cc/D4LE-8QYJ)

Casperson, N (2023) How Fintech can unlock the $31 trillion dollar female economy, Forbes, 22 August, www.forbes.com/sites/nicolecasperson/2023/08/22/how-fintech-can-unlock-the-31-trillion-female-economy/ (archived at https://perma.cc/X47U-D3HJ)

Deloitte (2022) Advancing more women leaders in financial services: A global report, www2.deloitte.com/xe/en/insights/industry/financial-services/gender-diversity-in-global-financial-services.html (archived at https://perma.cc/7A8V-W34H)

EY and Innovate Finance (2023) Changing the face of UK FinTech. From glass ceiling to open doors: championing equality and career progression for women in FinTech, https://assets.ey.com/content/dam/ey-sites/ey-com/en_uk/topics/banking-and-capital-markets/changing-the-face-of-uk-fintech.pdf (archived at https://perma.cc/KK7H-TNJG)

Federal Trade Commission (nd) Equal Credit Opportunity Act, www.ftc.gov/legal-library/browse/statutes/equal-credit-opportunity-act (archived at https://perma.cc/4GKG-7CRC)

Feingold, S (2022) What is the 'pink tax' and how does it hinder women?, World Economic Forum, https://www.weforum.org/agenda/2022/07/what-is-the-pink-tax-and-how-does-it-hinder-women/ (archived at https://perma.cc/3J67-QFPQ)

Financial Alliance for Women (2021) Gender-intelligent fintech design: how fintechs can capture the female economy, https://financialallianceforwomen.org/download/how-fintechs-can-capture-the-female-economy/ (archived at https://perma.cc/TD7M-96MH)

Financial Alliance for Women (2022) Tyme Group: Closing the banking gap with gender-intelligent digital services, https://financialallianceforwomen.org/download/tyme-closing-the-banking-gap-with-gender-intelligent-digital-services/ (archived at https://perma.cc/4XX2-92PA)

Fintech is Femme and Array (2023) Building your diversity, equity, inclusion, and belonging (DEIB) blueprint in fintech, https://workweek.com/wp-content/uploads/2023/05/Fintech-is-Femme-Array-DEIB-Report-2023.pdf (archived at https://perma.cc/65LQ-A4TC)

Fracica, A (2013) If you build it, they will come, Contracting Business, 8 May, www.contractingbusiness.com/residential-hvac/article/20866189/if-you-build-it-they-will-come (archived at https://perma.cc/7GPJ-JJ3Z)

Gopalakrishnan, K (2022) Financial Alliance for Women: Fintechs serving the female economy, https://financialallianceforwomen.org/download/fintechs-serving-the-female-economy/ (archived at https://perma.cc/KG4A-E8FM)

Government Equalities Office (2023) Gender pay gap reporting: guidance for employers, GOV.UK, 15 March, www.gov.uk/government/publications/gender-pay-gap-reporting-guidance-for-employers (archived at https://perma.cc/69DV-TL27)

Gupta, V (2023) Interview with Ellie Duncan, 23 January

Heinemeier Hansson, D (2019) The @AppleCard is such a f***ing sexist program. My wife and I filed joint tax returns, live in a community-property state, and have been married for a long time. Yet Apple's black box algorithm thinks I deserve 20x the credit limit she does. No appeals work. [Twitter] 7 November, https://twitter.com/dhh/status/1192540900393705474?lang=en (archived at https://perma.cc/V2KV-ANG8)

International Monetary Fund (2022) Financial Access Survey: 2022 Trends and Developments, https://www.imf.org/en/News/Articles/2022/10/04/pr22332-imf-releases-the-2022-financial-access-survey-results (archived at https://perma.cc/3GBW-CUU4)

Konish, L (2021) Men tend to have higher total credit limits than female borrowers, research finds, CNBC, 9 November, www.cnbc.com/2021/11/09/men-tend-to-have-higher-credit-limits-than-female-borrowers.html (archived at https://perma.cc/2CXS-K9N9)

Lau, T (2022) EXCLUSIVE: Have we really done well enough? – Theodora Lau in The Fintech Magazine, Fintech Finance News, 1 November, https://ffnews.com/newsarticle/exclusive-have-we-really-done-well-enough-theodora-lau-in-the-fintech-magazine/ (archived at https://perma.cc/6RU2-RWH3)

Lee, C (2022) Employers in Australia urged to close gender pay gap, HRM Asia, 13 December, https://hrmasia.com/employers-in-australia-urged-to-close-gender-pay-gap/ (archived at https://perma.cc/N9JF-MAJF)

Li, G (2018) Gender-related differences in credit use and credit scores, Federal Reserve, 22 June, www.federalreserve.gov/econres/notes/feds-notes/gender-related-differences-in-credit-use-and-credit-scores-20180622.html (archived at https://perma.cc/B7ML-PLCK)

McGurran, B (2020) Women and credit 2020: How history shaped today's credit landscape, Experian, 28 February, www.experian.com/blogs/ask-experian/women-and-credit/ (archived at https://perma.cc/84TM-CAHD)

Murray, C (2023) Gender pay gap: many of the UK's biggest employers fail to make progress, Raconteur, 5 April, www.raconteur.net/responsible-business/gender-pay-gap-uks-biggest-employers/ (archived at https://perma.cc/289F-5TU8)

New York City Department of Consumer Affairs (2015) From cradle to cane: the cost of being a female consumer, a study of gender pricing in New York City, Study-of-Gender-Pricing-in-NYC.pdf

New York State Department of Financial Services (2021) DFS issues findings on the Apple Card and its underwriter Goldman Sachs bank, Dfs.ny.gov 23 March, www.dfs.ny.gov/reports_and_publications/press_releases/pr202103231 (archived at https://perma.cc/NU9R-BZX5)

PwC (2023) Beyond the gender pay gap: Embracing broader diversity, equity and inclusion reporting to create meaningful change, Year 6 gender pay gap reporting 2022/23, www.pwc.co.uk/human-resource-services/assets/pdfs/year-6-gender-pay-gap-report-2022-2023.pdf (archived at https://perma.cc/LX4D-HR9C)

Rift Group (2018) Pink Tax today: How much extra do girls and women pay for everyday essentials?, https://www.riftrefunds.co.uk/blogs/pink-tax-today-how-much-extra-do-women-and-girls-pay-for-everyday-essentials/ (archived at https://perma.cc/L2W7-A95R)

Solal, I and Snellman, K (2023) For female founders, fundraising only from female VCs comes at a cost, *Harvard Business Review*, 1 February, https://hbr.org/2023/02/for-female-founders-only-fundraising-from-female-vcs-comes-at-a-cost (archived at https://perma.cc/2XQF-CMCQ)

Tilo, D (2023) Get ready: Govt plans to publish gender pay gaps, Human Resources Director, 10 February, www.hcamag.com/au/specialisation/diversity-inclusion/get-ready-govt-plans-to-publish-gender-pay-gaps/435881 (archived at https://perma.cc/J3B2-UDPE)

TymeBank (2023) TymeBank-TFG partnership opens a new front door to banking, TymeBank, 26 January, www.tymebank.co.za/press/tymebank-tfg-partnership-opens-a-new-front-door-to-banking/ (archived at https://perma.cc/JRF6-UFED)

Vigdor (2019) Apple Card investigated after gender discrimination complaints, *The New York Times*, 10 November, www.nytimes.com/2019/11/10/business/Apple-credit-card-investigation.html (archived at https://perma.cc/MAQ6-TWHF)

Workplace Gender Equality Agency (2012) What we do, Australian Government, www.wgea.gov.au/what-we-do (archived at https://perma.cc/8BTU-5M38)

World Bank (2022) Global Findex Database 2021: Financial inclusion, digital payments, and resilience in the age of COVID-19, www.worldbank.org/en/publication/globalfindex (archived at https://perma.cc/B76A-Q4N4)

Wozniak, S (2019) The same thing happened to us. I got 10x the credit limit. We have no separate bank or credit card accounts or any separate assets. Hard to get to a human for a correction though. It's big tech in 2019 [Twitter] 10 November, https://twitter.com/stevewoz/status/1193330241478901760 (archived at https://perma.cc/7RF8-FCJF)

Zippia (2023) Finance professional demographics and statistics in the US, Zippia, 21 July, www.zippia.com/finance-professional-jobs/demographics/ (archived at https://perma.cc/Z39H-6W8S)

Why are some countries yet to implement open banking?

07

Introduction

Open banking may still be in its infancy, but as some of the other chapters in this book have outlined, in many countries – both developed and developing – there are a growing number of examples and case studies where its potential to create a more equitable banking system is being realized.

However, there are also countries yet to implement open banking – even in jurisdictions where there is a will, there does not always appear to be a way. So, what needs to happen for countries to forge a path to open banking where there seems to be initial resistance?

CHAPTER OBJECTIVES

Questions to be answered in this chapter are:

- What is holding some countries back from implementing open banking?
- How important are political backing and regulatory intervention in getting open banking prioritized and over the line?
- What can be learned from Canada's experience of trying to adopt an open banking regime?

- How much does trust in the existing banking and financial services system play a part? Where there are high levels of trust, is there less urgency in adopting open banking?
- How important are advocacy groups in open banking implementations? What part have they played in getting buy-in for Australia's Consumer Data Right?
- Are there lessons to be learned from Europe's reticence? A closer look at the road to open banking in Bulgaria.
- Is the financial inclusion aspect getting overlooked in some countries? And if so, how can industry, government and regulators be convinced of the value in providing financial security for larger swathes of their population?

Where in the world?

Many countries worldwide are now live with open banking APIs – whether as a result of the industry participants having taken the initiative, or it has been mandated by a government body, the open banking movement is well underway. There are still many jurisdictions that, as yet, do not have open banking in any form. Many of the countries without open banking are in parts of Latin America, the Middle East and Africa, parts of Eastern Europe and Southeast Asia (Ozone API, 2023). What many of these countries have in common is significant numbers of unbanked individuals and an informal financial services system.

Given the evidence that open banking is an effective way to support a financially inclusive society, what is stopping some countries from implementing it?

Perhaps one reason is that because there is little widespread knowledge among consumers of open banking, governments and financial institutions do not typically come under pressure from the wider population to adopt it. Increasingly though, banks and financial institutions are required to answer to stakeholder and political pressure on a range of issues – in particular, those that come under a company's environmental, social and governance (ESG) policies. Open banking could certainly be said to come under the 's' in ESG, given that extending banking to unserved and underserved individuals has myriad social implications.

Can Canada overcome its inertia?

In some countries, open banking progress has stalled due to a lack of incentives, some of which are commercial and others more political or regulatory. In Canada, for example, the six largest banks have long engendered high levels of trust among consumers – that's CIBC, National Bank of Canada, Scotiabank, BMO, TD Bank and Royal Bank of Canada. In part, this is down to the enduring stability of Canada's banking system. During the 2007–08 financial crisis, which started in the US before spreading into the UK and Europe, some of the biggest US and European institutions collapsed after a huge run on the banks. Or, to prevent them from folding, many institutions required taxpayer-funded bailouts. However, there was not a single bank failure in Canada throughout what became known as the Great Financial Crisis. The last deposit-taking institution to have failed in Canada was back in 1996, when the Calgary-based Security Home Mortgage Corporation closed. According to the Canada Deposit Insurance Corporation (CDIC), which protects customers' bank deposits, the closure of that institution affected $42 million belonging to 26,000 depositors. Yet, within three weeks, all of its customers had received payouts from the CDIC. By comparison, the Federal Deposit Insurance Corporation (FDIC) reported that since 2001, 564 banks have failed in the US (Wells, 2023).

It is worth taking into consideration the size of those respective countries' banking industries. Canada has only 28 domestic banks and its six largest banking groups collectively control more than 85 per cent of domestic assets. The number of banks in the US runs into the thousands – there are more than 7,000 domestic banks in the US (Butterfield et al, 2023). See Chapter 2 for a fuller picture of the US banking industry.

High levels of trust in Canada's banks have translated into brand loyalty. When Canadians were asked how willing they would be to change their primary banking provider, 34 per cent answered 'very unlikely', and only 14 per cent and 9 per cent would be 'likely' or 'very likely' respectively (Statista, 2023). In other words, Canada's banks have a captive audience – so why would they want to risk losing that to other, challenger institutions or fintechs by adopting open banking APIs?

Reuben Piryatinsky, chief executive of Altitude Consulting, says that this has created a sense of 'inertia' among the banks. He suggests that 'knowing the vast majority of deposits is already held with the big FIs' there is little incentive for the largest banks to share customers' data. And there is certainly even less of an incentive to provide APIs for customers to export their data to 'shop around more easily and to facilitate moving from one financial institution to a different institution' (Piryatinsky, 2023).

On the other hand, the banks are in a highly favourable position, as they have already won the trust of consumers and have longstanding client relationships. As Piryatinsky observes, consumers have been able to shop around at other financial institutions for decades, in search of the best rates and products. 'Customers have been opening accounts, they have been moving money,' he says. 'So, essentially, open banking provides an opportunity for the big financial institutions to win – not only on the products they offer, but also on the customer service and how well they know the customer through richer data.'

Serving the underserved

Perhaps another incentive that is lacking in Canada is the number of unbanked. There are relatively few unbanked individuals in the country, which is certainly to be celebrated and is remarkable considering it welcomes so many immigrants annually. In 2022, Canada met its target of admitting 431,645 new permanent residents to the country – the largest number of people ever welcomed in a single year in Canada's history (Immigration, Refugees and Citizenship Canada, 2023). That same year, Immigration, Refugees and Citizenship Canada (IRCC) processed approximately 5.2 million applications for permanent residence, temporary residence and citizenship.

Meanwhile, between 2016 and 2021, more than 1.3 million new immigrants settled permanently in the country (Immigration, Refugees and Citizenship Canada, 2023).

An organization called Acorn Canada and the Canadian Centre for Policy Alternatives put the number of unbanked at approximately 1 million people, or 3 per cent of the population (Peesker, 2019). In some ways, then, Canada is already a financially inclusive society – or, at least, it would like to think it is. However, despite the low levels of unbanked individuals, it does not mean that those who are banked are being well served by financial institutions. The same organizations estimate that 15 per cent, or around 5 million, Canadians are underserved (Peesker, 2019). In Canada, the majority of those who are unbanked or underbanked are on low incomes, defined as a household or individual earning under 50 per cent of the median household income which, in 2018, was less than $18,380 (Banjoko, 2021).

Michelle Beyo, who is chief executive of Finavator and president of the Open Finance Network of Canada, says: 'We don't have very many unbanked, but we do have quite a few underserved Canadians that are just getting very basic banking.' She explains that individuals want a 'visualization of where all of their finances are' in a 'dashboard' format, which open banking could give them to help build an understanding of their finances. However, given that many of those underserved are not financially literate, Beyo says that requiring them to go to multiple websites and statements, and make an assessment on their savings or investments – if they have them – is 'very difficult'.

She asserts that open finance, when it is fully implemented, will give Canadians the opportunity to port their data over to a fintech or another bank 'so that you're getting the best product based on your behaviour, based on what you've done with your finances over the years'. Beyo says that this, in turn, will drive 'a new level playing field', encouraging consumers who might be 'paying more for the services they have and not getting very customized services' to bank, save or invest elsewhere. Of course, it will also ensure Canadians are not left exposed to the dangers posed by screen scraping – see Chapter 2 for an explanation of screen scraping.

Ultimately, the widespread adoption of open finance will encourage more fintechs to spring up, heralding an era of increasingly sophisticated banking, where personalized financial products and services, widening to include wealth and insurance, are the norm – all of which will combine to drive financial inclusion, Beyo adds (Beyo, 2023).

Five reasons why Canada – and other countries – are hesitant

High levels of trust among consumers in banking institutions and low numbers of unbanked individuals are certainly factors in Canada's tentative steps towards open banking and open finance. But they do not tell the whole story.

Altitude Consulting's Reuben Piryatinsky (2023) has identified five reasons Canada has been holding back when it comes to implementation:

1 'regulatory direction'
2 the solidity of the banking sector in Canada (as discussed previously)
3 liability
4 accreditation
5 monetization

Regulation

The absence of a 'regulatory requirement or imperative' initially, Piryatinsky argues, has resulted in 'a lack of clarity from some financial institutions as to what to do', with questions being asked about 'how do we get ready for open banking?'

It is true that a lack of clarity, or an explicit commitment or deadline for implementation is a barrier for banks and other financial institutions. After all, how are they meant to invest in the technology and infrastructure required for open banking when they do not even know if, or when, it will come into effect?

Let's go right back to the beginning which, in this case, is 2018. The Canadian Government's Department of Finance 'undertook a review of open banking', appointing an advisory committee to 'guide' said review. The findings from this initial review were released in early 2020, proposing that 'industry and government should collaborate to develop a framework' for 'the safe introduction' of open banking in Canada. The next stage – phase two – began in November of 2020, when the advisory committee held further stakeholder consultations, taking into consideration 'consumer privacy, security, access and recourse'. The FCAC fed into the design of a framework to ensure consumers are protected (Financial Consumer Agency of Canada, 2023).

The committee's final report was delivered to the Minister of Finance Chrystia Freeland in April 2021 (Financial Consumer Agency of Canada, 2022) and made publicly available in August the same year. At this stage, the recommendation was for a 'hybrid, made-in-Canada' approach to implementation and that the initial phase of this should ensure it is operational by January 2023. Speed was seen as a necessity to eliminate screen scraping, which the report identified as posing 'real security and liability risks' to Canadians (Duncan, 2021). Another recommendation out of the final report was the appointment of an 'open banking lead', whose responsibility it would be to convene industry and who reported to the Finance Minister.

It took until March 2022 for the open banking lead, Abraham Tachjian, to be appointed, by which point, another six months had passed without any further developments. Given that the entire process had begun back in 2018, Canada was now four years in and no further towards having a framework or regulatory roadmap in place. Finally, in November 2023, in the Fall Economic Statement, Freeland announced her intention to deliver 'consumer-driven banking', with the framework legislation due to be outlined in Budget 2024 (Duncan, 2023). It is worth comparing Canada's progress to the speed at which Brazil introduced open finance – see Chapter 4 – and at which the UK mandated open banking (see Chapter 5).

Piryatinsky says: 'Having no clear regulatory direction put the brakes on how fast the market was able to move and was ready to move because of the risks involved. Even in early 2023, the regulatory landscape [was] still being shaped for open banking through

Canada's open banking lead Abraham Tachjian and the working groups that he leads with the Department of Finance, as well as the industry.'

Liability

Interestingly, Piryatinsky believes that liability is the second blocker when it comes to progression. He explains: 'In an open banking ecosystem, there are multiple players – there are banks, fintechs, there are third parties as well – and the question of liability arises. Who's going to be liable for a data breach, for any kind of financial fraud?'

The issue of liability is, of course, not to be taken lightly and is one that has required serious consideration in jurisdictions where open banking is already live. In the US, where the market led open banking adoption, but where the Consumer Financial Protection Bureau has announced its intention to provide some regulatory oversight in due course, liability has been raised by the banks as an important issue (Weinberger, 2022). Steve Boms, executive director of industry group FDATA North America, has said that the organization and its members have been advocating for an open banking framework 'under which the entity responsible for a breach that results in financial loss to a consumer is responsible for making the consumer whole' (Weinberger, 2022).

The issue was also raised by Michael Hsu, acting Comptroller of the Currency in a speech in April 2023. He pointed out that banks, as data providers under an open banking regime, will have to 'interact with aggregators, fintechs, technology firms and competitor banks' and that, in doing so, this will likely 'raise accountability challenges when mistakes are made and consumers are hurt'. He suggested that the Office of the Comptroller of the Currency's (OCC's) third-party risk management expectations could 'provide a foundation for banks to assess those relationships', albeit with the caveat these will need 'some evolution and refinement' as the open banking and fintech 'landscape' evolves (Hsu, 2023).

Research conducted among Canadians by the FCAC reveals just how important liability is to consumers. When asked what protections they expect in open banking, and that would make them more likely to use it, 70 per cent – making it the most popular – cite 'full protection from any losses when something goes wrong', while 'requirements to report data breaches exposing consumer data' was chosen by 63 per cent of respondents (Financial Consumer Agency of Canada, 2023).

Accreditation and monetization

So, what other aspects of open banking are holding up Canada's implementation? Reuben Piryatinsky suggests that accreditation is one.

'Essentially, being in an open banking environment allows third parties to receive customers' personal and financial information, and the accreditation piece becomes important because any financial institution needs to be discerning with who that information can be disclosed to,' he explains. These could be the requirements that a fintech, for example, would need to meet to participate, including financial requirements, liquidity requirements, security requirements, technology requirements, insurance requirements, governance, 'and so on'.

The solution to this is an accreditation framework and a 'central party that enforces accreditation', says Piryatinsky. This central body would decide which third parties can take part in the ecosystem versus those that cannot, and 'what they need to do to participate'.

And the final reason for open banking's delay in Canada, according to Piryatinsky, is monetization. He observes that open banking – and, indeed, any kind of ecosystem implementation – requires 'a huge investment for financial institutions, in terms of opening up their data, in terms of getting their systems ready for external consumption'. It raises a number of questions, he says:

- After this big investment what's in it for us?
- How do we monetize it?
- When does this investment pay off, and in what ways?

These are questions that banks and other financial institutions need answers to – not only in Canada, but other jurisdictions – for them to truly commit to open banking.

'In terms of monetization, my view is it's important to focus on specific use cases that are directly related to customer needs – whether it is an individual consumer or a business and how they're going to use a specific product or service,' Piryatinsky explains, citing access to credit and expanded credit models as examples. He suggests that a portion of a company's return on investment might take longer to translate into revenue – factors such as growth in the number of customers, or share of wallet for the financial institution. Other non-monetary returns may include an increased net promoter score and a better overall customer experience.

The role of advocacy groups

Getting buy-in from across the ecosystem for open banking and open finance has so far proved challenging in Canada. Australia, which has opted for a Consumer Data Right (CDR) as opposed to open banking per se, is now a few years into its implementation. Perhaps Canada, and other countries, can learn from Australia's approach.

Mat Mytka, regional director at the Financial Data and Technology Association (FDATA) ANZ, calls open banking implementation 'large-scale systems change' and argues that, for systems change to come about, there needs to be 'a shared sense of purpose' (Mytka, 2023). That applies to participants and stakeholders at every level – government, policy, regulatory and industry, and not forgetting consumers.

FDATA is a not-for-profit organization that describes itself as 'advocating for robust international standards in open finance'. I asked Mytka, in countries where the financial services industry is not yet convinced of the value of open banking to them and to the wider population, can advocacy groups play a vital role in gathering disparate and opposing views to facilitate the move to open banking – or CDR – as one?

Mytka believes so: 'You need to cultivate a collective identity among all the stakeholders. If you're not operating towards some shared direction, it's really hard to get people to come into alignment.

So, collective identity is really important. As part of that, to get people to collaborate, you need to embrace all these different contexts and [the fact that] everyone is coming from different perspectives.'

He acknowledges there can be many different solutions to one problem – the same can be said for the way in which a country approaches open banking. Being able to listen to those different views and channel them into an outcome that all participants can get behind is a skill. 'Consumer advocates – as an example here in Australia – have a very different perspective than the banks might have, or the fintechs might have,' he notes.

However, Mytka cautions that when there are 'adversarial perspectives' being aired and expressed, this can result in an 'us versus them' mindset, or standoff. In turn, there can be energy and public money 'burned' on figuring out the answers, he says, stressing that this is why having a shared direction and sense of purpose is so critical to successfully implementing open banking.

It is a topic that came up for discussion during a roundtable as part of the Consumer Data Right Month in Australia, which took place across June 2023:

> One of the academics that we invited – and civil society and academia are important stakeholders in this whole process – reinforced that you need an independent non-government body to represent the collective interests of different stakeholders. And industry associations aren't the right form and function for that either, because they tend to lobby on behalf of the members and it becomes a little bit too biased towards what matters, ultimately, to the commercial interests of those organizations that are funding the association (Mytka, 2023).

For Mytka, that 'single body' or 'single voice' is particularly helpful when preparing a country to go beyond open banking and into open finance.

He cites the Open Banking Implementation Entity, or OBIE, in the UK as a good example: 'Despite some of the pitfalls and different constraints that were faced with open banking in the UK and the funding of OBIE, it served a really important role in the governance of open banking as a reform.'

Funding and support for Australian advocacy groups

One of the recommendations made following the independent Statutory Review of the Consumer Data Right, released in September 2022, is additional funding to support consumer advocacy groups specifically, on the basis that it found they are often 'under resourced' (Australian Government, 2023). In turn, this is found to diminish 'consumer input into the development of the CDR', as well as other government consultation processes. In its response to this particular recommendation as a result of the review, the Australian Government agreed the 'valuable role' that consumer advocacy groups play in the policy and design of CDR. It proposes a 'deliberately staged roll-out with fewer CDR-specific consultations' to help these groups better target their resources, noting that previous CDR consultations have been 'relatively frequent' (Australian Government, 2023). In other words, consumer advocacy groups had been spread too thin and, given they represent the very people that CDR is meant to benefit, there was a need to address this lack of resources.

Advocating for open banking in Canada

Some not-for-profit organizations in Canada took matters into their own hands in the absence of any open banking developments or announcements from government. In October 2023, Fintechs Canada, which is the collective voice for Canadian fintechs, launched a campaign called 'Choose More' that demanded the government 'upgrade Canada's financial system' by implementing open banking (Duncan, 2023). One of the claims made by Fintechs Canada in a post on its official LinkedIn page is that Canadians are 'paying thousands in banking fees over the course of their lives' and that businesses are losing out financially, too, due to a financial system that is 'lagging behind' (Duncan, 2023). It estimates that businesses in Canada are missing out on as much as $3 billion to $6.5 billion annually as a result.

In August the same year, Fintechs Canada drew up several recommendations as part of a request to government to renew its commitment, not only to open banking, but also to payments modernization. In its submission to the House of Commons Standing Committee on

Finance, the organization called for an amendment to the Canadian Payments Act in Budget 2024, or earlier, to give banks, credit unions and regulated payment service providers 'equal access' to Canada's real-time payments system, called Real-Time Rail (RTR). Fintechs Canada also wants to see a code of conduct that 'specifies the rules for data sharing' in the ecosystem and, furthermore, requires accredited participants to 'meet a common and transparent set of… standards' (Fintechs Canada, 2023).

The Open Finance Network of Canada is another not-for-profit organization established to promote the benefits of open banking and open finance in Canada. Its 'mission statement' is to bring together stakeholders 'from across financial services to advocate for data rights for Canadian consumers and businesses' (Open Finance Network of Canada, 2023). Members of OFNC's board speak regularly at North American and Canada-specific events on open banking and open finance, but they are also vocal at an international level, taking part in conversations on the global stage. By doing so, they are representing Canada and bringing to the fore some of the innovations and partnerships that have been forged in Canada, in spite of a lack of regulatory direction, at times.

Advocacy groups have a role to play in keeping the conversation going, even when there doesn't seem to be one happening at a national level, and being a collective voice that can help shape the policy and design of open banking.

How do you solve a problem like reticence?

Europe is widely considered as having successfully rolled out open banking via its second payment services directive, or PSD2 as it is better known. However, Europe is a diverse region and within the countries that make up this continent, there are huge variations in open banking readiness and willingness to adopt. This has resulted in what many in the industry refer to as fragmentation – the Nordic countries may have embraced open banking and are heading towards a cashless society (see Chapter 8), but this is not reflective of the entire region by any means.

Ghela Boskovich, founder of FemTechGlobal and head of Europe at the Financial Data and Technology Association (FDATA) observes that there is no 'single key' to adoption or buy-in of open banking (Boskovich, 2023). Instead, she acknowledges that there has been acceptance that it is 'not going away', that it cannot be 'swept under the rug' and that, 'globally, jurisdiction after jurisdiction and market after market have adopted a regulatory framework that opens up finance. The proverbial writing is on the wall and can no longer be ignored,' as she puts it. 'This also triggers a late adopter fear: fear of missing out and giving away market share to earlier adopters.'

Is that fear enough, though? It is likely that, in those countries where there has been a clear reticence to act, regulatory intervention is required. This has certainly been the case in Europe. Boskovich has witnessed a 'greater willingness' for regulators to start to enforce compliance across markets:

> We've seen this in the European Commission's PSD2 review consultation response: NCAs [National Competent Authorities] are now required to better harmonise a single interpretation of the directive, which will actually morph into a regulation – an actual law. This means that we'll start to see more supervision and enforcement of delivering the required open banking technical infrastructure.
>
> Greater alignment of economic incentives is also taking place: there is more discussion about how to make premium use cases a viable reality. In the EU, the SEPA [Single Euro Payments Area] SPAA [SEPA Payment Account Access] scheme is proof that all parties are willing to discuss commercial arrangements for enhanced data, which enables new approaches to product design and delivery (Boskovich, 2023).

Overcoming resistance to open banking in Bulgaria

Open banking and open finance are now live in Bulgaria, but it has taken a concerted effort to get to this point. The country comes under the European Union's PSD2 legislation and has adopted Berlin Group's NextGenPSD2 standard (Ozone API, 2023). However, both open banking and open finance were initially met with resistance by the country's existing banks – and, indeed, are still yet to be adopted widely by the population. The country has had numerous hurdles to overcome, least of all a regulator that 'has a reputation for being quite conservative', according to Ghela Boskovich. She adds that Bulgarian banks saw open banking as 'a threat, rather than an opportunity'.

In part, the key to getting banks onboard has been the monetization angle and ensuring those institutions realize the commercialization opportunities open to them. Speaking at an industry roundtable in 2022, Vasil Panchev, chief information officer at Postbank, explained that Bulgaria had initially been slow to adopt open banking because it was perceived by banks as a compliance issue (Konsentus, 2022).

Another perspective from the same roundtable was that of Merdihan Ismailov, chief digital information officer at IRIS Solutions, a third-party provider (TPP), who observed that, historically, Bulgarian banks had been 'resistant to change' but that now they view themselves as 'playing a valuable role in enabling the digital transformation journey'. Likewise, Panchev noted that 'attitudes are changing' (Konsentus, 2022).

IRIS Solutions has been one of many TPPs in Bulgaria to help banks see beyond the compliance angle and to 'monetize investments to extract value from open banking'. As a consequence, Ismailov explained that innovative use cases are now 'launching in market' and a greater number of TPPs are 'being approved to provide open banking services' (Konsentus, 2022).

Yet, challenges remain and any progress is, therefore, incremental. Ghela Boskovich explains: 'AISP/PISP licensing in Bulgaria is a lengthy process. There is no regulatory sandbox at the Bulgarian National Bank to help expedite the TPP licensing process, and according to the Open Banking Tracker, there are only five licensed TPPs in Bulgaria – 19 API aggregators, but only five licensed AIS/PISPs.'

The fintech scene in Bulgaria

Boskovich believes the success of open banking is 'also dependent upon the attractiveness and readiness of a market, especially in attracting fintechs to invest'. She observes that, in Europe, general fintech innovation associations started to spring up in 2013–14 in mature markets, while open banking-specific associations also started to form around 2015–16. However, she notes that some markets started to coalesce much later – Bulgaria being one:

> Bulgaria's first fintech association formed in 2020, and unlike other markets, there were no additional laws or regulations introduced to promote competition that require financial institutions to make customer or product data available to third parties. Without additional incentive to create an open banking framework outside of PSD2, the speed of adoption was set by the slowest mover in the market (Boskovich, 2023).

Since then, Bulgaria's fintech scene has thrived, it seems. There were 135 fintechs operating in Bulgaria in 2021, according to the Annual FinTech Report 2021 (FinTech Bulgaria, 2022). Other highlights from the report reveal that several educational initiatives had reached more than 300 people, while €32.2 million had been invested in Bulgarian fintech SMEs in the two years up to the report being published. The same report also revealed that, despite the Covid-19 pandemic, the industry's total and operating revenues continued to grow, reaching BGN 1.4 billion and BGN 1.06 billion in 2020, respectively.

However, as Boskovich points out, Bulgarian fintechs are 'still a relatively small group, with little political capital in comparison with some of their peers in other markets'.

Bringing consumers on the journey

Prior to the implementation of open banking in Bulgaria, it is fair to say that the country lagged its European neighbours in many aspects of digital adoption. Bulgaria ranked last out of the 28 EU countries in the European Commission Digital Economy and Society Index (DESI) for 2020 (European Commission, 2020). At the time, the majority of Bulgarians did not shop online, let alone bank online, which may be another reason the country's banking sector was in no rush to invest in open banking APIs. In 2020, only 29 per cent of the total adult population had 'basic digital skills', according to DESI, compared to an EU average of 58 per cent, while just 11 per cent had skills considered 'above basic'. When it came to online banking, 13 per cent of Bulgarians had used the internet for this activity in 2019, compared to the EU average that year of 66 per cent. Slightly more consumers used the internet to shop online (31 per cent), although this remained below the average across the EU in 2019 (71 per cent).

At the time, the index also recorded Bulgaria's integration of digital technology as 'well below average', given that just 7 per cent of its SMEs sold online – by comparison, the EU average was 18 per cent. Moreover, the 2020 index revealed that just 3 per cent of total SMEs made cross-border sales and only 2 per cent of their turnover came from the online segment (European Commission, 2020).

However, there has been a shift, according to a study published in 2022, which revealed that 43 per cent of Bulgarian consumers demonstrated an interest in receiving 'intelligent assistance' to manage payments, while 38 per cent showed an interest in having their data used to develop new and convenient payment methods (Ozone API, 2023).

The country is not without ambition, having introduced a 'Digital Transformation by 2023' plan, much of which involves education and training aimed at digitally upskilling the workforce. However, DESI 2022 showed little improvement in Bulgarians' basic digital skill level, with the percentage of the population with a basic knowledge still well below the EU average. The EU target is to have 80 per cent of the adult population with 'at least' basic digital skills by 2030, although the DESI report notes that the country needs to 'step up efforts' given that two-thirds of the population lack these skills (European Commission, 2022).

Bulgaria is a country where internet connectivity is patchy, although improving, and where a culture of shopping and banking in person persists. Bulgarian consumers are, typically, older and conservative. They also have low confidence in the banks, after a too-recent banking crisis that has left them scarred (Novinite, 2021). In 2014, Bulgarians experienced a banking crisis not unlike the Great Financial Crisis of 2007–08. Two of its biggest banking institutions saw a run on assets: Corporate Commercial Bank, known as KTB, had customers queueing at branches to withdraw their deposits and was placed in special insolvency; the country's then third-largest bank, First Investment Bank, also faced a run on its assets (Linhardt, 2014).

So, while open banking may be technically live in the country, Bulgarians are simply not demanding it. Open banking and open finance does have the potential to significantly improve levels of financial inclusion in Bulgaria if it were allowed to flourish. Yet, several investments are required for the country's population to reap the benefits in full. Firstly, the infrastructure needed to support its rollout needs investment, including internet connectivity. Then there needs to be a concerted effort and ongoing investment in education, to increase the digital skill levels of individuals and to familiarize them with online banking. Finally, Bulgaria's banks need to restore confidence in the banking sector – open banking could do that, if the financial services sector gets behind it.

Summary

As with any large-scale systems change, open banking is bound to encounter numerous challenges and barriers to implementation – whether that is outright opposition, lack of existing infrastructure, general hesitancy to change, how much investment it will require, or the likely return on investment, particularly for existing financial institutions. In addition, questions will arise relating to liability, accreditation and governance, as Canada can attest.

To realize the full potential of open banking and open finance as enablers of financial inclusion requires buy-in from all parts of the financial services ecosystem without exception. It also requires a bold vision and the ambition to understand the payoff in the long term. What is needed is a project manager, essentially. Where adoption has worked best is in countries where advocacy groups, government, or a regulatory body – a group with no commercial interests and without bias – have taken the initiative to lead on implementation.

No one said the road to open banking would be easy. As humans, we are naturally averse to change, after all. And people are – or should be – at the heart of open banking and open finance. What is apparent is that investment and infrastructure are, of course, hurdles, especially in developing economies. The biggest barrier of all, perhaps, is existing attitudes to the banks and banking sector. In Canada, exceptional trust and confidence in the six largest banks established over decades has made the ecosystem question what is to be gained from open banking. The banks already serve the majority of

Canadians and have proven their stability during times of acute stress. They have demonstrated immunity to the contagion of the Great Financial Crisis that affected so many US and European institutions. However, among those organizations in Canada advocating for open banking implementation, there are reasons to shake up the existing banking system – namely, the banking fees that consumers and businesses are paying and which can be exclusionary. Advocacy groups also argue that in failing to mandate open banking, Canada is falling behind other advanced nations.

By contrast, Bulgarians have little to no confidence in their banking system given that a far more recent crisis of 2014 lingers in the memory. Bulgaria also faces undeniable challenges related to financial and digital illiteracy among its population, but these can be overcome as long as there is willingness from government and the desire for change – with investment, of course. Losing consumers' trust can happen overnight, but winning it back can take years.

References

Australian Government (2023) Government statement in response to the Statutory Review of the Consumer Data Right, https://treasury.gov.au/sites/default/files/2023-06/p2023-404730-gs.pdf (archived at https://perma.cc/5PQX-V8H3)

Banjoko, M (2021) Combating the lack of financial inclusion in Canada – a case for open banking, Open Finance Network of Canada, 30 July, www.openfinancenetwork.ca/post/combating-the-lack-of-financial-inclusion-in-canada-a-case-for-open-banking (archived at https://perma.cc/EH6J-TEST)

Beyo, M (2023) Interview with Ellie Duncan, 13 February

Boskovich, G (2023) Written comment to Ellie Duncan, 7 August

Butterfield, K, Ragas, C and Onesi, A (2023) Mitigating risk in the Canadian banking industry – and how it differs from the US, Fasken, 17 March, www.fasken.com/en/knowledge/2023/03/mitigating-risk-in-the-canadian-banking-industry-and-how-it-differs-from-the-us (archived at https://perma.cc/AV8H-VF5E)

Duncan, E (2021) Final report on Open Banking in Canada sets 2023 deadline, Open Banking Expo, 5 August, www.openbankingexpo.com/

news/final-report-on-open-banking-in-canada-sets-2023-deadline/
(archived at https://perma.cc/S3YL-XBJX)

Duncan, E (2023) Fintechs Canada campaigns government for Open
Banking, Open Banking Expo, 5 October, www.openbankingexpo.
com/news/fintechs-canada-campaigns-government-for-open-banking/
(archived at https://perma.cc/K3NW-93E6)

Duncan, E (2023) Canadian government commits to 'consumer-driven
banking' in Fall Statement. Open Banking Expo, 22 November,
www.openbankingexpo.com/news/canadian-government-commits-to-
consumer-driven-banking-in-fall-statement/ (archived at https://perma.cc/
2D22-28CC)

European Commission (2020) Digital Economy and Society Index (DESI)
2020: Bulgaria, https://digital-strategy.ec.europa.eu/en/policies/desi-
bulgaria (archived at https://perma.cc/H8ZM-AZ8B)

European Commission (2022) Digital Economy and Society Index (DESI)
2022: Bulgaria https://digital-strategy.ec.europa.eu/en/policies/desi-
bulgaria (archived at https://perma.cc/H8ZM-AZ8B)

FDATA (2023) FDATA Global Homepage, https://fdata.global/ (archived
at https://perma.cc/8VJF-DZX2)

Financial Consumer Agency of Canada (FCAC) (2022) Open banking,
Government of Canada, 31 August, www.canada.ca/en/financial-
consumer-agency/services/banking/open-banking.html (archived at
https://perma.cc/6TYM-USZL)

Financial Consumer Agency of Canada (FCAC) (2023) Open banking
and consumer protection: Canadians' awareness and expectations,
Government of Canada, 5 June, www.canada.ca/en/financial-consumer-
agency/programs/research/open-banking-consumer-protection.html
(archived at https://perma.cc/VKE2-CXF5)

FinTech Bulgaria (2022) Annual FinTech Report 2021, https://
fintechbulgaria.org/annual-fintech-report-2021-is-here-download-it-
now/ (archived at https://perma.cc/4YYC-USPU)

Fintechs Canada (2023) Fintechs Canada calls for renewed commitment to
open banking, payments modernization, 3 August,
https://fintechscanada.ca/resources/fintechs-canada-calls-for-renewed-
commitment-to-open-banking-payments-modernization/ (archived at
https://perma.cc/6SRD-43RC)

Hsu, M (2023) Acting comptroller of the currency Michael J. Hsu, remarks
at FDX Global Summit, 'Open Banking and the OCC' OCC.gov,
19 April, www.occ.gov/news-issuances/speeches/2023/pub-speech-2023-
38.pdf (archived at https://perma.cc/J6Y7-8GAV)

Immigration, Refugees and Citizenship Canada (2023) Canada welcomes historic number of newcomers in 2022, Government of Canada, 3 January, www.canada.ca/en/immigration-refugees-citizenship/news/2022/12/canada-welcomes-historic-number-of-newcomers-in-2022.html (archived at https://perma.cc/J8SD-GS7X)

Konsentus (2022) From resistance to collaboration: open finance in Bulgaria, 13 April, www.konsentus.com/insights/articles/from-resistance-to-collaboration-open-finance-in-bulgaria/ (archived at https://perma.cc/T2BY-FNYG)

Linhardt, S (2014) Crisis leaves Bulgaria's banks in limbo, The Banker, 1 September, www.thebanker.com/World/Central-Eastern-Europe/Bulgaria/Crisis-leaves-Bulgaria-s-banks-in-limbo (archived at https://perma.cc/Q7EG-RGMX)

Mytka, M (2023) Interview with Ellie Duncan, 11 July

Novinite (2021) Bulgaria in Europe: Why Bulgarians do not use online banking? Novinite.com (archived at https://perma.cc/JCN4-L3TV), 22 September, www.novinite.com/articles/211341/Bulgaria+in+Europe per cent3A+Why+Bulgarians+Do+Not+Use+Online+Banking per cent3F#google_vignette (archived at https://perma.cc/D8YG-3KGZ)

Open Banking Tracker (2023) Open Banking in Bulgaria, Openbankingtracker.com (archived at https://perma.cc/7LVU-NNQQ), date unknown, www.openbankingtracker.com/country/bulgaria (archived at https://perma.cc/24UG-ENDN)

Open Finance Network of Canada (2023) Who We Are, www.openfinancenetwork.ca/ (archived at https://perma.cc/5P54-U33V)

Ozone API (2023) The Global Open Data Tracker: Innovation Atlas, https://ozoneapi.com/the-global-open-data-tracker/atlas/ (archived at https://perma.cc/3GF4-JM3B)

Peesker, S (2019) The Globe and Mail: In a cashless world, society's most vulnerable are being left behind, Acorn Canada, 25 March, https://acorncanada.org/news/globe-and-mail-cashless-world-societys-most-vulnerable-are-being-left-behind/ (archived at https://perma.cc/PJ4H-7F6R)

Piryatinsky, R (2023) Interview with Ellie Duncan, 28 February

Statista (2023) Willingness to change primary bank in Canada as of March 2023, Statista, 7 June, www.statista.com/forecasts/998490/willingness-to-change-primary-bank-in-canada (archived at https://perma.cc/KQG4-4BVV)

The Global Open Data Tracker (2023) Bulgaria, Ozone API, https://ozoneapi.com/the-global-open-data-tracker/atlas/bulgaria/ (archived at https://perma.cc/G4QE-H7WE)

Weinberger, E (2022) Banks seek guidance on who's liable for open banking data fraud, Bloomberg Law, 31 October, https://news. bloomberglaw.com/banking-law/banks-seek-guidance-on-whos-liable-for-open-banking-data-fraud (archived at https://perma.cc/ K6RT-U7MD)

Wells, V (2023) Posthaste: Canadians are worried about the health of the country's banks after U.S. failures, *Financial Post*, 10 May, https://financialpost.com/news/people-worrying-health-canada-banks-wake-us-failures (archived at https://perma.cc/KG8N-TC2F)

Being part of the financial system – is it for everyone?

08

Introduction

There are individuals and organizations firmly against moving to an entirely cashless society. One of the arguments against the digitalization of financial services is that bringing the financially excluded into the wider financial system exposes them to products and services that could see them accumulate debt, or be mis-sold to.

For individuals who have spent almost their entire lives unbanked, the prospect of becoming part of the 'system' is not only a daunting one, but it may even clash with the very principles by which they choose to live.

CHAPTER OBJECTIVES

Some of the questions to be answered are:

- Might some consumers always want to remain outside of the system?
- What are some of the reasons or arguments for spurning a cashless society? Why is financial inclusion one of them?
- Can open banking restore individuals' trust in financial services and banking?
- If not, what does that mean for open banking's prospects and long-term success?

The move to a cashless society – for and against

The use of cash is in decline, globally – that much is clear. It is not surprising to know that fewer people are using cash. Contactless payment with a card, either online or in person, or via a digital wallet, has become a quick, easy and reliable method of payment. Even when individuals are still required to use a PIN for a card payment, there is a level of security as well as speed that cash does not match. Online payments tend to offer more flexibility, too – for example, with instalment payment methods such as buy now, pay later.

In contrast, carrying cash can be fraught with risks, making people more vulnerable – as explored in Chapter 1. Cash as a payment method is far less convenient for many people because it requires, possibly, finding a cash machine to withdraw money from and being able to take out the right amount. During the Covid-19 pandemic, cash payments were, at many retailers and businesses, actively discouraged in line with social distancing rules. Cash became seen as another way for Covid-19 to be passed on, as it was a less sanitary way of paying for goods and services given that it required direct contact with another person.

On the other side of the argument are those who say cash is more convenient, perhaps because it can be easier for some individuals to keep track of their money, especially if they are paid in cash. Others may simply have a personal preference – after all, change is always hard for humans, so if cash is all someone has known, they might like it to stay that way. For many individuals, cash is perceived as a store of value – read on to find out more about how this view proliferates in the UK.

There are also many governments and organizations that believe a financially inclusive society should continue to offer access to cash, and enable cash payments to remain in use. Going entirely cashless is often considered another form of financial exclusion. So, how does cash fit into an open banking/finance world?

Paying with cash in the UK

Even prior to the pandemic, cash use among Britons had been declining, as documented by the Bank of England. It reports that in 2019, 23 per cent of payments were made in cash, down from around 60 per cent a decade earlier (Caswell, 2022). During 2020, when the pandemic and subsequent nationwide lockdowns were underway, cash accounted for 17 per cent of all payments in the UK. Covid-19 accelerated the decline of cash as a payment method – having dropped by approximately 15 per cent each year since 2017, this increased to a 35 per cent reduction in 2020. Following the lifting of pandemic restrictions, cash use bounced back a little, with an estimated 73 per cent of all UK consumers saying they had used cash in January 2022, compared to half of consumers in mid-2020.

So, the pandemic simply sped up a trend that was well underway in the years prior to 2020 – the Bank of England estimates that it brought forward cash decline by over five years (Caswell, 2022). Interestingly, though, cash remained the second most frequently used payment method in the UK in 2021, behind debit cards, and accounted for 15 per cent of all payments (UK Finance, 2022). The same year, 23.1 million consumers used cash only once a month or not at all, which was a huge leap from the previous year's 13.7 million. However, that leaves 1.1 million people who mainly used cash, particularly when paying for daily shopping, but not so much when it came to paying household bills (UK Finance, 2022).

Trade body UK Finance (2022) predicts that by 2031, only 6 per cent of all payments will be made in cash – or fewer than 3 billion cash payments. But that figure does suggest that there will still be a proportion of the population for whom this will be their preferred method of payment, even by the start of the next decade. As UK Finance states, cash will become 'less important than it once was', but will remain 'valued and preferred by many'. It points out that, historically, one of the advantages of using cash was that it could be a 'budgeting tool' for those, in particular, with 'limited budgets'. This is somewhat less the case now, given that budgeting tools are widely available within online banking apps, or as a separate app to download. The advent of open banking in the UK has triggered the

creation of personal financial management – or PFM – apps and platforms, while subscription management tools are also increasingly
available to the masses.

Cash as a store of value

So, where does that leave cash? What appeal does it still hold for
some Britons?

The Bank of England has conducted research into the notion of
cash as a way of preserving value. Its survey of 5,000 adults in
England and Wales reveals that 60 per cent held cash 'in reserve',
with the median amount held totalling £167. Around one-third of
respondents kept less than £100 in cash on them or at home. This led
the Bank of England to 'have a high degree of confidence' that £10
billion is being held in reserve by households (Caswell, 2022).

It is interesting to note that while cash as a form of payment fell
out of favour during the pandemic, more people actually stockpiled
cash at home throughout this period – even households that hadn't
previously done so. The Bank of England found that this applied to
'a cohort of people' – 17 per cent of respondents – who increased
their cash holdings.

This prompted another line of questioning: why do people feel
they need to keep some of their money as cash? And even more so,
why did this reasoning increase during the pandemic? The Bank of
England identified two main reasons among those individuals who
now hold cash in reserve but who had not done so in the past (16 per
cent): 32 per cent are 'worried about an emergency' and 22 per cent
said it was because they wanted to 'feel more in control' of their
money.

This trend is not confined to the UK, though. Sweden's central
bank, Sveriges Riksbank, calls this phenomenon the 'cash paradox'
and suggests it is most evident in 'advanced' economies – the paradox
being that demand for cash is growing, but the share of cash payments is actually in decline (Sveriges Riksbank, 2022). It attributes
this to the 'public's desire to have cash as a means of saving', in
particular during times of crisis or uncertainty. As a consequence,
the Riksbank has observed that the amount of cash in higher

denominations tends to increase, given it is being kept in savings rather than to pay for goods. Therefore, there is a drop in the amount in circulation of smaller denominations of cash. Notably, Sweden is one of few countries where this paradox does not apply – see section further on in this chapter for an explanation of why the country is bucking the trend.

Which countries' populations are reliant on cash

It is unsurprising to learn that high cash use is typically prevalent in countries with a fairly high or very high unbanked population. So, which countries are those?

As Table 8.1 shows, many of the countries where cash is still king are defined as emerging economies. They may not yet have the infrastructure to support online banking and widespread contactless payments, or even card payments. They are likely some years behind the developed economies that are well on their way to becoming cashless societies.

According to analysis by Merchant Machine, Romania is the most reliant on physical cash, with more than 70 per cent of payments in the country made with cash (Wright, 2022a). Its research also shows that 42 per cent of the Eastern European country population is unbanked, explaining why cash payments remain high in Bulgaria, Ukraine and Hungary, as well as Romania (Wright, 2022a).

Merchant Machine's ranking of the countries most reliant on physical cash takes into account several factors, in addition to percentage of cash transactions, including how much of the population is unbanked, the number of ATMs per 100,000 adults and internet use among adults.

From cash to cashless in Japan

Not all developed economies are prepared to leave cash behind, though. In Japan, for example, the shift to fewer cash-based payments has required government intervention.

Table 8.1 The top 10 countries most reliant on cash

Country	Ranking	Population unbanked (%)	Internet users (%)	Cash transaction (%)	No. of ATMs per 100,000 adults
Romania	1	42%	64%	78%	64
Egypt	2	67%	45%	55%	20
Kazakhstan	3	41%	76%	60%	86
Bulgaria	4	28%	63%	63%	94
Ukraine	5	37%	57%	60%	96
Morocco	6	71%	62%	41%	29
Philippines	7	66%	60%	37%	29
Peru	8	57%	49%	22%	127
Hungary	9	25%	77%	45%	61
Vietnam	10	69%	66%	26%	26

SOURCE Wright, 2022a

The Japanese Government's Ministry of Economy, Trade and Industry revealed its 'Cashless Vision' for the country in 2019, in an effort to keep up with many of its neighbouring countries which have embraced cashless payments, including Singapore, South Korea and China. Under the government's 'vision', it aims to increase cashless payments as a total share of payments to 40 per cent by 2025 (Buchholz, 2020). Since the government set out its ambition, cashless payments in Japan have been growing – in part due to the pandemic, as in so many countries. Data from the Bank of Japan, the Japan Consumer Credit Association and the Payments Japan Association shows cashless payments grew to account for more than one-third of all spending in the country (Mishima and Iwata, 2023). A 17 per cent annual increase saw cashless purchasing reach 111 trillion yen – breaching 100 trillion yen for the first time, as reported by Nikkei Asia. Within that figure, credit cards are the most popular form of cashless transaction, up 16 per cent in 2022 on the previous year, to 93.7 trillion yen. However, QR code payments climbed 50 per cent to 9.7 trillion yen, which means they were more popular than debit card payments among Japanese consumers, which rose to 3.2 trillion yen (Mishima and Iwata, 2023).

Notably, the cost of the infrastructure required to enable cash payments has been on the rise, according to the country's Ministry of Economy, Trade and Industry, which estimated the annual cost has climbed to 2.8 trillion yen (Mishima and Iwata, 2023). Another reason to hasten the country's move to cashless payments is that Japan now welcomes millions of tourists each year, and they will typically expect to be able to pay by card or digital wallet.

A significant part of Japan's 'Cashless Vision' is the introduction of a system that pays salaries to workers digitally, without having to go through bank accounts. The system will allow companies to pay their employees using smartphone payment apps and has been positioned as a positive for foreign workers in the country, given the difficulties they are often faced with to open a bank account. However, there has been some resistance from corporate Japan to the proposed system – namely, higher system and operational costs have been cited as a barrier (Kutty and Tochibayashi, 2022).

Japan's 'Digital Salary Payment' system officially came into effect on 1 April 2023, with payment service providers able to apply to deliver the service – so it will be a few more months before the service is rolled out fully (*The Japan News*, 2023).

Which countries are nearly cashless? A closer look at Sweden

The Nordic countries are some of the closest to becoming entirely cashless – 4 out of the 10 most cashless countries in Europe are in the Nordics (Doherty, 2022). Of those, Norway and Sweden are fighting it out (not literally) to be the first cashless society, although it looks like Sweden is the closest to achieving this status. The country's central bank, Sveriges Riksbank (2020) reports that between 2010 and 2020, the percentage of people who paid with cash for their last purchase declined from 39 per cent to just 9 per cent. So, Sweden is following the same trend as seen globally, which is hardly surprising. But even in a country which is, by all accounts, so close to cashlessness, opposition can be found and it's worth examining which groups feel most opposed to a cashless society and their reasons why.

Data from the Riksbank shows that it is older members of society who are the most negative about the decline in the use of cash. More than half (54 per cent) of Swedes aged 65 to 84 expressed a negative view on the decline in physical cash, compared to 19 per cent of those aged 18 to 24. As well as age being a factor, location also shapes Swedes' views on moving to a cashless society, as those living in rural areas said they would find it harder to cope without cash than those in more urban or metropolitan areas – see Table 8.2. As the central bank puts it, cash can act as a 'good back-up alternative' in the event of electrical outages and technical issues with internet access, which can leave people more vulnerable in rural parts of the country (Sveriges Riksbank, 2020).

So, how did the pandemic affect the prevalence of cash in Sweden? As mentioned earlier, in the UK, cash rebounded a little post-pandemic, following a sharp drop in 2020. Sweden did not follow this trend, however. A survey by the Riksbank of Swedish people's

Table 8.2   Could you cope without cash the way society looks today?

Answer	Metropolitan region	Larger urban areas/ intermediate areas	Rural areas
Yes	77%	69%	58%
No	20%	27%	37%
Don't know	3%	3%	4%

SOURCE Sveriges Riksbank, 2020

spending habits in 2022 revealed that the country's population continued to shift away from cash and towards digital payments,
although card use remained largely unchanged – see Table 8.3. In
fact, the central bank reports that during the pandemic, paying digitally, or paying with Swish – a mobile wallet payment system used
widely in Sweden – received something of a boost during the pandemic, particularly among the country's elderly population. Like so
many countries, in Sweden, online shopping increased during Covid-
19 and people chose not to use cash if they did have to pay in person,
in order to minimize contact (Sveriges Riksbank, 2022).

Table 8.3   Percentage of people who paid by cash, card or Swish in the last
30 days

Year	Cash	Bank card	Swish
2016	79%	93%	52%
2018	61%	93%	62%
2020	50%	92%	75%
2022	34%	90%	82%

SOURCE Sveriges Riksbank, 2022

CASE STUDY
The story of Swish in Sweden

What is Sweden's Swish? The mobile payments system began life in 2012, the result of a cooperation or working group formed by the Swedish Bankers Association between six of Sweden's largest banks – Dankse Bank, Handelsbanken, SEB, Nordea, Länsförsäkringar, and Swedbank and Sparbankerna (Getswish AB, 2023a). Those six banks jointly own Getswish AB – although other banks have since connected to the payments system, including Sparbanken Syd, Skandia and ICA Banken. Swedes use the word 'swisha' as a colloquial term for making a payment on the Swish app (Fawthrop, 2019).

What started out as a mobile app designed for individuals in Sweden to pay one another soon piqued the interest of businesses. By 2014, Swish had been expanded to work for businesses, according to Gunilla Garpas, Swish product portfolio manager at Nordea. The appeal for businesses lies in the fact that the system provides real-time processing of funds for companies, whereas other payment systems can take up to seven days to move funds between different accounts. Swish typically charges businesses a flat fee of two kronor per transaction, although this can vary depending on size of company and for non-profits there is no fee at all. Garpas points to fast uptake of Swish once a business starts using the payment system, noting that, in some cases, businesses have reported that Swish accounted for half of their total sales within two to three months of introducing it (Garpas, 2019).

Swish's rise to prominence has been rapid. In 2019, the payments system exceeded 7 million users and became the preferred payment method among 18- to 40-year-olds in Sweden. By 2022, the number of Swish users had surpassed 8 million, with more than half of all Swish payments made to companies. In August 2023 alone, 325,000 companies were offering payments via Swish, while just over 85 million Swish payments were made. During the same month, SEK 44.4 billion was sent via Swish and, among private users, 93 per cent send or receive a Swish payment every month (Getswish AB, 2023b).

Is cash still king?

There are other arguments against going cashless, though, that are surprisingly prevalent in some developed economies. Analysis by

Merchant Machine has revealed sentiment towards going cashless in countries around the world and across individual US states. The findings were based on a calculation of the proportion of negative and positive tweets about cashlessness in each country and US state. The majority of countries (54) want to go cashless, which leaves 32 countries that 'reject the idea' (Wright, 2022b).

The US, Canada, Russia and Australia were all found to be pro-cashless societies. In the US, all states bar two – Alabama and Delaware – want to go cashless, according to Merchant Machine's analysis. It concluded that the most pro-cashless states are those with low levels of unbanked individuals, such as Iowa, where just 2.6 per cent are unbanked but where 38.48 per cent of tweets are positive about the issue. Meanwhile, in pro-cash Alabama, 7.6 per cent of the population is unbanked (Wright, 2022b). This makes sense, of course – people without a bank account will feel entirely excluded from society should their cash not be accepted as a form of payment anywhere. They will be left vulnerable, and this vulnerability is exposed as fear.

In the UK, anti-cashless views are gaining ground, even as much of the population believes the country is heading firmly in the direction of becoming cashless. Back in 2017, a YouGov survey that asked consumers whether the country they live in will 'make the transition to a fully cashless society', found that 21 per cent think it will take 11 to 20 years for the UK to become cashless. However, 17 per cent thought it would happen in the next 10 years and 22 per cent in more than 20 years, leaving 29 per cent who think the UK will never 'discard physical currency' (Harmston, 2017).

Official figures have shown that approximately 8 million people in the UK still rely on having access to cash and that one in five UK adults lack 'essential' digital skills (Statham et al, 2020). It is not only the UK where cash is still king, to a certain extent. Given that a country's physical money forms part of its cultural identity, there is an attachment to cash that is proving hard to wean populations off. Just prior to the pandemic, Americans paid with cash about one-third of the time and used cheques as often as digital payments (Bellens, 2020).

Some of the fears being brought up about moving to a cashless society are entirely justified. In the UK and elsewhere, concerns have been voiced about the groups of people who might feel excluded or left behind should they no longer be able to use cash in shops, including the elderly and other vulnerable groups, such as those on lower incomes, as well as those in very rural locations. The worry is that older individuals in particular may not have the technology to do their banking online or to facilitate digital transactions, and that even if they did, they would not have the skill set to make full use of it. As such, they may be further isolated from society. This has been exacerbated by the closure of bank branches and ATMs nationwide over the past few years.

As touched upon earlier, there are those who simply prefer to use cash to keep track of their spending – the seamlessness of tapping a contactless card, or using a mobile wallet on a smartphone to pay, can cause some people to lose track of how much is leaving their account. Cash is tangible – people can physically see how much they are handing over to pay for goods and services.

In all likelihood, cash will continue to be in circulation, albeit to a lesser extent in future. It is important that consumers have choice at checkouts, whether physical or online. However, it is vital that when it comes to discussions around the shift to a cashless society that any scaremongering is avoided. Equally, proponents of digital banking and the move to open banking must tread carefully to ensure that those with genuine worries and concerns are listened to and given longer to come round to the concept of possibly living without, or with less, cash.

To allay fears in the UK about people's ability to access and then use cash, in 2022, the government enacted new legislation (HM Treasury, 2022). It granted the Financial Conduct Authority (FCA), the UK's financial regulator, powers over the UK's largest banks and building societies to ensure that 'cash withdrawal and deposit facilities are available in communities across the country'. Yet 96 per cent of the UK's population are within two kilometres of a free-to-use cash access point, including ATMs, Post Office branches and bank branches, which suggests fairly comprehensive coverage remains in place nationally.

Rachel Statham, a senior research fellow at IPPR Scotland, believes there are some individuals for whom it is vital they retain access to cash in the UK, because it is a 'lifeline', including families with a very tight financial budget, individuals who are reliant on carers to help them manage their money, and those working in the informal economy (Statham, 2020). How the transition to a cashless society is managed and handled will be critical in the coming years, and open banking will play a key part in ensuring that some of the most vulnerable in society are given the digital skills they need and ongoing support to feel comfortable moving away from cash eventually.

India's attempt at demonetization back in 2017 provides a lesson in how not to withdraw cash from society. In November 2016, India's government, led by Prime Minister Narendra Modi, took the decision to withdraw, with almost immediate effect, the majority of rupees in circulation. The demonetization applied to India's 500- and 1,000-rupee notes, representing 86 per cent of the currency in circulation at the time (Saberin, 2016). The government's justification for such an action was that it was tackling corruption, helping to expose money that had remained undeclared for tax purposes (Chakravorti, 2017). The population was given a deadline to exchange their notes at banks for newly minted currency. But, given their reliance on cash and, in many cases, the long distance to their nearest bank branch, media reports at the time suggested that all the policy did was cause anguish for individuals, especially those on lower incomes (Saberin, 2016). However, this exercise in demonetization was something of a boon for India's mobile wallets and digital payment companies. Paytm is reported to have seen a 435 per cent increase in traffic and a 250 per cent surge in overall transactions and transaction value (Chakravorti, 2017).

It is something of a cautionary tale, although it is hard to imagine another country attempting anything on such a scale. Denying people the choice to use cash, leaving them unable to pay for basic supplies, and watching as, at the same time, digital wallet providers are able to gain new business, will erode trust. This type of policy approach feeds into the idea that banks and financial institutions exist to make big gains from those with so much to lose.

In Delaware, cashless stores have been prohibited as part of an effort to ensure that the demographic groups most excluded by the shift to a cashless society are still able to pay for goods and services. Delaware joins Massachusetts, New Jersey and Rhode Island, as well as cities in the US such as Philadelphia and New York City, in banning cashless retail outlets (Delaware House Democrats, 2022). Delaware House Democrats passed the bill in May 2022, citing the fact that approximately 20 per cent of residents are un- or underbanked – primarily young people, those who are homeless and low-income households that still rely on cash. House Bill 299 'would prohibit the seller of consumer goods or services from refusing to accept cash payment at a retail store through an in-person transaction'. Where businesses continue to accept cash payments, they must not charge more for doing so. The Bill does not apply to utilities companies providing households with gas and electricity, and neither does it apply to telephone, mail or internet sales.

In a press release announcing the passing of the measure, Representative Franklin Cooke, who sponsored House Bill 299, said that cashless stores can have 'a discriminatory effect' on residents who use cash to purchase 'basic necessities'. He observed that there is 'a decent chance a person who doesn't have a credit card doesn't have a vehicle', meaning that if their local store does not accept cash, they are 'left without easy access' to purchase even basic goods.

Senator Jack Walsh is also quoted in the press release as saying that 'it can be easy to forget' that more than 8 million US households do not have bank accounts, and are also not able to obtain either a debit or credit card. He said that for those individuals and households, 'cashless stores make navigating an increasingly unequal economy that much harder'(Delaware House Democrats, 2022).

Do some individuals want to remain unbanked and excluded by choice?

Using cash is no marker of being financially excluded, though – people can be banked and even well-served by the financial services sector and still choose to retain some savings in cash, and use physical money occasionally to pay for goods and services.

However, the choice to remain unbanked, and removed from banking and the wider financial services system completely, is representative of a totally different belief system. Chapters 1 and 4 have explored the reasons that individuals worldwide are unbanked or underserved, with circumstance, immigration status, gender and the historic credit scoring system all potential factors.

Without wanting to stray into the social media-fuelled world of conspiracy theories, there are some people who have a deep distrust of the financial services industry and wish to remain entirely free from what they see as its influence.

The survey conducted by YouGov and referred to earlier in this chapter offers some insight into a few of the deeper fears that people express about the system – while some are misplaced, others are not. Of those surveyed, 65 per cent said they feel that using mobile or cashless payments increases 'the chance of suffering fraud or theft'. When asked further about mobile payments and deposit systems or apps, 31 per cent do not think they are secure, and a much smaller but still significant 16 per cent said they do not trust the providers operating the systems (Harmston, 2017).

While these findings are a few years old, the rise in cases of fraud and identity theft online is not likely to have assuaged these fears. Also, a lack of trust in institutions and in large-scale systems is not uncommon – at its extreme, it can cause people to shun society and all its trappings entirely, and to choose to live 'off grid', as it were. But at the other end of the spectrum, it may mean that individuals remain almost in a state of limbo – neither feeling like they belong or that they want to, nor that they can achieve a certain quality of life without some of the technology and financial services that make life easier and more convenient.

The Great Financial Crisis of 2007–08 did irreparable damage in this respect. The notion that fairly well-off people and families could lose their home and savings almost overnight was really an alien concept to those in the developed countries that were most affected, like the US and UK. The fact that this happened, and people queued outside bank branches in a desperate bid to retrieve their assets, is an abiding memory for some – it is a period that will not be easily forgotten. At the same time as people's homes were being repossessed, and the institutions they had banked with for years suddenly ran out of money and were declaring bankruptcy, those at the very senior levels of management at those institutions appeared to have more wealth than ever. For those who had worked and saved hard for their home and lifestyle, and who were now seeing it ebb away, watching the bankers who had triggered the crisis and caused such lasting damage walk away seemingly unscathed was insulting. The fact that some in the banking industry had profited from others' demise, or were able to walk out of one company and into another extremely well-paying job at another banking organization, was enough to send trust in bankers and banking plummeting.

Undoing the damage wreaked by the Financial Crisis

What can open banking do for the people who have felt let down and disappointed by the financial system ever since the financial crisis? It seems a big ask to assume that open banking can right the wrongs. But, given that open banking is such an overhaul of a system that has been seen as antiquated, or averse to change, there is a chance that it could alter people's views of banking and financial services. The crucial detail about open banking is that it's about the ownership of data moving away from the banks and into the hands of the people whose data it is.

Ghela Boskovich, founder of FemTechGlobal and head of Europe at the Financial Data and Technology Association, says some people's 'distrust' of the financial system is 'understandable'. However, she asks of individuals who choose to remove themselves, 'where are they going to go?'. For Boskovich, there is no alternative – or at least none with any proven longevity or stability, referring to DeFi and crypto-currency (Boskovich, 2023).

She says that much of the impetus for implementing open banking and for the entrepreneurs who have started up fintechs is wanting to change the bias and discrimination in the system, while realizing they have to work within the constraints of the existing financial system. 'How do I change the system as it is, if I can't set up a new one? I think that's where the fintech revolution really happened,' says Boskovich. 'I can't break it, I can't set up a new one. But I can fight this little corner and that's why it's happened. I think open banking is partly a result of the need to get access to the data in that corner.'

As she sees it, open banking is about changing the nature of ownership around the information and the intelligence within banking, using technology to facilitate the flow of that information. 'You're still doing the same thing, pulling all the insights together, you're still aggregating the data across a market set, you're still doing analysis on budgeting, you're still balancing an investment portfolio – you're just doing it openly within a discrete legal and security framework,' she explains. 'And you're doing it with the consent of the actual data subject, who "owns" their data. The explicit ownership of the data is at the heart of these new open regimes.'

Summary

Open banking is probably not a 'cure' for all of the financial system's ills. It is likely that there will always be individuals who wish to remain outside of a system that they do not trust and never intend to.

'Those who have been excluded may not trust the previous regime, they may not trust the system under an open regime, either,' Ghela Boskovich notes. 'But the one thing that they will have in an open regime is an assurance that the information is theirs to direct. That is the fundamental difference between the previous and open regimes. If they understand that, then there's a different way of ordering off the menu.'

If the fintechs and challenger banks that have proliferated globally can continue to appeal to people who have found the prospect of banking daunting, or too corporate even, then some trust could yet be restored.

As Boskovich observes: 'Trust in an institution is always a challenge, especially when you've been on the fringes and you've been excluded. I also think open banking is a softer, more gentle introduction to formal finances than the traditional system. Primarily because the consumer has a perception of choice and they have an actual real choice, and therein lies the difference.'

The consent required by open banking from consumers for their banking data to be shared is also, she suspects, 'improving the trustworthiness of the providers'.

I think Boskovich hits the nail on the head when she says: 'There's a lot more explaining in open banking than there is in traditional finance and I think that will improve the perception of trustworthiness. But it will take time.'

Indeed, only time will really tell if open banking and open finance have been able to convince sceptics of the financial system that there is a form of banking that exists to serve their interests and not purely those of the institutions.

References

Bellens, J (2020) Why the potential end of cash is about more than money, EY, 7 January, www.ey.com/en_ro/banking-capital-markets/why-the-potential-end-of-cash-is-about-more-than-money (archived at https://perma.cc/XYD2-XGAQ)

Boskovich, G (2023) Interview with Ellie Duncan, 16 February

Buchholz, K (2020) Where cash is still king, Statista, 10 August, www.statista.com/chart/19868/share-of-cash-payments-in-different-countries/ (archived at https://perma.cc/HB93-7B2K)

Caswell, E (2022) Knocked down during lockdown: the return of cash, Bank of England, 14 October, www.bankofengland.co.uk/quarterly-bulletin/2022/2022-q3/knocked-down-during-lockdown-the-return-of-cash (archived at https://perma.cc/VGQ5-LU56)

Chakravorti, B (2017) Early lessons from India's demonetization experiment, *Harvard Business Review*, 14 March, https://hbr.org/2017/03/early-lessons-from-indias-demonetization-experiment (archived at https://perma.cc/6DSL-XXE8)

Delaware House Democrats (2022) House passes Cooke Bill to prohibit cashless stores. Housedems.delaware.gov, 19 May, https://housedems.delaware.gov/2022/05/19/house-passes-cooke-bill-to-prohibit-cashless-stores/ (archived at https://perma.cc/3K9V-Q87L)

Doherty, M (2022) The Nordic countries ready to say goodbye to cash, Ingenico, 7 June, https://ingenico.com/en/newsroom/blogs/nordic-countries-ready-say-goodbye-cash (archived at https://perma.cc/35EW-FSG8)

Fawthrop, A (2019) What is Swish? The mobile payments system used by more than two-thirds of Swedes, NS Banking, 15 July, https://www.nsbanking.com/analysis/swish-payments-sweden/ (archived at https://perma.cc/8ZER-83WB)

Garpas, G (2019) The benefits of Swish for businesses in Sweden, Nordea, 20 February, www.nordea.com/en/news/the-benefits-of-swish-for-businesses-in-sweden (archived at https://perma.cc/KN7J-ZQPE)

Getswish AB (2023a) Our Story, Swish.nu, www.swish.nu/about-swish (archived at https://perma.cc/M6UG-NRGV)

Getswish AB (2023b) Swish in numbers, Swish.nu, www.swish.nu/about-swish (archived at https://perma.cc/M6UG-NRGV)

Harmston, S (2017) A third of Brits expect this to be last generation using cash, YouGov, 6 July, https://yougov.co.uk/topics/consumer/articles-reports/2017/07/06/third-brits-expect-be-last-generation-using-cash (archived at https://perma.cc/NWC6-KRDJ)

HM Treasury (2022) New powers to protect access to cash, Gov.uk, 19 May, www.gov.uk/government/news/new-powers-to-protect-access-to-cash (archived at https://perma.cc/5AY7-TGXG)

Kutty, N and Tochibayashi, N (2022) How Japan is moving towards a cashless society with digital salary payments, World Economic Forum, 20 September, www.weforum.org/agenda/2022/09/japan-cashless-society-digital-salary-payment/ (archived at https://perma.cc/FSN5-AZL8)

Mishima, D and Iwata, N (2023) Cashless payments in Japan top one-third of spending, Nikkei Asia, 4 April, https://asia.nikkei.com/Business/Finance/Cashless-payments-in-Japan-top-one-third-of-spending (archived at https://perma.cc/7DZR-7NEG)

Saberin, Z (2016) India discontinued 86 percent of its circulated currency – and the poor are in crisis, Vice, 1 December, www.vice.com/en/article/a3j5ng/india-discontinued-86-percent-of-its-circulated-currency-and-the-poor-are-in-crisis (archived at https://perma.cc/UX69-M9HU)

Statham, R (2020) Who benefits from the shift away from cash? FCA, 27 March, www.fca.org.uk/insight/who-benefits-shift-away-cash (archived at https://perma.cc/VC5C-9N6C)

Statham R, Rankin L and Sloan, D (2020) Not cashless, but less cash: economic justice and the future of UK payments, Ippr.org, 24 January, www.ippr.org/research/publications/not-cashless-but-less-cash (archived at https://perma.cc/J5QE-P5WR)

Sveriges Riksbank (2020) The payment market is being digitalized, Riksbank.se (archived at https://perma.cc/93GA-K33S), 29 October, www.riksbank.se/en-gb/ayments--cash/payments-in-sweden/payments-in-sweden-2020/1.-the-payment-market-is-being-digitalised/cash-is-losing-ground/credit-cards-are-now-also-more-common-than-cash/ (archived at https://perma.cc/L5VF-RR99)

Sveriges Riksbank (2022) In Sweden, we prefer to pay digitally, Riksbank.se (archived at https://perma.cc/93GA-K33S), 15 December, www.riksbank.se/en-gb/payments--cash/payments-in-sweden/ payments-report-2022/trends-on-the-payment-market/-in-sweden- we-prefer-to-pay-digitally/payment-habits-from-the-pandemic-persist/ (archived at https://perma.cc/B34N-6A6B)

The Japan News (2023) Application process begins for Japan digital salary payment service providers, 2 April, https://japannews.yomiuri.co.jp/ business/economy/20230402-101095/ (archived at https://perma.cc/ 26TR-T93T)

UK Finance (2022) UK Payment Markets Summary 2022, https://www.ukfinance.org.uk/system/files/2022-08/UKF%20 per%20cent20Payment%20per%20cent20Markets%20per%20 cent20Summary%20per%20cent202022.pdf

Wright, I (2022a) The countries most reliant on cash, Merchant Machine, 17 November, https://merchantmachine.co.uk/most-reliant-on-cash/ (archived at https://perma.cc/Y2GX-H9HR)

Wright, I (2022b) The countries & states that most want or reject a cashless society, Merchant Machine, 20 November, https:// merchantmachine.co.uk/cashless-society/ (archived at https://perma.cc/ WRA4-495J)

What comes next? The move to open finance

09

Introduction

In documenting the adoption of open banking in countries through-out the world in the rest of this book, it is clear that it does not stop at banking. Open finance is already underway in Brazil and in Australia, albeit gradually and with mixed results so far.

Open finance points to a far more ambitious movement globally, whereby the entirety of people's financial lives is 'open'. It heralds a move away from financial services operating in silos, to an intercon-nectedness that has the potential to transform the way individuals live. If that sounds dramatic then it is likely that, in reality, it would be less so. Let's face it, the implementation of open banking has moved quickly in some jurisdictions and at a snail's pace in others, so the introduction of open finance is likely to take time and be phased.

The advent of open finance begs many questions, and the industry does not have all the answers just yet. Nevertheless, its prospects are thrilling.

CHAPTER OBJECTIVES

The main questions to be answered are:

- What is open finance? Is there a working definition?
- Where open finance is already being rolled out, where are the stumbling blocks? And what can the industry learn from these early challenges?

- How has Australia approached open finance through its Consumer Data Right? What is required for its success?
- What has open banking taught us about large-scale systems change that can be applied to open finance?
- How will open finance promote sustained financial inclusion, including in Colombia? How is it already doing so elsewhere in Latin America?

Defining open finance

The UK's financial services regulator, the Financial Conduct Authority, defines open finance as the 'extension of open banking-like data sharing to a wider range of financial products' – which is a neat summary, in my view. That means it extends to include people's investments, pensions and insurance, but also mortgages, energy/utilities, and telecoms. The FCA also explains what's in it for consumers – who are, and always should be, the ultimate beneficiaries – pointing to 'increased competition, improved advice and improved access to' financial services and products (Financial Conduct Authority, 2021).

The Inter-American Development Bank offers its own definition of open finance, explaining it in the context – and yet distinct from – open banking, which it states 'limits its ecosystem to banking services and products'. The IDB defines an open finance ecosystem as providing 'a secure and efficient mechanism' for consumers to 'grant authorized TPPs' access to their financial data so that they, in turn, can offer products and services that 'align with the consumers' specific requirements' (Herrera et al, 2023).

When we think about those who are unbanked, though, the likelihood is they will remain so under open finance. This is why it is so critical that countries use open banking to make banking services accessible to the masses. Then, and only then, can open finance take effect – those same people who have become banked, and indeed anyone who is underserved, will then be fully served across all aspects of their financial lives.

Will open finance be mandated?

It seems likely that in those jurisdictions where open banking has been mandated, open finance will also be driven by regulation. The UK is one such example. According to Deloitte, the UK intends to 'mandate open finance by law in the same way' that the second Payment Services Directive and the Retail Banking Market Investigation Order 2017 (as detailed in Chapter 5) mandated open banking (Gallo et al, 2022).

The FCA has acknowledged that 'appropriate regulation' will be necessary on the basis that open finance is likely to 'create or increase risks and raise new questions' around data ethics. The regulatory body views regulation as not only essential to being able to manage those risks, but also in instilling confidence in consumers 'to use open finance services'. Crucially, the FCA recognizes that open finance is in the best interests of consumers and, back in 2019, issued a 'call for input', inviting stakeholders to respond. On publishing the results of this call for input, the FCA found there is 'a degree of consensus' around the 'building blocks' needed for open finance to develop in consumers' best interests. One such building block identified is 'a legislative and regulatory framework' (Financial Conduct Authority, 2021).

In the UK, open finance is part of the Government's Smart Data initiative, which aims to 'enable secure and consent-driven cross-sector data sharing with TPPs, starting with communication, energy and finance' (Gallo et al, 2022).

In Latin America, open finance is already mandated in Brazil (see Chapter 4), while some other countries in the region have lagged behind. In this region, open finance is widely seen as fostering financial inclusion. A study by the Inter-American Development Bank (IDB) and the Financial Data and Technology Association (FDATA) found that 80 per cent of public sector actors it surveyed in Latin America and the Caribbean believe that 'some form of regulation is necessary for open finance'. The organization also surveyed 38 companies in the fintech sector, and discovered that 94 per cent think that the pre-existence of financial data-sharing regulation 'positively impacts the growth and maturation' of open finance (Fonseca, 2023).

Susana Cordeiro Guerra, manager of the Institutions for Development Sector at the IDB, says that due to the complexity of implementing open finance ecosystems, it 'requires regulations and rules to operate for the benefit of financial consumers'. She goes on to say that 'appropriate' regulatory frameworks can aid the creation of public-private alliances for implementation, and hand consumers 'power' over their data (Cordeiro Guerra, 2023). Richard Prior, chief executive of FDATA Global, agrees that regulation is a requirement – in fact, he calls it 'critical for the delivery and healthy evolution of these new financial ecosystems'. Prior adds that open finance needs 'clear rules and guidelines that afford protections around access to, and use of, consumer-owned data' (Prior, 2023).

Regulation can unite a bloc of countries within a region – by all working towards the same set of standards and laws, it ensures that an open banking or open finance ecosystem is interoperable and can help individual countries move at speed towards a single vision. Without this – as other jurisdictions have found to their detriment – there can be fragmentation and a lack of commitment or willingness to reach an end point.

So, the publication of proposed joint open finance regulation by four Latin American fintech associations in May 2023 is significant and may even provide a blueprint for other regions. The Open Finance Standard for the Pacific Alliance was delivered at the Chile Fintech Forum in Santiago on 17 May 2023 (Open Banking Exchange, 2023). Its significance lies in the fact that, by implementing joint regulation, Chile, Colombia, Mexico and Peru recognize the potentially transformative effect open finance could have on people's lives. The countries also realize that only by working together can that potential be harnessed and eventually come to fruition in the form of financial inclusion. Additionally, joint standards adopted by several countries within a region provide a level playing field that encourages healthy and fair competition among industry participants.

Lauren Jones, director, market development at Open Banking Exchange explains that the joint proposal has been delivered to the fintech associations' respective regulators, adding that 'much of the detail is still to be worked through'. She observes that the proposed joint standard has a place in the history books, too. While the

European Economic Area (EEA) became the first region to implement 'regional' open banking, Jones observes that the EEA also has a 'continuous and harmonized' regulatory and legislative framework landscape – this is not something shared with the Pacific Alliance. So, the joint open finance standard between Colombia, Chile, Mexico and Peru is truly the first of its kind in that respect. So far, what is known is that the group of countries will use the Financial-grade API, known as FAPI, and also OAuth 2.0 and OpenID Connect 'as a base to define technical requirements for the financial sector and other sectors' (Jones, 2023).

In each of the four countries where the joint open finance proposal was presented, law firm Dentons collaborated. Ignacio Pera Rivas, partner at Dentons Chile and one of the authors of the document, acknowledged that 'generating a common standard' for a concept 'as complex' as open finance might seem to be a difficult task. However, he asserts that the situation in each of the countries that form the Pacific Alliance 'generates an ideal and timely environment for both regulators and actors in the fintech industry' to work together on a common standard (Estrada, 2023).

Playing catch-up in Colombia

Colombia has looked to both Brazil and Mexico to inform its own approach to open finance. Geographically, it makes sense to follow in their footsteps, but demographically too, given that nearly one-quarter of the country's population was unbanked in 2020 (Open Banking Exchange, 2023). Financial inclusion is imperative in rolling out open finance in the country. It is against this backdrop that Colombia's Ministry of Finance and Public Credit issued a consultation on a draft decree to regulate open finance in October 2021. In July the following year, the Colombian government published a final decree, with a clear purpose to promote 'competition, inclusion and efficiency' in the provision of services (Open Banking Exchange, 2023).

In issuing the decree, the government's intention was to 'clarify the rules' governing the transfer of consumer data between financial institutions, as well as to 'promote access to such information in favor of the development' of new financial products and services.

One of the main 'pillars' of Colombia's open banking and open finance implementation is the 'initiation of payments as an activity within the payments ecosystem' (Adarve and Acosta, 2023). Much like its neighbours across Latin America, and Brazil in particular, Colombia has sought to focus on the payment initiation aspect of open banking, over data access (Open Banking Exchange, 2023). Essentially, the Colombian government has recognized the success of Brazil's Pix payments system and seeks to replicate it.

Pix is not the only payments system success story in the region, by any means. Mexico has its own Interbank Electronic Payment System (SPEI), which is used by banks and fintechs to reconcile and settle customer payments. Elsewhere, Argentina has Transferencias 3.0 – an open and universal digital payment system which was introduced in November 2021 and is backed by its central bank, Banco Central De La Republica Argentina, or BCRA (Pinedo, 2023). It uses QR codes to facilitate transactions between banks, electronic wallets and fintechs, requiring neither the use of cash, nor a debit card. Within two months of having launched the system, the central bank reported that 2.01 million transactions had been completed, mobilizing 3,509 million pesos (BCRA, 2022). Bolivia's QR BCB instant payment system is still early in its development and is available only to customers of lender Banco Union, but is expected to be fully operational in 2024 (Pinedo, 2023). El Salvador's Transfer365 was launched by the country's central bank in June 2021, and is used by commercial banks, savings and credit associations (Pinedo, 2023). In its first year of operating, the system moved some $7.9 billion.

Although Brazil can be said to have implemented open finance already, Colombia could be considered a fast follower, in the sense that having seen other countries – not only in Latin America, but globally – implement open banking and open finance frameworks, it shows signs of being able to catch up with the progress made elsewhere, at pace. In particular, Colombia has witnessed the limited success of Mexico's Fintech Law (see Chapter 3) where, despite its best efforts to tackle financial exclusion head-on through what is best described as a 'hybrid approach', the country has not been able to make significant inroads into banking the large numbers of unbanked among its population. This contrasts with the relative success of open finance in Brazil – see Chapter 4 for a detailed overview of Brazil's implementation – which has taken a phased approach from open banking to open finance, and where there is evidence of a reduction in financial inequality in the country. Pix was Brazil's answer to a population that had been largely reliant on cash – and Colombia will be hoping it, too, can wean its population off cash and onto digital payments with a similar system. Around 7 out of 10 payments are paid in cash in Colombia (Open Banking Exchange, 2023). However, there are signs that the population is embracing the digital transformation of financial services – evidence for which can be found in its fintech ecosystem.

Colombia already has a thriving fintech sector, which has grown rapidly in the space of a few years. Back in 2017, there were 84 Colombia-based fintechs, but now the country boasts the third largest fintech sector in Latin America, accounting for 11 per cent of all fintech companies in the region (Feliba, 2023). Colombia Fintech, the association of fintech companies in Colombia, puts the number of fintechs in 2023 at 322, creating 9,308 jobs (Feliba, 2023). According to the association, 76 per cent of Colombia's 'digitally active' population uses fintech solutions. Luis Miguel Zapata, vice president, digital ecosystems at Bancolombia, has described how the partnerships between banks and fintechs are 'extremely healthy' (Open Banking Exchange, 2023). He suggested that the secret to effective collaboration is to remember that it is 'an ecosystem, not an egosystem'.

CASE STUDY
Belvo's ecosystem partnerships in the spotlight

Partnerships between fintechs and payment services providers (PSPs) are also proving fruitful. Colombian payments and financial services platform MOVii formed a strategic alliance with open finance platform Belvo in 2023 to help tackle fraud and authentication in online payments – an issue that is by no means exclusive to Colombia (Belvo Communications, 2023). However, payment fraud affects approximately 20 per cent of online payments in the country. According to Belvo, its open finance technology means that an individual can verify their identity via their financial institution when making a payment online, reducing the risk of fraud in transactions by as much as 80 per cent (Belvo Communications, 2023).

Belvo is also working to increase adoption of Pagos Seguros en Linea (PSE) in Colombia (Rojas, 2023). PSE stands for 'Secure Online Payments' when translated into English, and is described as the 'preferred alternative payment solution' in the country (Ebanx, 2023). Colombians use PSE to make real-time payments – when they choose it as their payment method, the PSE interface redirects the user to their online banking, where they can authorize the payment instantly and securely (Ebanx, 2023). It does seem that this bank-to-bank payment method is gaining traction in Colombia, where Belvo reports it is accepted by more than 20,000 merchants (Rojas, 2023). What Belvo has done is create a solution that makes the process of paying with PSE even more streamlined, by taking it from a 10-stage process down to four, encouraging Colombians to complete the payment. Another feature of Belvo's solution is the ability for an individual to only have to register their bank details once, ready for future recurring transactions.

Colombian fintech Monet provides instant salary advances to employees via an app (Belvo, 2023). It uses Belvo's open banking technology as the 'base infrastructure' for its solution, so that it can access users' real-time financial data and build more accurate risk profiles of its users. In turn, users of Monet can share their banking credentials, knowing they are doing so safely and securely. Belvo's single integration, which means it can access data from any of the countries in which it operates, has enabled Monet to expand into Mexico. According to Belvo, many Colombian employees require their salary in advance due to a lack of liquidity in the region more widely, as well as lack of access to formal credit services. It also points out that some industries in Colombia do not have the ability to provide their workers with 'on-demand wage payments'.

Initial hurdles to overcome

Much like open banking, open finance – or smart data – rests on the idea of handing consumers control of their data and, in doing so, delivering services that really and truly improve the quality of their lives, through ease, speed and personalization. Unlike open banking, open finance does not apply to only one type of dataset, but to a much broader and therefore wide-ranging set of financial services data, spanning investments, insurance, pensions, utilities and many more verticals and sectors.

In a speech in March 2023, Mairead McGuinness, European Commissioner for Financial Stability, Financial Services and the Capital Markets Union spoke about the transition from open banking to open finance. She explained that open finance is not just about sharing a 'much broader range' of data, but doing so with the 'consent and understanding' of the individual. She cited several examples of how that data might be used, so that a consumer can get a 'bespoke insurance product', or so that switching providers might become 'more seamless'. However, she also acknowledged that people are 'concerned' about who has access to that data and 'what that information is being used for' (McGuinness, 2023).

This issue of trust – which I have returned to throughout this book – is problematic if open finance is to be a success, particularly given that a lack of trust remains a barrier to widespread adoption of open banking. McGuinness put it in quite stark terms in the same speech, when she said that even though the EU's second Payment Services Directive (PSD2) 'entered into force' in 2018, by 2021, less than 5 per cent of consumers in the EU 'were using open banking'.

Lack of trust is not only a barrier in the UK and Europe, but in Australia too, where mistrust is deeply ingrained. Research by Frollo, an open banking platform, conducted among 1,066 Australians across varied ages, genders and locations, found that only 51 per cent trust their banks enough to 'share financial information with them by linking their accounts' (Fennell, 2022). That leaves half of the population who do not trust their bank enough to do this. The same research, which took the temperature of consumer attitudes towards sharing financial data, also revealed that the overwhelming majority, at 91 per cent, identified privacy as the most important aspect, ahead of security and transparency, at 88 per cent (Fennell, 2022).

Stumbling block

It is clear that, even when consumers are given the ability to consent to sharing their data, their misgivings about the financial services industry are so entrenched that they remain cautious and hesitant. Mairead McGuinness set out in her speech that privacy and security are concerns for people, saying that 'consumers are wary of what a company might learn about them' and then whether those same companies will 'manage your data with your best interests in mind' (McGuinness, 2023).

Certainly, if open finance is to achieve the broad reach it seeks to – both in terms of verticals and among individuals – trust needs to be restored.

One idea being considered by the EU is 'permission dashboards', which McGuinness describes as 'an interface' giving individuals 'a simple overview of their own data that they might want to share'. Through their dashboard, a consumer could 'grant and revoke permissions to share information' (McGuinness, 2023).

Australia's Consumer Data Right

It is well known and documented that Australia opted to implement a Consumer Data Right (CDR), which means the country essentially leapfrogged open banking and chose to establish a regime that bore more resemblance to an open finance ecosystem. The Australian Government describes it as 'an economy-wide reform that will be rolled out sector by sector', with banking the obvious starting point (Australian Government, 2023a). At time of writing, CDR had been rolled out to the banking and energy sectors, with the intention to include non-bank lending as the third sector, according to the government's website. The Australian Government plays a central role in CDR, having designed the system which it now oversees. As stated on its website, providers go through a 'rigorous accreditation process' to be able to provide CDR services to the population, with the process of accreditation ultimately managed by the Australian Competition and Consumer Commission, or ACCC.

CDR is being offered as an 'opt-in' service to Australian consumers and businesses so that they have control over whether to share their data, 'with full visibility of who it's being shared with and the purpose for sharing it' (Australian Government, 2023a).

CDR timeline

The Consumer Data Right officially launched in July 2020, but the work began back in July 2019, when Australia's four largest banks made their 'product reference data for their standard products publicly available' to businesses, such as comparison sites (Australian Government, 2023b). At this stage, it included standardized, general information on interest rates, fees and charges. The four biggest banks are:

- Australia and New Zealand Banking Group
- Commonwealth Bank of Australia
- National Australia Bank
- Westpac Banking Corporation

In February 2020, those banks made their product reference data for mortgages and loans publicly available (Australian Government, 2023b). For clarification, the government states that only businesses can access product reference data. It was only in 2020, when CDR went live in July, that customers of those banks could choose to share their banking data, initially from a range of personal accounts, before expanding to include a greater range of products, such as home loans and personal loans. Jump to February 2021, and the four major banks had gone live with all of their banking data, including information on overdrafts and business finance – what is known as 'Phase 3 data' by the government (Australian Government 2023b).

Mat Mytka, regional director at the Financial Data and Technology Association (FDATA) ANZ, says that with CDR, Australia was 'trying to do something a little bit differently' from open banking in the UK. 'But, we also adopted a similar mindset by going, let's start with the whole sector and mandate that the banks create these standardized APIs and do the digital transformation to enable that to take place,' he explains. Mytka adds that, consequently, there has been 'an extraordinary amount of energy and resources – and public and private money – poured into standing that up' (Mytka, 2023).

Indeed, May 2021 saw an additional $111.3 million dedicated to the rollout of CDR, as part of Australia's $1.2 billion Digital Economy Strategy (Australian Government, 2023b). Later that same year, customers of the non-major banks began to be able to share banking data from personal savings and credit card accounts, and by November of that year, they could share their banking data from home loans and personal loans. By February 2022, those same customers who banked with the non-major banks could share information about overdrafts and business finance (Australian Government, 2023b).

Mytka points out that CDR has its 'limitations', given that payments initiation is yet to be enabled. 'It's only read access at the moment, so you can share your banking data with a fintech that can help you manage your finances, or understand what you can afford on a loan, or understand your spending,' he explains. 'There are limitations for its adoption and use because that write access – the ability to move money or update the data that sits within our bank – isn't quite there yet, we don't have the framework in place. That's coming with action initiation' (Mytka, 2023).

The Australian Government committed a further $88.8 million to invest in CDR over 2023–24, specifically to support its rollout across banking, energy and non-bank lending sectors, and some of which will be used to fund the design of action initiation (Australian Government, 2023b). To clarify, payment initiation is a type of action initiation under CDR, but it also refers, more broadly, to 'a new, secure channel for consumers to instruct a firm to initiate actions' with their consent (Australian Government, 2023c). The development of CDR to include action initiation is seen as a significant next step in Australia, which recognizes the part that payment initiation has played in 'the success of open banking in the UK' (Australian Government, 2023c).

Open energy

November 2022 marked the start of consumer data sharing for customer data held by the following energy retailers (Australian Government, 2023b):

- Australian Energy Market Operator
- AGL Energy Group
- Origin Energy Group
- Energy Australia Group

Open Finance Advisors defines open energy as a 'regulatory and technology framework' that enables Australian consumers to 'easily share their own energy data with accredited third parties' (Charnley, 2022). In other words, much like with open banking, consumers can get a full picture of their energy usage, how much they're paying and whether they will be better off by switching to another provider. One of the several use cases that have emerged since November 2022 is the opportunity to install an alternative supply of power, such as solar (Charnley, 2022).

FDATA ANZ's Mat Mytka sees a whole series of use cases emerging already from open energy, including solar panel installations on properties.

While it looks like the rollout of open energy might have had a slow start, the staggered approach is intentional and those four organizations that have already commenced with open energy are considered the largest players in the market (Frollo, 2023a). It is worth explaining that the Australian Energy Market Operator, or AEMO, is not an energy retailer but that it manages electricity and gas systems and markets across the country. In November 2023, consumer data sharing for what open banking provider Frollo calls 'larger retailers' – those with more than 10,000 customers – will commence. This is when smaller retailers, with customer numbers below 10,000, will also be able to sign up to CDR (Frollo, 2023a). In its State of the Nation report 2024, Frollo confirms that in November, it is expected that more than 20 larger retailers will come on board, including Red Energy, Powershop, Dodo and Alinta Energy. By this point, it would cover around 89 per cent of the National Electricity Market customers in Australia. Finally, when a provider called Ergon joins as expected in July 2024, coverage will be up to 99 per cent (Frollo, 2023a).

Can CDR restore trust in Australia's biggest banks?

Australia's major banks and other financial institutions suffer from a lack of consumer confidence, which partly stems from some banking controversies. In this way, Australia has much in common with the UK, with open banking and open finance seen, perhaps, as an opportunity for banks to improve their behaviours and culture amid a more competitive market, thereby restoring levels of trustworthiness.

Table 9.1 Trust in traditional banks across major APAC markets

Country	Completely trust	Somewhat trust	Neither trust nor distrust	Somewhat distrust	Completely distrust
Australia	40%	35%	19%	3%	2%
India	32%	40%	26%	2%	1%
APAC	29%	44%	21%	4%	2%
Singapore	29%	49%	19%	2%	1%
Indonesia	27%	55%	16%	2%	1%
Hong Kong	23%	51%	22%	3%	1%
China	23%	42%	23%	9%	3%

SOURCE Tan, 2022a

Table 9.2 Trust in digital-only banks across major APAC markets

Country	Completely trust	Somewhat trust	Neither trust nor distrust	Somewhat distrust	Completely distrust
Australia	27%	35%	26%	8%	4%
India	15%	36%	36%	11%	1%
APAC	13%	31%	38%	13%	5%
China	11%	24%	39%	15%	10%
Hong Kong	8%	29%	45%	14%	4%
Indonesia	7%	31%	43%	15%	4%
Singapore	5%	32%	42%	16%	5%

SOURCE Tan, 2022a

Interestingly, though, Australians are just as, if not more wary of digital-only banks. According to data from YouGov, less than half (44 per cent) of consumers in the APAC region say they trust digital-only banks, while 73 per cent trust traditional banks (Tan, 2022a). However, among the major APAC countries – others being Singapore, India, China, Hong Kong and Indonesia – Australians demonstrate the highest levels of trust in both types of banking model. Clearly, the industry is doing something right.

Once again, similarities can be drawn between Australia and the UK – despite the incumbent banks' past failings having dented consumer confidence, those same consumers are reluctant to bank with challenger or digital banks, commonly citing their relative novelty as a reason. Inertia is another factor at play, however. While the longevity of the major banks often works in their favour, it also stifles innovation and competition. Regulators in the UK and Australia have recognized that, mandating open banking and CDR, respectively, in response.

Further research by YouGov delves into Australian consumers' priorities when choosing a financial service provider, whether that's a bank, insurer, or payment service provider. Their main preference is for low or no fees to pay, while the safety and security of their money is also a top concern.

Has CDR delivered?

A report published early in 2023 by Open Finance Advisors took stock of CDR developments in Australia and found it had, perhaps, not quite delivered on its early promise in terms of participation and reliability of data. The Australian Open Banking Ecosystem Map and Report in collaboration with FDATA ANZ, FinTech Australia and Open Finance ANZ, concluded that 'data reliability and completeness issues' are holding open banking back 'from really taking off' (Charnley, 2023). At this point, Australia was two-and-a-half years into open banking implementation. The report revealed that 95 per cent of authorized deposit-taking institutions were sharing data – equivalent to 114 brands – with 88 data recipients of all access model types.

Table 9.3 Which of the following are important to you when choosing a financial company for a new product or service?

Considerations	Australia	APAC
Low or no fees	68%	54%
Safety and security of my money	67%	65%
Good customer service	65%	57%
Good interest rates	58%	54%
Access to digital services	52%	48%
Company's ethical values	37%	33%
Company's stance on environmental sustainability	30%	32%
Attractive incentives to switch/take out a product	25%	32%

SOURCE Tan, 2022b

Interestingly, though, of those 88 data recipients, fintechs made up 40 per cent. Meanwhile, those companies that might be labelled technology 'intermediaries', such as Frollo, Basiq, Yodlee and Adatree, accounted for 15 per cent of accredited participants and are, therefore, 'playing a key role in enabling the growth of the Consumer Data Right' (Charnley, 2023).

Until this first phase is complete, with open banking fully live and operational, CDR cannot 'accelerate'. Brenton Charnley, one of the authors of the report and founder of Open Finance Advisors, said Australia had 'high consumer bank coverage' but that the data being shared also needed to be reliable for CDR to really get underway, in terms of 'speed, completeness and accuracy of data' (Charnley, 2023).

Open banking provider Frollo's report on the state of open banking in Australia states that open banking APIs have 'generally been fast and reliable for a few years'. However, it asserts that a 'more useful' performance metric is the conversion rate, calculated as the percentage of 'successful attempts to complete the consent process' (Frollo, 2023b). Here, the report suggested there is 'room for

Table 9.4 Percentage of consents that do not succeed on the data holder side

	Percentage
Bank 1	33%
Bank 2	32%
Bank 3	29%
Bank 4	29%
Bank 5	29%
Industry average	27%
Bank 6	18%
Bank 7	17%
Bank 8	16%
Bank 9	11%
Bank 10	7%

SOURCE Frollo, 2023b

improvement', with issues concerning consent conversions in particular. Analysis of consent conversion collected in the Frollo consumer app found that 27 per cent of consent attempts failed on the
data holder side, after the data recipient had collected the consent,
between January and August 2023. So, Frollo dug a little deeper in an
attempt to uncover why this was happening. For nearly half the users
who did not successfully link their account, the reason was identified
as not being able to log into their bank – mainly issues with the one-
time password issued by banks.

In what is, ultimately, good news for banks and consumers alike,
in Australia, the Frollo report concluded that while the failures are
'frustrating' on the consumer side, they are 'a fixable problem' if data
holders take action to address these issues in their system.

Table 9.5   Why consents do not succeed

Reason	Percentage
Can't login to bank	48%
Issue after logging in	35%
Can't select accounts	12%
Other	5%

SOURCE Frollo, 2023b

What next for Australia?

One particular concern highlighted by the Open Finance Advisors report was 'low' adoption of CDR among consumers so far, made even more challenging by the lack of publicly available statistics to verify the number of customers 'that have consented to use data' through CDR. Given that 'consumer usage is the ultimate validation' of CDR, this is something of an oversight. FDATA ANZ's Mat Mytka is quoted in the report as saying that the 'number of consumer consents are a good proxy and interim success measure' of Australia's CDR until it is able to 'accurately measure consumer and SMB outcomes' (Charnley, 2023).

So, what needs to happen for Australia to make the leap to true open finance? Some believe that leadership needs to come from the top. The Open Finance Advisors report called on the ACCC and Treasury to 'provide some clear goals and broader transparent metrics about consumer participation' to 'drive the ecosystem forward' (Charnley, 2023).

Mytka acknowledges that measuring consumer outcomes is hard and that Australia 'defaults to how many API calls get made, and how many startups are involved' as proxies. These figures fail to get to the 'important social outcomes' that he believes any policy reforms should focus on, such as, 'how many people have we enabled to be more financially literate... and manage their finances better?' Or, indeed, asking the question, 'how are we improving the financial wellbeing of our citizens?' given that CDR has been such a significant financial investment (Mytka, 2023).

With CDR having been rolled out to the energy sector, the telecoms, insurance and superannuation industries are next. The Australian Government's Treasury department has stated that expanding CDR to telecommunications is likely to drive more competition and 'allow consumers to better leverage their internet and mobile data when choosing products and bundle solutions that suit their needs'. It also expects the combination of banking, energy and telecoms data to 'generate cross-sectoral use cases' (The Treasury, 2023).

However, the brakes have since been applied and expansion into the telecoms, pensions and insurance sectors is now firmly on pause. The Treasury has confirmed that a 'strategic assessment' is planned for the end of 2024, which will 'inform future expansions and the implementation of action initiation'. This is a setback for Australia but, one would hope, only a minor one. In terms of maintaining momentum in the meantime, there is plenty of scope in the energy sector, and still work to be done on data reliability in open banking.

Tony Thrassis, chief executive of Australian open banking provider Frollo, believes that the pause in rolling out CDR, rather than giving open banking a chance to mature, actually gives it 'an opportunity to accelerate' (Thrassis, 2023). Certainly, the banking and energy sectors have breathing space, as it were – time to take stock now that initial rollout among banks is near completion, and to iron out any issues that remain. As of 18 August 2023, Frollo reported that 76 data holders were active in banking, totalling 115 brands, with six brands still to become active. Meanwhile, the sectors yet to join the open ecosystem have a chance to learn what works and what doesn't, and to work on CDR use cases. It has also been confirmed that buy now, pay later products – a type of non-bank lending – will come under the CDR, with banks also obliged to share data for these products if they offer them.

Yet, Mytka observes that the delay points to a more deep-seated issue with CDR and Australia's approach to bringing on board other sectors and industries, which is 'a lack of vision... What outcomes are we actually designing for? And what future does that create for Australian society?' he asks. He suggests CDR has lacked that from the very beginning of the project, adding that 'there's no clear vision about what we're actually working towards' (Mytka, 2023).

It is a huge learning curve for Australia and one that other countries would do well to take note of before they embark on anything on the scale of Australia's CDR. There needs to be a mission statement, in effect. In Australia, as in the UK, open banking was implemented first, with a view to promoting effective competition in an otherwise little-trusted banking system comprising a small number of larger players – financial inclusion was not the original aim, but rather has been a happy by-product.

CASE STUDY
Ofwat

Australia's Consumer Data Right has now rolled out to the country's energy sector – in fact, it is blazing a trail. Will it inspire utilities companies in other jurisdictions to follow suit? Is there any evidence of other energy or utility suppliers prioritizing open finance or smart data? On the face of it, there are few instances of energy and other utility companies having recognized the imperative of data sharing.

However, the body that regulates the water industry in England and Wales, Ofwat, appears to be leading the charge. In 2021, Ofwat published a report outlining its views on how open data can potentially enable water companies to create more value for their customers, and also allowing customers to consider the environmental benefits. It laid bare some of the work already being done in this area, with open data sharing underway in some areas of the industry (Ofwat, 2021).

By now, the concept of financial institutions opening up data and the various use cases that can be sparked by doing so are familiar. But what does that look like for water companies and consumers? In the context of this book, how might it help those customers who are more vulnerable?

As Ofwat points out in its report, the water industry 'is host to a wealth of data and information' and, by opening up access to this data, the regulator sees three areas of opportunity in particular, namely innovation, efficiency and transparency (Ofwat, 2023). One such example of innovation is the development of 'new products and services such as apps' that, ultimately, improve the customer experience. When it comes to transparency, Ofwat believes that by making data 'freely available… to access, use and share', trust in water companies can be established. The regulator also identified that open data is an opportunity for collaboration across the industry, 'facilitating the linking and merging of data to create larger datasets' and enabling water companies to work together to address 'shared' challenges. This data could also feed into future policymaking at the government level.

The types of data held by the water industry that could be shared under an open data regime include operational data, asset data, customer (including personal) data and financial data (Ofwat, 2021). Some datasets are already being shared among water companies (although they are not widely available), including Priority Services Register Data, which holds information on vulnerable customers' addresses and contact details. However, the Environment Agency flood risk mapping is open and available to all participants in the industry. But Ofwat suggests there is more value to be gained by making industry data 'as open as possible'.

In its report from 2021, Ofwat states that at that time there were 'very few' water companies providing 'open access to their data sets', although it also points to some individual open data initiatives that had emerged from hackathons and pilots. These have produced some fascinating and, in some instances, groundbreaking case studies. United Utilities, for example, took part in a hackathon with external partners to make use of open data sets from Public Health England on the location of food service establishments. Ofwat reported that the data 'hack' found a 'strong correlation' between these establishments and an 'increased risk of wastewater flooding' (Ofwat, 2021). Utility provider Anglian Water accessed mobile phone data from telecoms provider BT 'to predict water consumption hotspots' and specifically how 'per capita consumption might have been impacted by more people living at home during Covid-19' (Ofwat, 2021).

Ofwat outlines how data sharing can help water companies better serve their more vulnerable customers – typically those who struggle to pay their water bill. At the time of the report, United Utilities was making use of open banking technologies to 'verify customer income in real-time', allowing it to 'streamline its process' for considering whether a customer might be eligible for 'reduced-rate social tariffs' (Ofwat, 2021).

Despite the many benefits set out in the Ofwat report, and the data-sharing initiatives already in evidence across the industry, the regulator felt obliged to issue a call to action in 2023. In a press release, Ofwat urged water companies to 'unleash' the benefits of open data, given that it found 'little progress' had been made in water utilities opening their data. To ensure that tangible progress is made, Ofwat announced the development of a 'licence condition that will provide new powers to ensure companies deliver' (Ofwat, 2023). In short, the water regulator expects companies to 'embed a stronger data culture' and collaborate to 'speed up' delivery.

OVO Energy and open banking – how to reassure consumers

In the UK, one energy supplier has begun using open banking technology. OVO Energy has launched what it claims is the 'industry's first open banking digital tool' (OVO Energy, 2022). The tool allows OVO Energy to create 'bespoke repayment options' by building up 'an accurate picture of affordability' among customers who may be struggling to pay or manage their energy bills. OVO Energy is able to offer its open banking tool by working with credit reference agency Experian to 'pull through' a customer's financial information from bank accounts and other bills 'quickly and securely' (OVO Energy, 2023).

The company also provides its customers with an explanation of open banking, and best demonstrates its benefits by comparing the time it would take to use open banking to provide all the required financial information, versus the length of time it takes for them to manually input it. According to OVO Energy, for customers who choose to share their bank statements with them through Experian – in other words, using open banking – the process will take 15 minutes. It states that, should a customer wish to fill in the required details manually, it will take them 45 minutes and they will need all their bank statements, receipts and online banking details 'to hand' (OVO Energy, 2023).

By using this 'frequently asked questions' section, OVO Energy explains what exactly the consumer gains from using open banking and also helps to allay any concerns they may have about its safety and security. This is one of the best examples I have seen of an open banking use case that provides the consumer with a relatively simple explanation of open banking, free of jargon, and makes the benefits immediately clear. By pre-empting the questions its customers will likely have about open banking and Experian, OVO Energy – rather cleverly, in my view – uses it as an opportunity to educate them without being patronizing, and in the process, reassures people that the technology is there to help them, not trick them.

Summary

This chapter has taken in approaches to open finance from Latin America to the UK and Europe via Australia. What stands out is that while there are some exciting developments and progress being made, there is still much that needs to be smoothed out, particularly given that open finance requires buy-in from so many different industries and their respective regulators.

Open finance, where it is being rolled out, is being stymied by lack of open banking progress or, more accurately, incomplete open banking implementations. Get open banking right, and there is a chance that those same jurisdictions may well find it easier to make the transition to implementing data sharing in the energy, investment, pensions and telecoms sectors.

Interestingly, the doubts expressed by consumers about open banking, namely security, privacy, and trust and transparency, also plague countries' open finance implementations. But, as OVO Energy in the UK demonstrates, there is no reason why the benefits of consenting to share data cannot be communicated easily and without the need for prior industry knowledge.

Whether open finance can promote financial inclusion depends largely on whether that is its intended aim from the get-go. Open finance needs to have a purpose if it is to be adopted by industries other than banking, as Australia has found out to its detriment. Delaying the rollout of CDR to telecoms companies, as well as to the pensions and insurance sectors, may be more beneficial in the long term, if once it does come, there is clarity around what is in it for the customers of these sectors. By the time these industries join Australia's open ecosystem, it is likely the earlier issues around data quality in banking and energy will have been resolved and any lessons learned can be passed on.

The region where it seems most likely that open finance will have the most positive impact on financial inclusion is in Latin America, given the strides many of the countries in this region have made so far in banking the unbanked. Because the numbers of unbanked and underserved are so huge, there is more at stake for Latin America and also, potentially, more opportunity. The hope is that the historic alliance between Mexico, Colombia, Chile and Peru does not get watered down, or lose its focus along the way.

So, can open finance promote financial inclusion? The answer, in my mind, is a resounding yes – but it requires leadership, regulation, investment, ambition and vision. It also needs a certain amount of commitment from government, regulators and all concerned to see it through to 'completion' and to really reap the rewards across industries and throughout populations.

References

Adarve, L H and Acosta, J (2023) Changes and novelties in the field of Data Protection 2022, Dentons, 24 January, www.dentons.com/en/insights/articles/2023/january/24/changes-and-novelties-in-the-field-of-data-protection-2022 (archived at https://perma.cc/H3VN-QTBM)

Australian Government (2023a) What is CDR? Cdr.gov.au, www.cdr.gov.au/what-is-cdr (archived at https://perma.cc/BEG7-8GP5)

Australian Government (2023b) Rollout, Cdr.gov.au, www.cdr.gov.au/rollout (archived at https://perma.cc/H7E3-3QPG)

Australian Government (2023c) Government statement in response to the Statutory Review of the Consumer Data Right, https://treasury.gov.au/sites/default/files/2023-06/p2023-404730-gs.pdf (archived at https://perma.cc/5PQX-V8H3)

Banco Central De La Republica Argentina (BCRA) (2022) Transfers 3.0: more than two million interoperable transactions made in less than two months (translated), 22 January, www.bcra.gob.ar/Noticias/Transferencias-3-0-millones-de-transacciones-realizadas.asp#: (archived at https://perma.cc/R3B6-BTB8)

Belvo (2023) Instant salary advances with your smartphone from Monet, https://belvo.com/es/casos-de-exito/monet/ (archived at https://perma.cc/958C-ADBM)

Belvo Communications (2023) Belvo and MOVii seal alliance to solve
    fraud with Open Finance in online payments in Colombia, Belvo,
    23 October, www.latamfintech.co/articles/belvo-y-movii-sellan-alianza-
    estrategica-para-solucionar-el-fraude-en-los-pagos-en-linea-en-colombia
    (archived at https://perma.cc/X3P4-84WR)

Charnley, B (2022) What is Open Energy in Australia? Open Finance
    Advisors, 23 December, www.openfinanceadvisors.com/blog/what-is-
    open-energy-in-australia (archived at https://perma.cc/Z9BZ-72QU)

Charnley, B (2023) Launch of the Australian open banking ecosystem map &
    report, Open Finance Advisors, 27 January, www.openfinanceadvisors.
    com/blog/australian-open-banking-ecosystem-map-launch (archived at
    https://perma.cc/GZB3-X8V3)

Colombia Fintech (2023) Key Figures, https://colombiafintech.co/
    (archived at https://perma.cc/2C4E-4F5X)

Cordeiro Guerra, S (2023) Regulations and Institutional Capacity needed
    to advance open finance in Latin America and the Caribbean: Study,
    Inter-American Development Bank, 7 June, www.iadb.org/en/news/
    regulations-and-institutional-capacity-needed-advance-open-finance-
    latin-america-and-caribbean (archived at https://perma.cc/RJ8X-BV2Q)

Ebanx (2023) PSE – Secure online payments, Business.ebanx.com, date
    unknown, https://business.ebanx.com/es/colombia/metodos-de-pago/pse
    (archived at https://perma.cc/N5WE-TWZM)

Estrada, S (2023) Fintech of the Pacific Alliance propose to standardize
    Open finance (translated), El Economista, 17 May, www.eleconomista.
    com.mx/sectorfinanciero/Fintech-de-la-Alianza-del-Pacifico-proponen-
    estandarizar-Open-finance-20230517-0093.html (archived at
    https://perma.cc/5NQL-CR5S)

Feliba, D (2023) Colombia edges closer to Open Finance, Fintech Nexus,
    23 March, www.fintechnexus.com/colombia-edges-closer-to-open-
    finance/ (archived at https://perma.cc/JWN3-WY3Z)

Fennell, J (2022) Only half of Australians trust their banks, study reveals,
    Broker News, 27 May, www.brokernews.com.au/news/breaking-news/
    only-half-of-australians-trust-their-banks-study-reveals-280286.aspx
    (archived at https://perma.cc/9KSX-MC3Y)

Financial Conduct Authority (2021) FCA publishes feedback to Call for
    Input on open finance, 26 March, www.fca.org.uk/news/news-stories/
    fca-publishes-feedback-call-input-open-finance (archived at https://
    perma.cc/QCL7-XN7T)

Fonseca, D (2023) Open finance in Latin America and the Caribbean:
    great opportunities, large challenges, https://publications.iadb.org/

publications/english/viewer/Open-Finance-in-Latin-America-and-the-Caribbean-Great-Opportunities-Large-Challenges.pdf (archived at https://perma.cc/8LRH-KTFC)

Frollo (2023a) Open Energy: Innovating for a competitive advantage, Blog.frollo.com.au (archived at https://perma.cc/W8NU-JYYP), 17 October, https://blog.frollo.com.au/open-energy/ (archived at https://perma.cc/3EN7-3WZS)

Frollo (2023b) The State of Open Banking 2024, https://blog.frollo.com.au/ (archived at https://perma.cc/4ERC-AHBY)

Gallo, V, Nair, S, Hill, C, Bailey, S, Thornhill, B and Jardine, J (2022) Open Finance: preparing for success, Deloitte, 28 March, https://ukfinancialservicesinsights.deloitte.com/post/102hlis/open-finance-preparing-for-success (archived at https://perma.cc/4FCQ-JAJ6)

Herrera, D, Pereira, W, Volochen, L and Zarate Moreno, A M (2023) Open finance in Latin America and the Caribbean: great opportunities, large challenges, https://publications.iadb.org/publications/english/viewer/Open-Finance-in-Latin-America-and-the-Caribbean-Great-Opportunities-Large-Challenges.pdf (archived at https://perma.cc/8LRH-KTFC)

Jones, L (2023) Latin America to make history with regional open banking initiative, Open Banking Exchange, 24 May, www.openbanking.exchange/latin-america-to-make-history-with-regional-open-banking-initiative/ (archived at https://perma.cc/4EFA-VFRJ)

McGuinness, M (2023) Keynote speech by Commissioner McGuinness at event in European Parliament 'From Open Banking to Open Finance: what does the future hold?', European, https://ec.europa.eu/commission/presscorner/detail/en/SPEECH_23_1819 (archived at https://perma.cc/QR3D-DEZ9)

Mytka, M (2023) Interview with Ellie Duncan, 11 July

Ofwat (2021) H2Open – Open data in the water industry: a case for change, www.ofwat.gov.uk/publication/h2open-open-data-in-the-water-industry-a-case-for-change/ (archived at https://perma.cc/8AF9-3NKU)

Ofwat (2023) Ofwat calls on water companies to act now on open data, Ofwat.gov.uk, 8 June, www.ofwat.gov.uk/ofwat-calls-on-water-companies-to-act-now-on-open-data/ (archived at https://perma.cc/2CNT-AZYK)

Open Banking Exchange (2023) Open Banking in Colombia: The True Trailblazers? Open Banking Exchange Insight, 19 October, www.openbanking.exchange/resources/insights/open-banking-in-colombia-the-true-trailblazers/ (archived at https://perma.cc/46YH-KPMJ)

OVO Energy (2022) OVO wins Energy Supplier and Net Zero Innovation Technology at the Energy Awards 2022, 30 June, https://company.ovo.com/ovo-wins-energy-supplier-and-net-zero-innovation-technology-at-the-energy-awards-2022/ (archived at https://perma.cc/2CV2-GVDC)

OVO Energy (2023) Support with your energy payments, Ovoenergy.com, www.ovoenergy.com/payment-support (archived at https://perma.cc/6MQT-HH9X)

Pinedo, A (2023) These are Latin America's instant payment systems, Iupana, 13 February, https://iupana.com/2023/02/13/these-are-latin-americas-instant-payment-systems/?lang=en (archived at https://perma.cc/5QBV-YFBE)

Prior, R (2023) Regulations and institutional capacity needed to advance open finance in Latin America and the Caribbean: study, Inter-American Development Bank, 7 June, www.iadb.org/en/news/regulations-and-institutional-capacity-needed-advance-open-finance-latin-america-and-caribbean (archived at https://perma.cc/RJ8X-BV2Q)

Rojas, M (2023) Belvo transforms bank-to-bank payments in Colombia with open finance, Belvo, 22 February, https://belvo.com/blog/belvo-transforms-bank-to-bank-payments-in-colombia-with-open-finance/ (archived at https://perma.cc/B4BU-XW5C)

Tan, S (2022a) Consumer trust in traditional versus digital-only banks in APAC, YouGov, 30 May, https://au.yougov.com/news/2022/05/30/consumer-trust-traditional-vs-digital-banks-survey/ (archived at https://perma.cc/BP45-C46V)

Tan, S (2022b) What do Australia's consumers most consider when choosing a financial service provider? YouGov, 6 May, https://business.yougov.com/content/42428-australia-choose-financial-service-provider-2022 (archived at https://perma.cc/JD5L-6Y22)

The Treasury (2023) Consumer Data Right rules – expansion to the telecommunications sector and other operational enhancements, Treasury.gov.au (archived at https://perma.cc/QV97-UN5C) https://treasury.gov.au/consultation/c2022-315575 (archived at https://perma.cc/Y7N7-BLZG)

Thrassis, T (2023) The State of Open Banking 2024, https://blog.frollo.com.au/ (archived at https://perma.cc/4ERC-AHBY)

Final thoughts on open banking, open finance and financial inclusion

10

Introduction

In this final chapter, I want to bring all the strands together to draw some conclusions about open banking and financial inclusion, with a few calls to action along the way.

CHAPTER OBJECTIVES

The main questions to be answered are:

- What are the main learnings, having spoken to a wide range of voices from across the open banking, fintech and open finance industries?
- Has the book busted any misconceptions about being unbanked?
- What needs to happen now to continue to transform the financial services industry and bring people from around the world into a system that has previously excluded them?
- How do we all – including those who are already banked – benefit from a financial ecosystem that works for everyone?
- Is there enough momentum industry-wide to see it through to open finance and beyond? What will it take to get there?

First-hand accounts

Is there a common thread running through the stories of the people I spoke to for this book? I'd say there are several, including:

- Recognition that the traditional banking, lending and payments systems are not serving everyone in the way they should and that barriers remain to financial equality that can be overcome.
- An ambition and vision to see how open banking or consumer-permissioned data sharing can bring about a new era of banking and access to credit, and the determination to make it happen.
- An understanding of the long-term ill effects of failing to address financial exclusion, not only on the individual, but on society as a whole.
- Why it will take collaboration on so many levels to encourage widespread adoption – at the national, global, and public and private sector levels, as well as in the form of partnerships between banks and fintechs. The sharing of different approaches to implementing open banking between countries means that those working in the industry are always learning and striving for best practice.
- That women have been disproportionately affected by financial exclusion, despite their increased participation in the workforce and their growing wealth.
- Seizing the opportunity – all the people I spoke to for this book have seen an opportunity to start their own fintech business, advocate for open banking, or record and track the progress of global financial inclusion.
- A passion for open banking, or financial inclusion, or both.

That last one – the passion displayed by these individuals – is the one that binds all those threads together. It is a word that is often overused to the point of being meaningless. However, in this case, all the people I interviewed demonstrated a passion and commitment that rings true. Many of them believe in open banking and its ability to transform the financial lives of those who remain on the peripheries of society.

The individuals who shared with me their very personal experiences of being financially excluded, understand first-hand what it means to be on the outside looking in. They watched as their peers, relatives and other people around them gained access to the most basic banking services, and yet were not provided the opportunity to join them themselves. Moreover, once they had worked out how to gain entry, they wanted to leave open the doors to other marginalized groups, whether that be women, immigrants, or those with a black mark against their credit history. Both Vrinda Gupta and Rob Pasco founded their respective companies, Sequin and Plend, to remedy some of what they experienced and have gone on to deploy open banking to overturn traditional credit scoring and decisioning systems.

Exclusion to inclusion

I hope that defining financial exclusion and detailing how many people are affected globally has informed your understanding of the scale and size of the issue. But I was also keen to dispel any myths there might be surrounding financial exclusion. I wanted to challenge pre-conceived ideas of who is most commonly referred to as being unbanked or underserved – by speaking directly to people who had, at one time, fallen into these categories or possibly still do. It was vital that this book painted a picture of what it means to be unbanked or underserved by the banking system, and documented the demographics most typically affected. Only then could I begin to explore how open banking can promote and foster a far more equitable financial system.

Inroads have been made when it comes to financial inclusion; the pandemic proved to be something of a catalyst for change, with more people banked now than at any other time, as Chapter 1 showed. While Covid-19 raged on, confining people to their homes, households began familiarizing themselves with online banking and digital payments. Previously unbanked members of households – particularly women – received financial support from the state directly into an account in their name. It normalized online banking and, as such, there should be no looking back. However, while it has been encouraging to see some positives emerge from the global tragedy, it does not mean we should be complacent. Many people may have had to open an online current account for the first time to receive government handouts, but as I have discovered in writing this book, without education and support, they have continued to withdraw the money as cash.

I reiterate my call to banks, fintechs, governments, regulators and central banks to build on the progress made during the pandemic. Financial inclusion is one of the UN's Sustainable Development Goals – it is an imperative that it be prioritized. Financial exclusion is a stain on society and should be considered a global emergency. In the 21st century, access to basic financial services and products is not a 'nice to have', it is a 'need to have', regardless of income.

The trust issue

Speaking at an FDX Global Summit in April 2023, the acting US Comptroller of the Currency, Michael J Hsu, concluded his remarks with a statement about trust. He asserted that 'an open banking culture' which recognizes how hard-won trust is in banking and puts it above other objectives 'including growth and profit' will, in fact, 'succeed over time' (Hsu, 2023). I have to agree.

While carrying out my research for this book, trust was the one issue that came up time and again. I have referenced several different studies across various regions that show consumers report low levels of trust in their banks – and, also, in digital-only banks. However, it is not always a lack of trust – in the case of Canada, consumers typically exhibit high levels of trust in the country's largest banks (see Chapter 7). Either way, trust is somewhat of a barrier to wider adoption of open banking in many jurisdictions. Too much trust, as it were, and people see little need to shake up the system because the incumbent banks are meeting their needs. Too little trust and consumers question or doubt the need to share their data – other, newer financial institutions are sometimes tarred with the same brush.

If we turn that on its head, then open banking is an opportunity to either reward that trust, or to restore it among populations. The more people feel like the financial services industry is genuinely willing and able to serve them, the more trust is likely to be established. Crucial to this is getting the message to people that open banking only works when they consent to sharing their account or transaction data – the data that was previously owned by the banks is now in their hands.

Key to establishing trust in open banking probably comes down to not marketing it as open banking, but rather as a new way of doing banking in the digital, information age. See the example of UK energy supplier OVO Energy in Chapter 9 – keep any explanation of open banking brief and relate it to consumer-permissioned data sharing. Then explain in the most straightforward language, avoiding any terminology, the immediate benefits to them. Finally, address any security and privacy concerns directly but concisely, pointing people to the fact that open banking is regulated and overseen by certain industry bodies.

Maybe it is the phrase itself that is the issue – open banking seems to put the onus on banks to deliver the messaging, when actually it is incumbent on the entire financial services, payments and fintech industry to inform and educate. In that case, open data or open finance better encapsulate the end goal and might even help to bypass trust as a barrier. After all, many people's first experience of consumer-permissioned data sharing might not be through their bank, but via a transaction. Digital payments are, increasingly, a 'way in' to the broader concept of open banking – this has certainly proven to be the case in Latin American countries, such as Brazil (see Chapter 4). Australia probably has what I consider to be the most accurate and least problematic name: Consumer Data Right. Because that is, essentially, what open banking, open finance and open data are – and in using a broader term, it becomes about far more than banking and, even, financial services. Any organizations that require consumer data or have significant volumes of our data – and let's face it, that is most industries now – come under that heading. They all have a responsibility to serve individuals and to ensure people have access to essential services, whether that is credit, energy, telecoms or a water supply.

Regulation or market forces?

One question I posed – and, indeed, sought to find the answer to in Chapter 3 – is whether it is possible to have an open banking ecosystem or framework that is designed with the sole aim of fostering financial inclusion. Certainly, as was covered in Chapter 3, there are pros and cons to a market-driven approach versus a regulation-led implementation. Which one of these approaches a country adopts may well depend on their existing financial services industry, including its track record, product offering and target market. I like to think that open banking implementations reflect a country's culture as much as anything else. That the US has relied on market forces to implement open banking, and its regulator is only contemplating oversight several years in, seems a natural fit, for example.

It does lead me to believe that regulation and ongoing oversight or governance are required to ensure standardization and create a level playing field. Having a regulatory body to convene an industry around a single aim or outcome is more likely to achieve financial inclusion than simply relying on market participants to take the initiative. This is why regulation is an imperative – when serving consumers' interests and needs is mandated, it will happen. If it is left up to market forces, consumers may feel they are being sold to, or there is an ulterior motive at play. It also leaves room for a private company or corporation to market their technology as the industry standard, but I question whether any market-driven approach can truly have the consumer's best interests at heart. What it does lend itself to is a highly innovative market and that is something that will be to the benefit of individuals.

It comes down to that tricky balancing act between innovation and regulation – how do you regulate without stymying innovation, for instance? Is it even possible? I would venture that it is and, perhaps, a crucial element of any regulated open banking implementation is a regulatory sandbox – one that is provided by the financial services regulator and that can act as a testing bed for new ideas and propositions.

Leadership and ownership are vital for open banking to be implemented with any success, and the same applies to open finance. Ambition and vision have also emerged as crucial attributes – there is no point in approaching open banking as a 'one and done' project. It is part of the ongoing digital transformation of banking as we know it, and the eventual transition to an 'open everything' world. It is not a case of if we get there, but when – and no one, or rather no institution, wants to be the laggard.

The need for digital identity: does India hold the answer?

What has become increasingly clear to me as I've been working on this book is the part that nationwide digital identity schemes can and should play in enhancing open banking and open finance ecosystems, as initially discussed in Chapter 5. Or, to put it another way, it is worth questioning how effective open banking can be without a digital identity system in place. It is also of vital importance that these digital identity schemes talk to each other at a global level – they must be interoperable.

National Australia Bank and NatWest addressed this requirement in a joint white paper, in which they concluded that there is a need for 'an economy-wide mechanism to identify and authenticate individuals and businesses reliably and safely' across what they call the digital ecosystem in both Australia and the UK (Carr et al, 2023). The white paper's authors suggest that, together, government and the private sector will need to deliver such a solution and that it will also require collaboration between industry and the public sector, which have the 'expertise'.

Meanwhile, the Australian Government forged ahead with its Digital ID system in the second half of 2023, as detailed in Chapter 5. Cybersecurity incidents have been something of a driving force for getting digital identity legislation off the ground there. The government has stepped up the pace of delivery and has also made a commitment to identity 'resilience' – there is a real sense of urgency, which other countries would do well to adopt. Two of Australia's largest banks have also begun to offer their customers a digital identity solution, ConnectID. The wording and positioning of this offering, I think, have been well thought through – the solution aims to stop people 'oversharing' when it comes to having to prove their identity, by ensuring that only the data required is shared with the organization requesting it, and only with the customer's consent. Proof of identity is, finally, going paperless – eliminating the need to carry around documentation to verify your identity, or scan and send proof via an unsecured personal email. By offering this solution, Commonwealth Bank and National Australia Bank are also saying to their customers, 'you can trust us to only share the necessary data in order to prove that you are who you say you are'. ConnectID makes it clear that it is a conduit for the data, and that it does not see or store an individual's data – another important clarification that will need to be well communicated to Australians.

Chapter 1 scrutinized India's digital identity framework, known as Aadhaar, which has been largely successfully rolled out. In fact, Aadhaar has been one piece of a larger digital infrastructure puzzle in India that has had a significant impact on levels of financial inclusion in the country.

Digital public infrastructure and financial inclusion

As I approached the final month of working on this book, one headline caught my eye as it claimed that India had 'hit its financial inclusion goal 41 years early' (FinTech Global, 2023). How had a country with such a large population, and much of it unbanked, managed to achieve such a feat? Was open banking involved in this target being reached?

The answer lies in a G20 report which reveals that India has seen ownership of transaction accounts increase from around one-quarter of its adult population in 2008 to more than 80 per cent today (Global Partnership for Financial Inclusion, 2023). In other words, having originally estimated that this level of progress would take up to 47 years, instead it took only a few. The reason? India's digital public infrastructure, or DPI. The report defines DPI as 'interoperable, open, and inclusive systems supported by technology' for the provision of both public and private services that can accelerate digital transformation 'in an inclusive way'. Digital ID, digital payments and data exchange in the financial sector all constitute a DPI, according to the Global Partnership for Financial Inclusion (2023). The organization points to several examples of DPIs that are advancing financial inclusion in countries, including India's Aadhaar, Brazil's Pix payments system, and data exchange platforms such as Australia's Consumer Data Right and Open Banking in the UK. The report concludes that, without DPIs, it would have taken India the full 47 years to achieve financial inclusion.

On the subject of digital ID, the report suggests that different use cases can 'facilitate access to and usage of financial services', mainly for account opening and authentication purposes. It also acknowledged that effective digital identity ecosystems can take the form of centralized systems, such as India's Aadhaar, or they can be based on 'federations of public- and/or private-sector ID providers', or even be entirely decentralized.

The Global Partnership for Financial Inclusion also recognizes that within the move to digital payments, government-to-person payments, or G2Ps, have scaled significantly and present another opportunity for the advancement of financial inclusion. Specifically, the report mentions the role of G2P payments in contributing to the 'economic empowerment' of women, as discussed in Chapter 6. The positive effect these payments have had on women is undeniable, providing them with a digital means to run their household and even, in some cases, to seek employment. This is the kind of public sector approach to digital payments and open banking that, once underway at scale, has a long-lasting and transformative impact on the financial lives of many millions of people and from which there is no looking back.

Finally, the report nods to the shift from open banking 'efforts' to open finance initiatives which, in turn, are 'motivating discussions on open data' and are 'another framing for data exchange' (Global Partnership for Financial Inclusion, 2023).

India has shown how true financial inclusion can be achieved and offers a possible blueprint that other countries – particularly those developing economies with significant numbers of unbanked and underserved – could adopt. The good news is that, according to the G20 report, digital infrastructure requires input from both public and private sectors, creating opportunities and new forms of revenue for all.

Digital upskilling and financial literacy

In countries where open banking is live, there is an ongoing debate about consumer awareness and understanding of the technology. The argument is often that consumers need to know what it is and then they will consent to it. But surely that is not the point. I suspect that rather than investing in resources and materials that attempt to explain to consumers what open banking is, expecting them to grasp it, and for adoption rates to soar, there is another way. To me, it makes much more sense for governments to offer their citizens the means to improve their financial literacy and provide them with the digital skills that will become necessary as we all continue to adapt to a cashless society. After all, that is a form of financial inclusion – being able to understand how formal financial services work can be hugely empowering.

In Chapter 6, the effect of giving women their own money in the form of government-to-person payments straight into an online account transformed their way of thinking about and spending money. They began making investments in products for their household and considered themselves valued members of society who could enter the workforce.

For so many people who continue to use cash and rely on informal financial services, they are not necessarily doing so because it is a preference. Instead, this method of paying and this way of living is all that they know. Show people a safer, more secure and easier way to pay for goods and services, or to budget and save, and they will do it. Also, people cannot be expected to trust institutions or technology that they do not understand or are unfamiliar with. What they will trust are real-life examples of open banking that make a difference to their everyday lives – the industry must demonstrate what open banking can do through use cases, not tell people how the technology works.

The need for an implementation entity

Given that there is an increasing preference around the world for regulatory-driven open banking, establishing an entity to ensure the rollout of open banking seems like a logical and necessary aspect of that approach.

In Chapter 5, I detailed the role that the UK's Open Banking Implementation Entity, or OBIE, played in delivering open banking. It was formed by the Competition and Markets Authority (CMA) to act as a supervisor of the country's open banking ecosystem rollout. Part of the OBIE's remit was to convene the industry, including regulatory bodies, fintechs and the largest nine current account holders among others, to get the financial services industry moving as one towards an agreed outcome – what it called the roadmap. It had a role distinct from that of the financial regulator, but the OBIE was answerable to the Financial Conduct Authority, the CMA and HM Treasury. Other countries have often looked to this structure as one that could help them get open banking implemented effectively, and within budget. Certainly, it is a model that can and should be replicated.

The creation of an implementation entity was deemed such a successful approach that once the UK's Open Banking Roadmap had been completed, and the OBIE itself was considered to have met its obligations in that regard, it was agreed by the Joint Regulatory Oversight Committee that a future entity should be formed to oversee the next phase. Any successor to the OBIE will be operating under an entirely new mandate and roadmap, as open banking becomes open finance and, eventually, open or smart data. In the meantime, the Joint Regulatory Oversight Committee, which is made up of the FCA, CMA, HM Treasury and the Payment Systems Regulator, gave the OBIE – or Open Banking Limited as it is better known – a mandate to continue during what has been dubbed the 'transition phase'.

Having a body that oversees delivery and holds ecosystem participants accountable is necessary, in my view, for a successful open
banking regime. An entity should be created specifically to carry out
this role and, as in the UK, it works well if that entity reports into the
overarching financial services regulatory body. However, let's face it,
the cost of standing up such an entity may be too burdensome for
some countries, particularly the developing economies. The OBIE
was funded by the UK's nine biggest banks – also known as the
CMA9 (see Chapter 5 for a further explanation). Any future UK
entity is, therefore, likely to be funded in a more sustainable way,
with backing coming not just from the banks, but also from third-
party providers and other members of the ecosystem.

Australia opted for a similar open banking-focused entity that is
also considered to be a useful model for countries to consider following. It is called the Australian Competition and Consumer Commission,
or ACCC, and is perhaps best described as an amalgamation of the
OBIE and the CMA. In that sense, it differs from the OBIE, in that
the ACCC 'sets and regulates' open banking, as well as administers
competition (EY, 2019). It, too, has been a costly exercise for
Australia's incumbents, running into hundreds of millions of dollars,
as established in Chapter 3.

Back in 2021, Canada proposed the creation of a similar body or
entity. In its final report, the Government of Canada's Advisory
Committee on Open Banking recommended appointing an Open
Banking Lead initially, who would eventually 'transition to become a
government entity' that would go on to serve as Canada's 'Open
Banking authority' (Open Finance Network of Canada, 2021). This
'purpose-built' governance entity would be responsible for the 'ongoing administration' of open banking, the advisory committee said in
its report, picking up from the lead at the conclusion of their mandate (Duncan, 2021). Whether this will come to fruition remains to
be seen, particularly as Canada seems to favour a 'hybrid' approach
that straddles the regulation-led open banking model, as seen in the
UK, Brazil and Australia, and the commercial partnerships-based
approach of the US.

I would argue that an implementation entity can be a practical
way to get open banking over the line, particularly in countries where

some parts of the ecosystem could potentially be laggards – this type of entity can be a positive driving force. Perhaps the biggest lesson learned from the UK is to have an entity already positioned to take over once the initial mandate concludes. So, if a country opts for a regulatory-driven approach, then be prepared to maintain a certain level of governance and oversight for the sake of continuation. This is what Canada seems to have accounted for in its recommendations for open banking – the advisory committee wording appears to make it clear there would be a transition from the Open Banking lead to the entity.

The UK, unfortunately, lacked this joined-up approach, which resulted in a period of uncertainty for the industry. With the roadmap having been completed by January 2023, as announced by the CMA, the ecosystem was left feeling directionless and unsure of what to do next. Having been reliant on the OBIE's oversight for so many years and without a clear vision outlined for the following phase, there was widespread concern that the UK was at risk of losing its international standing. Momentum ebbed in the early part of 2023, although the Joint Regulatory Oversight Committee was able to steer the industry back on track with its report on the next phase of open banking in the UK. It will have been approximately one year since the OBIE delivered its roadmap – a timeframe that is not ideal. Yet, so passionate are those that work in open banking and payments that even while time has been lost, the intention remains.

What is not yet clear is how an implementation or governance entity might work in a country that is pushing towards a broader concept, like open data, which involves multiple industries, each with its own regulator. Whichever country comes up with a blueprint for that – and it could still be the UK – will be onto something.

The finish line

Getting there will not be easy – it has not proved so up until now. For open banking to be implemented with any degree of success and then increasing adoption requires several things to happen: consumers' trust in banks and other financial institutions must be restored or maintained, and there must be a willingness on the part of individuals to share their data and to do so across most areas of their financial lives – but, crucially, to recognize that, in doing so, they are in control of their data. This is a huge mindset change, given that people assume – rightly, in some cases – that banks and other organizations or corporations own their data.

The onus is not all on the individual, though. Banks and existing institutions must play their part. They must embrace the move to open banking and place their own trust that the technology behind it will create a fairer financial system. They must trust that the rise of fintechs does not sound the death knell for the incumbents. In fact, as numerous studies have shown and which I have referred to throughout this book, people do entrust the banks with so much of their everyday banking and savings needs.

Open banking can be a force for good – it is already proving to be so in many ways and in many different countries. Is it possible that financial exclusion could be extinguished entirely? That there will come a time when not a single person is unbanked? It may sound impossible, but aim high and we might well come close.

References

Carr, B, Abeyratne, A and Melling, C (2023) Lessons learned from Australia and the United Kingdom: the Consumer Data Right and Open Banking, https://openapi.ulsterbank.co.uk/bankofapis/v1.0/dynamic-content/content/assets/community-articles/NatWest_ebook_OpenBanking_Design.pdf (archived at https://perma.cc/F3FT-VJSJ)

Duncan, E (2021) Final report on Open Banking in Canada sets 2023 deadline, Open Banking Expo, 5 August, www.openbankingexpo.com/news/final-report-on-open-banking-in-canada-sets-2023-deadline/ (archived at https://perma.cc/S3YL-XBJX)

EY (2019) How Canada should approach Open Banking, https://assets.ey.com/content/dam/ey-sites/ey-com/en_ca/topics/open-banking/ey-how-canada-should-approach-open-banking.pdf?download (archived at https://perma.cc/P987-CPZ2)

FinTech Global (2023) How India hit its financial inclusion goal 41 years early, 11 September, https://fintech.global/2023/09/11/how-india-hit-its-financial-inclusion-goal-41-years-early/ (archived at https://perma.cc/SRB7-YVYW)

Global Partnership for Financial Inclusion (2023) G20 policy recommendations for advancing financial inclusion and productivity gains through digital public infrastructure, https://documents.worldbank.org/en/publication/documents-reports/documentdetail/099092023121016458/p178703046f82d07c0bbc60b5e474ea7841 (archived at https://perma.cc/G3AC-GBCP)

Hsu, M J (2023) Remarks at FDX Global Summit 'Open Banking and the OCC', Occ.gov, 19 April, www.occ.gov/news-issuances/speeches/2023/pub-speech-2023-38.pdf (archived at https://perma.cc/J6Y7-8GAV)

Open Finance Network of Canada (2021) A step forward for open banking in Canada, Openfinancenetwork.ca, 11 August, www.openfinancenetwork.ca/post/a-step-forward-for-open-banking-in-canada (archived at https://perma.cc/3NBZ-2ZST)

INDEX

The index is filed in alphabetical, word-by-word order. Numbers in main headings are filed as spelt out in full excepting for product phases and payment services directives, which are filed chronologically. Acronyms and 'Mc' are filed as presented. Page locators in *italics* denote information contained within a table.

Looking for another book?

Explore our award-winning
books from global business
experts in Finance and
Banking

Scan the code to browse

www.koganpage.com/finance

Also from Kogan Page

ISBN: 9781398608962

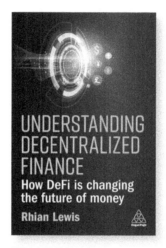

ISBN: 9781398609372

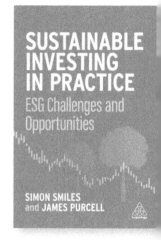

ISBN: 9781398607903

ISBN: 9781398610538

ISBN: 9781398612938

ISBN: 9781398613874

www.koganpage.com